Psychoanalytic Theory for Social Work Practice

Written by practicing social workers and social work educators, this is the first book in over twenty years to introduce psychoanalytic theory to social work practitioners. The loss of psychoanalytic theory has left social work without a model to fully understand the impact of trauma and deprivation on the inner world of their clients and to make sense of behaviour which may be disturbing and self-destructive.

Psychoanalytic Theory for Social Work Practice analyses psychoanalytic and psychosocial approaches to social work and relates them to current practices and values. Focusing on working with children and families, the text covers salient issues in social work practice including risk assessment, dealing with patients with drug and alcohol problems, and supervision and management of emotional stress. It also examines the research evidence for this approach.

With psychoanalytic and psychosocial approaches becoming increasingly popular this text will be a welcome addition for both professionals and students in the social work field, promoting analytical thinking and presenting practical examples of how psychoanalytic theories can be applied in practice. It offers a new perspective on understanding clients and discusses realistic ways in which clients can be helped to change.

Marion Bower is a Senior Clinical Lecturer in Social Work in the Child and Family Department at the Tavistock Clinic. She has worked in child, adolescent and adult mental health services for over twenty years. She is on the editorial boards of the *Journal of Social Work Practice* and the *British Journal of Psychotherapy*. She is co-editor of *The Emotional Needs of Young Children and Their Families* published by Routledge. She is an Associate Member of the Lincoln Clinic and works in private practice as an adult psychotherapist.

Psychoanalytic Theory for Social Work Practice

Thinking under fire

Edited by Marion Bower

Routledge
Taylor & Francis Group

LONDON AND NEW YORK

First published 2005
by Routledge
2 Park Square, Milton Park, Abingdon, Oxfordshire, OX14 4RN

Simultaneously published in the USA and Canada
by Routledge
29 West 35th Street, New York, NY 10001

Routledge is an imprint of the Taylor & Francis Group

Typeset in Sabon
by J&L Composition, Filey, North Yorkshire
Printed and bound in Great Britain by TJ International Ltd, Padstow, Cornwall

British Library Cataloguing in Publication Data
A catalogue record for this book is available from the British Library

Library of Congress Cataloging in Publication Data
A catalog record for this book has been requested

ISBN 0-415-33799-2 (hbk)
ISBN 0-415-33800-X (pbk)

Contents

Contributors

Dick Agass, formerly a mental health social worker, is a BCP-registered psychoanalytic psychotherapist in private practice and a part-time consultant psychotherapist in the Bradford District NHS Care Trust. He is an associate member of the Lincoln Clinic and Centre for Psychotherapy.

Marion Bower is a senior clinical lecturer in social work in the Child and Family Department at the Tavistock Clinic. She is co-editor of *The Emotional Need of Young Children and their Families* (Routledge, 1995). She is also an adult psychotherapist in private practice.

Stephen Briggs is a senior clinical lecturer and Vice Dean in the Adolescent Department of the Tavistock Clinic. He is the author of *Growth and Risk in Infancy* (Jessica Kingsley, 1997), *Working with Adolescents; a contemporary psychodynamic approach* (Palgrave, 2002).

Ron Britton was a consultant child psychiatrist and Chair of the Child and Family Department at the Tavistock Clinic. He is a training analyst of the British Psychoanalytic Society.

Andrew Cooper is professor of social work at the Tavistock Clinic/University of East London. He is also an adult psychotherapist.

Gwyn Daniel is a senior clinical lecturer in social work and systemic psychotherapist at the Tavistock Clinic and Co-Director, Oxford Family Institute. She is the author (With Charlotte Burck) of *Gender and Family Therapy* and (with Gill Gorell Barnes, Paul Thompson and Natasha Burchardt) of *Growing up in Stepfamilies* as well as articles (with Kirsten Blow) on therapeutic court assessments and (with Bernadette Wren) on children and parental mental illness.

Maureen Fox is a consultant clinical psychologist in the Child and Family Department at the Tavistock Clinic and the convenor of the Refugee Workshop. She is an adult psychotherapist.

Judith Freedman is consultant psychiatrist in psychotherapy at the Portman Clinic. She regularly serves as an expert witness in family court proceedings. Dr Freedman is a Fellow of the Royal College of Psychiatrists and a psychoanalyst.

Naz Keval is a consultant clinical psychologist and adult psychotherapist in a primary care setting for Hertfordshire Partnership NHS Trust. He also runs a private practice and does some medico-legal work.

Julie Long is a child psychotherapist who has worked for a number of social services departments and is also in private practice.

Gillian Miles (now retired) was employed at the time of the research study on sexually abused girls as a senior clinical lecturer in social work at the Tavistock Clinic, working with families in a multidisciplinary setting, and involved in training and research. She was centrally involved in the work with the parents within the study. She is a psychotherapist in private practice.

Jo Mishan is a psychoanalytic psychotherpist and mental health nurse and works at St. Anns Hospital in the outpatient department of the Halliwick Psychological Therapies Department. For six years he was the unit manager of the Day Hospital which specialises in the treatment of personality disorders.

David Simpson is joint head of the Tavistock Learning and Complex Disabilities Service. He is a consultant child and adolescent psychiatrist at the Tavistock Clinic. He is a member of the British Psychoanalytic Society and works in private practice as a psychoanalyst.

Olive Stevenson CBE is Professor Emeritus of Social Work Studies at the University of Nottingham. She studied at Oxford University, the London School of Economics and the Tavistock Clinic. She began her career as a child care officer and has researched and published widely on child welfare, latterly particularly in relation to child abuse and neglect. She has also undertaken work on the protection of vulnerable adults.

Judith Trowell is a consultant child psychiatrist in the Child and Family Department of the Tavistock Clinic. She is also a psychoanalyst.

Martin Wegmann is a consultant clinical psychologist and group analyst. He worked at the Gatehouse Drugs Service, Southall, Middlesex. He now works at the Henderson Hospital.

Gianna Williams is a consultant child and adolescent psychotherapist at the Tavistock Clinic. She founded the Eating Disorders Workshop at the Tavistock Clinic and has written and lectured extensively on these themes.

Biddy Youell is a child psychotherapist based in the Child and Family Department of the Tavistock Clinic. She is also head of training at the Northern School of Child and Adolescent Psychotherapy in Leeds. A former teacher, Biddy retains a particular interest in the application of psychoanalytic thinking in nonclinical settings.

Foreword

I am pleased to have been asked to write a foreword to this book. Yet it is a challenge and not without discomfort. It involves a journey back to the 1950s when social work was establishing itself as a profession and when education was seeking appropriate theory on which to ground practice. I am conscious of the extent to which the theories and assumptions underpinning this book are unfamiliar to many of today's qualified social workers, including those in child welfare.

This foreword explores the reasons for this unfamiliarity and poses four questions. These are:

- Should psychoanalytic theory have a place in the practice of contemporary social work in child welfare?
- How important was psychoanalytic theory in the early years of British social work?
- What contributed to its continuing fall from favour?
- What now needs to be done?

Should psychoanalytic theory have a place in the practice of contemporary social work in child welfare?

This question has been carefully phrased; to argue, as I will, that such theory should have 'a place' in child welfare practice does not imply that it should be exclusive or even that it should hold a dominant position. In my career as a social worker educator, I have always believed that social workers need to understand and utilise a range of theories. The very nature of the work, in which social workers move between the external and inner worlds of the child and his/her parents, makes it essential to build practice on theories which embrace these different understandings. To present to social work students these diverse and sometimes conflicting views of human interaction is a formidable task for social work educators and one which is often not done well. Yet it is integral to the task. Within that context, psychoanalytic theory has an essential contribution to make to practice, for reasons discussed below.

The wording of the heading also refers to '*conscious* practice'; ideas deriving from psychoanalytic theory have become part and parcel of our collective understanding of human behaviour; even if they are not consciously expressed in terms of that theory. The obvious example concerns ideas about the unconscious mind – however loosely used – and its effect on behaviour. It is no longer contentious, or even adventurous, to hypothesise that a person's actions may be driven by emotional forces which he or she is unaware of. Furthermore, it is frequently assumed that those forces have their origins in earlier childhood experiences. Yet, without precision and a clear focus, the impact and significance of such assumptions are not used constructively to help the person manage their feelings.

So why is it so important that this body of theory – ever-changing and developing – should be a key element in social work? I am not expert in particular aspects of theory which the different authors address in this book. But, in general, this way of looking at human behaviour speaks deeply to me as it is one, very important, way to understand the more profound dynamics of human behaviour which so affect interaction. In the field of child welfare, in which social workers deal with some of the most troubled and damaged children and their families, it is imperative to have some basis for understanding the strange, often destructive, reactions of those caught up in the misery, this is not to say it is all misery or to discount the observable evidence that some children (and indeed adults) are amazingly resilient (Daniel 1999, Gilligan 1999, Werner 2000).

No doubt some of this resilience is due to basic personality traits. But psychoanalytic theories of child development do not only offer explanation for negative outcomes, they suggest a rationale for positive 'against the odds' outcomes. For example, the internalisation of past good experiences can be kept intact even when a child has been deeply hurt.

As I write this, I am thinking of a microscope; the analogy is at once attractive and repugnant. The social worker does not want to peer at another human being, as at a collection of cells. The process of engaging with another human being (usually in difficulty) is in some ways the opposite of microscopic examination. But (as this book illustrates so graphically), this process of engagement necessitates intense concentration on the feelings and actions of the 'client' at certain moments. Only in this way can the worker begin to grasp what is going on. The process is 'microscopic' in the sense that it looks in enlarged detail at what is being presented. These observations can then be used for reflection about the meaning of what is seen. Thus, in one particular way, a good social work interview should be analogous to a psychoanalytic encounter. The listening should be attuned and refined to the feelings being presented, whether it is in the rough drawings of a child or the apparent ramblings of an angry mother. There are many differences between these two modes of professional interaction and the analogy should not be taken too far. It is used here to emphasise the critical need in child welfare practice for *concentrated empathy*, which includes detailed observations. This has to be grounded in a suitable body of theory, if we are to make sense of what we observe and feel.

In my view, the varied, and sometimes conflicting, theories which form part of the psychoanalytic family tree offer the best basis for understanding what is going on beneath the surface of the troubled waters in which deprived and damaged children swim and sometimes sink. (Do we see when they are 'not waving but drowning'; as Stevie Smith put it?) Such theories are neither infallible nor complete. They are part of the search for meaning in what is said and what is done. But they are good enough to improve practice and much, much better than the present atheoretical stance adopted by many social workers. Such a stance may be a consequence of poor education or it may be a kind of cover for hidden assumptions – which can be dangerous.

There are a number of assumptions based on psychoanalytic theories, which are indispensable to good practice in child welfare.

Past experiences affect current attitudes and behaviour

This is now commonplace, even platitudinous. Yet, as Howe (1997) has argued the importance of such links is all too frequently passed over. For example, the crucial work of assessment, these links are too often missing. Whilst there is room for detailed argument as to the ways the past and present interact, it is flying in the face of a substantial body of evidence if the story of an individual's life journey is not taken into account.

We are not always consciously aware of the ways in which experiences affect behaviour

Again, this may seem self evident; it is part of the discourse of a sophisticated society. But, in reality, most of us have only limited self-awareness of the ways in which the past has affected us. The turmoil and disruption surrounding the past lives of children and adults with whom social workers work makes it inevitable that many of them will have little awareness of the interaction between experience and behaviour in their own lives. It is sometimes part of the social workers' task to facilitate such awareness. This is a sensitive area, requiring the use of professional judgement. Awareness in itself is not 'a good'; the goal is to enable a greater degree of control over behaviour. This is not achieved simply through 'awareness'; it is achieved through facing the pain of past experiences, understanding something of its effects and being supported in the process to move on. Social workers cannot always work in this way but it remains a key element in the role; for example, when a child or young person is fearful, angry or desolate at the prospect of going to a foster home because of unacknowledged and unresolved mourning about past losses. Revisiting feelings about the past may be essential to move forward.

Client may have feelings about the worker that derive from other (sometimes unconscious), unconnected experiences

This is a looser formulation of the psychoanalytic concepts of transference and counter transference. It is often essential to examine the dynamics of the worker–client relationship in which fundamental, primitive and sometimes explosive emotions are embedded. Whilst this is true to an extent of all social work, in child welfare practice in particular, there is much basic pain. There are open wounds and there are angry scars, from rejection, abuse and neglect. There is guilt, anger and depression in abundance. It is inevitable that feelings on both sides, however contained or hidden, are powerful. The worker cannot and should not be immune and has a profound responsibility to manage these transactions ethically and sensitively. In my opinion, opportunities to examine and reflect upon these processes are as essential in social work in this field as in psychotherapy, even if they are differently focused and organised.

In sum, in child welfare practice, social workers need theory and skills which help them understand the complex emotional dynamics affecting the attitudes and behaviour of the parties involved, workers included. Only in this way can they begin to grapple with the dilemmas and dangers which routinely confront them. psychoanalytic theories, and the ways of thinking which they foster, provide an extremely important context, within which to practice safely and creatively.

How important was psychoanalytic theory in the early years of British social work?

The period in question spans about twenty years, 1950–1970. During that time, there were major developments in social work and in social work education. The establishment in 1948 of Childrens' Departments in local authorities, following the passing of the Children Act in 1948, was a major step in consolidating statutory services for deprived children. It was primarily concerned with 'children in care' (or 'looked after' as we now say) but led to a focus also on services for children in need, or in danger, in their own homes. One impetus for the creation of these departments came from the inquiry into the death of Dennis O'Neill, a foster child, at the hands of his foster parents (Monkton 1945). But of greater significance was the Curtis Committee which reported on the position of children 'in care' and found it wanting (Curtis 1946). This report itself should be seen in the context of wartime experiences with evacuated children, large numbers of whom were sent to the country from London and other large urban centres. In these years, psychoanalytically orientated people played significant roles. For example, Anna Freud's work with children in a Hampstead nursery made a significant contribution to the growing awareness of the effects of separation on young children. In terms of their impact on social work, the work of Clare and Donald Winnicott, rooted in psychoanalytic theory, was crucial. Their work with evacuated children in Oxfordshire during the war has recently been well documented in a biography of Clare (Kanter 2004). From this point until the 1970s, Clare, herself a psychiatric social worker, gained a unique position of influence on social work. She directed the first child care course at the LSE and worked within the Home Office on a programme of expansion of training courses. She worked with huge energy (and was whole heartedly supported by Donald) and had a national voice at numerous professional conferences.

It should be remembered that, in the very early days, there were only three such 'child care courses'. The major expansion began in the mid-1960s. In the UK, Clare was the symbol of progressive child care practice. It was, however, a 'home-grown' movement, which took little account of the parallel developments of social work in the USA at that time. (The influence of those big players in the USA on the British scene was to come later.) It is important to understand Clare's teaching was firmly located in the daily reality of child care social work. This is well confirmed in the recent reprinting of her work in Kanter's biography. There is no sense in that writing that the external realities were disregarded or devalued. These early images of the early child care officers were of sturdy practical women, in small untidy cars, packed with dismantled cots, battered toys and potties; a world away from their clinical sisters.

Yet, somehow, the myth was propagated that social workers in child care were 'analysts manqué'. It was simply not true. But it was the case that a significant part of the basic education of child care social workers was based on this body of theory and that there was little attempt to present alternative theory. That is not to say that the importance of other factors relevant to a child's development were ignored: childrens' health and the ill effects of poverty on family life, for example, were well to the fore. What was lacking was a coherent body of knowledge, such as that derived from sociology, to complement the psychoanalytic insights.

Into that incomplete and insecure world of social work came, in the mid-1960s, an onslaught from sociologists and others, such as social policy theorists, who increasingly came to teach directly on social work courses as they rapidly expanded. The late Baroness Wootten launched a preliminary attack in the 1950s (Woolton 1959), 'The social worker has no need to pose as a miniature psychoanalyst or psychiatrist . . . Rather than search for something deeper underneath . . . the social worker would do better to look for something more superficial on top when she is confronted with problems of behaviour'. There was often intense discomfort between these two worlds. Whilst the child care workers rushed about, busy and practical 'in the field', back in the universities and polytechnics there was intense mutual ideological distrust. The influence of Marxist theory, with a world view which appeared to be opposed to psychoanalytic theory was an important element in this. Essentially, social workers were seen by their enemies as papering over the cracks of an unjust and unequal society. Social work, especially that part of it described as 'casework', was seen as a conservative, counter-revolutionary element.

Kanter (2004, pp. 48–51) describes well the difficulty and pain which Clare Winnicott experienced when she went back to the LSE from the Home Office in the early 1970s. She was, one suspects, ill prepared for that ideological turmoil. But the description of those experiences should not be taken as unique or unusual. It was merely played out with a ferocity typical of that institution. What happened at the LSE was mirrored, in more or less similar degree, across the country and during the years until the end of the 1970s. The sad part of this story is that social work teachers were unable to convince critics or sceptics that social work must draw on a range of theories to underpin the nature of their work, which requires them to move between the internal and external worlds of those they seek to help. My own (unsuccessful) attempt to open up this dialogue can be seen in an early article (Stevenson 1971).

> 'The concept of role in sociology and its relationship to the personality of the individual is an area which merits further investigation by social work teachers . . . It is the point at which we must help our students look at the interaction between theories which are complementary. It is this interaction between the social expectation from the individual and his unique capacities which is so significant for understanding certain problems. But this interaction needs to be studied when the essentials of each theoretical position are understood. They are different but they relate to each other. This interaction is at its most subtle in the sphere of family relationships. In family functioning, the models of male and female role and of parenthood are laid down in childhood. Thus individual traits are inextricably bound up with the norms and values which are embodied in concepts of role in a particular society.' (p. 229)

In sum: early social work in child care in the UK was greatly influenced by psychoanalytic ideas. These were not presented in opposition to other theories of individual and social behaviour. However, other theory which can be seen as complementary' was not adequately formulated and incorporated into training at that time. The presentation of psychoanalytic concepts met with angry distrust and misunderstanding – perhaps also fear – on the part of some of those who taught in courses. This was also exacerbated by a sociological critique of social workers' aspirations to professionalism. In hindsight, it can be seen that several factors, some of which are further explored in the next section, conspired to push psychoanalytic theory away from social work before there had been time for an emerging profession to use it appropriately.

What contributed to its continuing fall from favour?

Thus far, the analysis has concentrated on the impact of theoretical or ideological dispute on the development of social work. But that is only a small part of the story; 1970 was a landmark in the development of social services. Childrens' services were amalgamated with other social services in local government into 'social service departments' (Seebohm 1963). Many of us supported the model of a generic social work service, believing that there were common elements which made this professionally feasible and desirable. However, as is so often the case in radical reform, there was little understanding of the skills and resources needed to translate this goal into effective reality. Social service departments struggled with frequent structural change which absorbed the energy of all concerned.

Local government proved inhospitable to an emerging profession; there was growing criticism of social work courses by employers who alleged that they were out of touch with the realities of practice. The mechanisms set up to achieve 'partnership' between training courses and agencies often felt more like power struggles, in which theoretical debate had little place. (The exception was the important but confused 'anti-oppressive' agenda.) The notion of planned professional development for social workers was not translated into reality. (In contrast, nurses ongoing registration depended on such continuing education.)

Into this uncertain and confused world of local government, came, in 1973, the bombshell of the Maria Colwell inquiry (DHSS 1974) which examined the case of this six-year-old child, murdered by her step-father. For the first time, there was a spotlight on social work, as an emerging profession. The report was deeply critical and had a profound effect on social workers. It was to be the first of many inquiries between 1974 and the present. The response of local government management to the anxiety created by these events was to tighten control. This process, explored by Menzies (1970) in a seminal paper in relation to nurses in hospitals, has been profoundly significant. Elaborate systems and structures have been put in place designed to reduce risk of harm to children. Many of these measures can be seen to be sensible and beneficial and it is no part of my argument to deny the necessity for procedures and protocols in the complex world of intra- and interprofessional work in child welfare. However, we have reached a point, perhaps marked by the outcomes of the Victoria Climbié inquiry (2003), at which it is imperative to recognise that these systemic and procedural techniques are not in themselves sufficient to protect children from harm or, indeed, the social workers from damaging censure. As Reder and Duncan (2003) have recently shown, there is a pressing need to examine issues of communication and cooperation at deeper levels and to use theories which illuminate the darker places of our attempts to work with others and, of course, with the families, who our concern is focused. We neglect such theory at our peril.

The challenge is, however, a major one, because social services generally – not just its child welfare services – has been increasingly bureaucratised and managerialised in recent years. Neither of these terms should be read as necessarily negative in connotation. An agency such as a social service department has important and positive bureaucratic characteristics in the sociological sense. There has to be a hierarchy for decision making, accountability for resources and, crucially, systems for the fair allocation of those resources. Similarly, it soon became apparent after 1970 that social service departments were woefully ill-equipped to provide effective and efficient management of (suddenly enlarged) organisations. It was necessary to put in place managerial controls.

So what is wrong? The focus on improvement of performance by procedures, regulation and measurable indicators (a 'tick box culture') has consumed psychic (and physical) energy almost to the exclusion of energy for reflection on the judgements which have to be made. It has also increased anxiety to dangerous levels. The anxiety of the field worker about cases is compounded by the anxiety of managers about targets. There has to be space for thinking about the meaning of what is being seen, heard and experienced. It is within that space that psychoanalytic contribution is so valuable.

In sum: as we moved into the 1970s, the psychoanalytic contribution to child welfare practice was further undermined by the surge of, and pressure towards, the improvement of the techniques of organisational control. Paradoxically, these (usually) sincere attempts to change things for the better have to an extent increased the tension and fear because there has been so little attempt to provide opportunities for understanding the impact of the work and its agency context. There is a real danger that the better local authority workers in child care will seek to deploy their skills in an environment, such as voluntary agencies, where they hope to be better supported and respected as professional people.

What now needs to be done?

There are two inter-related aspects of this question. The first concerns the context within which social workers are educated. Various important changes are taking place at present, including those at post-qualifying level; there is consequently substantial curriculum change. I would like to think that we have come far enough to accept that the ideological battles, fascinating and important as they are to the cognoscenti, should not, and need not, divert us from the sensible use of this group of psychoanalytic theories as one, important element in the development of the skills of social work. Surely we have enough agreed ground on which to base our teaching in this area? If we cannot move forward on this, from what theory are our students going to try to understand some of the most complex feelings and actions of their clients? Without such an attempt, intervention to improve their lot is unguided. Furthermore, workers' awareness of their own reactions will be inadequate. A particular example of this is to be found in a number of cases in which the overt or covert hostility of a parent or care-giver towards the worker has affected the behaviour of the workers and their capacity to ensure the safety of the child. (See for example, the case of Jasmine Beckford (1985).)

Thus, I am arguing for a way of examining peoples' behaviour which takes us 'a layer down'. This is not always necessary or appropriate; for example the widespread use of cognitive behavioural techniques in certain kinds of emotional disturbance is demonstrably valuable. However, it is my contention that this type of approach is not adequate for many of the situations in which a worker in child welfare routinely finds his- or herself. This book offers valuable introduction to a wide range of theory from this family tree. Could it be the precursor to a timely debate on how these valuable insights can be incorporated into the corpus of social work education and how they are to be utilised in practice?

The second aspect of 'what needs to be done' lies not in education but in the agencies. It is useless to promote an approach to theory, which involves reflection and the raising of awareness of the self and others, unless the host agency respects its importance and facilitates its development. This is a huge agenda, at first sight very daunting. What we have to think about is how to create a climate and culture which allows this way of thinking to flourish. Much-used words like 'space' and 'reflection' immediately suggest 'time' to the managerially challenged. But maybe we have reached a point when it must be acknowledged that time needs to be used differently if the goal of better practice (and fewer disasters) is to be met.

There are a number of strategies and changes which could make a substantial difference to the organisational culture. Of particular significance is the use of supervision as a tool for performance development, not simply for managerial control. (I do not dispute the need for the latter.) It may be that these two elements in supervision could be separated. For example, work which I undertook in one local authority suggested the possibility of increased peer group consultation for experienced workers, with focused case discussion at its heart. A second, essential, requirement for improvement lies in tailored plans for individual professional development – one strand of which should be learning about aspects of psychoanalytic theory. A third way of introducing these reflective processes is through interprofessional case-focused meetings, with facilitation. This was very successfully achieved in Nottingham, in relation to cases of serious neglect (Glennie et al. 1998).

The well-worn maxim of 'where there's a will there's a way' is, of course, central to this discussion. Difficult as the situation is for many agencies, especially local authorities in urban areas, a willingness to offer some opportunities for a changed style of working might pay dividends in terms of staff morale. Staff recruitment and retention are critical to organisational effectiveness. As agencies seek to address these problems, one vital component will be the development of a culture which is underpinned by respect for professional development. This entails the creation of opportunities for the continuing integration of theory and practice. Close scrutiny of practice from the perspective of psychoanalytic theory could be a particularly valuable element in such processes.

In conclusion: a 'changed style of working' must be underpinned by the use of concepts and theories designed better to understand what is happening to workers and their clients. There has been much talk about 'evidence based practice' in recent years. That is a laudable objective, provided we are clear as to what we consider to be 'evidence'. Those who believe, as I do, that there are substantial aspects of psychoanalytic theory which can be 'evidenced', must be prepared to make explicit their grounds for so believing.

I hope that this book will be taken seriously by those who are committed to the improvement of child welfare practice and – importantly – to the re-energising of its work force. It deserves to be.

Olive Stevenson

References

Beckford J (1985) *A child in trust: report of panel of inquiry*. London, London Borough of Brent.

Curtis Committee (1946) *Report on the care of children committee*. London, HMSO. Cmnd. 6922.

Daniel B (1999) A picture of powerlessness: an exploration of child neglect and ways in which social workers and parents can be empowered towards efficacy. *International Journal of Child and Family Welfare* 4(3): 209–220.

Department of Health and Social Security (1974) *Maria Colwell Inquiry: Report into the care and supervision provided in relation to Maria Colwell*. London, HMSO.

Gilligan R (1999). Enhancing the resilience of children and young people in public care by mentoring their talents and interests. *Child and Family Social Work* 4(3): 187–196.

Glennie S, Cruden B, Thorn J (1998) *Neglected Children: Maintaining hope, optimism and direction*. Notts County and City Area Child Protection Committees.

Howe D (1997) Psychosocial and relationship-based theories for child and family social work: political philosophy, psychology and welfare practice. *Child and Family Social Work* 2: 161–169.

Kanter J (ed.) (2004) *Face to face with children. The life and work of Clare Winnicott*. London and New York, Karnac.

Lord Laming (2003) *The Victoria Climbié Inquiry*. London; The Stationery Office. Cmnd. 5730.

Menzies IEP (1970) reprinted in *Containing Anxiety in Institutions*. London, Free Association Books (1988).

Monkton W (1945) *Report on the circumstances which led to the boarding out of Dennis and Terence O'Neill*. London, HMSO. Cmnd. 6636.

Reder P, Duncan S (2003) Understanding communication in child protection networks. *Child Abuse Review* 12(2).

Seebohm Report (1968) *Report of the committee on local authority and allied personal social services*. London, HMSO. Cmnd 3703.

Stevenson O (1971) Knowledge for social work. *British Journal of Social Work* **1**(2): 225–238.

Werner E (2000) Protection factors and individual resilience. In Schonkoff J, Meisels S (eds) *The Handbook of Childhood Intervention*. Cambridge University Press.

Wootton B (1959) *Social Science and Social Pathology*. London, Routledge.

Preface

It gives me great pleasure to write a preface for this book, which I hope will make a significant contribution to the further development of social work in Britain and other countries. The book is published at an important moment in the history of the social work profession in Britain. For the first time social care workers are now part of a registered profession. In past decades the question of professional registration was often a subject of heated debate between those who were convinced of its need if social work was to establish itself within the multidisciplinary professional field, and those who saw this as a kind of betrayal of the marginalised and often powerless people who use our services. In my view this is a false antithesis. To be professionalised does not imply blind conformity, or complacency. Service users need professionals to be politically and professionally potent if they are to work, and advocate, successfully in their interests.

Those who use our services also need, and all the evidence suggests want, us to be competent at what we do while also refusing the role of distanced expert. The therapeutic specialisms within social work have not always managed this tension as well as they might have done. Psychoanalytically based social work practice is rooted in a complex and highly developed theoretical base that can attract suspicion and hostility. We have not always been astute in finding ways to render these ideas more accessible and familiar. This is despite the fact that, as Olive Stevenson notes in her foreword, many psychoanalytic concepts have passed into our ordinary language and understanding of human nature. One strength of this book is that it aims to communicate about psychoanalytic theory and practice in an accessible and grounded way. Its central purpose is to show that psychoanalytic social work and clinical practice is both a useful and a necessary part of the repertoire of any modern social work service.

But, in a climate shaped by the demands of evidence-based practice, the sceptic may legitimately ask about the empirical justification for including psychoanalytic theories and methods in both the core training of social workers and in the range of service provision offered by hard-pressed commissioners. Here we enter more complicated territory. Social work in common with the profession of psychoanalytic psychotherapy, has been reluctant and slow to engage with this new culture. This is to be explained partly by the familiar (but again largely phoney) cultural tension between the clinical and practice 'arts' and the research and social policy 'sciences'. Good experimental research designs in the applied social sciences are notoriously hard to achieve, but this is not a reason to abandon the quest. Equally, there is much we need to know about social work and psychotherapeutic practice that cannot be quantified. A rich and diverse tradition of qualitative, descriptive and clinically based research methodologies has evolved in recent decades. For good philosophical reasons but also for reasons that have more to do with intellectual defensiveness, creative interchange between different research paradigms has been hard to achieve. We need to advance beyond this state of affairs, and the present book offers some indications of the basis on which this might be achieved.

At the level of theory, there are some extremely encouraging developments that support the possibility of progress, and provide a real basis for demonstrating the central relevance of psychoanalytic social work practice in modern welfare programmes. Advances in the neurosciences have shown that early human development is a matter of two-way interaction between the brain and the socio-emotional environment. The brain is, quite literally, a 'social organ' and does not develop in the absence of the right emotional and psycho-social conditions; equally, well-conducted studies have shown that early impairments to organic and hence emotional and relational functioning (as a result of child neglect for example) can be wholly or partly repaired through later therapeutic and environmental provision. This has led one researcher and clinician to spell out the implications for social policy like this: 'Communities shape experiences that change brains'. The role of well-trained and supervised psychoanalytic social work practitioners in a vision of welfare provision founded on these insights is self-evident – or one might hope that it would be.

The fact that it is not self-evident raises questions about how the social work profession as a whole can re-assert its rightful place within the panoply of modern mental health and welfare delivery. Research is part of the answer, but a confident relationship to theories that are useful for practice, and tested in practice, is another. The present book is a powerful contribution to re-establishing the possibility of a social work profession that is less afraid of theoretical depth, confident but not doctrinaire about the role of psychoanalytic practice in relation to other methodologies, and above all open to the fact of social, professional and policy change without fear of loss of professional identity.

Andrew Cooper
Professor of Social Work,
The Tavistock Clinic and the
University of East London

How to use this book

Marion Bower

The purpose of this book is to introduce social workers to some key psychoanalytic theories particularly those of Freud, Klein and Bion and some of the modern British psychoanalytic thinkers. It is not intended as a blueprint for all aspects of childcare social work. However, all the chapters cover issues which are bread and butter to social work practitioners. This includes the assessment of risk to self or others, communicating with vulnerable and disturbed people of all ages, working with people who have been abused or traumatised, and working with families and professional systems. These familiar topics will be approached from a new perspective.

Each chapter can stand on its own, however, reading the book is intended to be a cumulative experience as the reader will encounter the same ideas in different contexts which I think is a helpful way of learning them, and I will suggest which chapters can helpfully be read together.

There has been no consistent attempt to use psychoanalytic thinking in mainstream social work for over 25 years, and much of the work described takes place in specialist settings. However many of the authors are social workers and all have many years experience in working with social services.

Some of the work described in the book, particularly assessment, short term interventions and the role of supervision (Chapters 4, 5, 9, 14 and 15) can be translated very directly into mainstream social work practice. Some chapters which describe psychotherapy or the working of more specialised therapeutic services do not have the same equivalence. I am not advocating that social workers act like psychotherapists, each has something to offer and our clients need what social work has to offer. However readers will have to do more work to link these ideas to their role and task as social workers. I have included the chapters on therapy for two reasons.

Firstly, because they throw light on issues which are very central for social work. This includes the effects of deprivation and trauma on the inner world, understanding identity and the impact of disability on families. These ideas have implications not only for direct work with clients, but also for agency policies.

The second reason for including accounts of therapeutic work is to look in detail at the process of change in individuals and families. There is very little discussion in contemporary social work literature about how people can be helped to change, and what sort of change can realistically be expected. A distinction needs to be made between behavioural change or compliance, and internal change, which is harder to achieve. Social workers often refer to therapeutic services and they need to know when this is appropriate, what to expect and how to support the work. *Even more importantly social workers need to know how their own work brings about personal change and how this can be recognised.*

Most of us go into social work because we want to improve peoples' lives. Society and our employers expect this of us. These expectations are often unrealistically high, driven by conscious and unconscious guilt about how our society treats its most vulnerable members. The difficulties in meeting these expectations can touch on powerful *unconscious* anxieties in ourselves. This is often felt not only as a fear that we might not be able to help, but also as an anxiety of causing damage. These wishes and anxieties were described by Isabel Menzies in a piece of research on the difficulties in retaining nursing staff. (Another aspect of Menzies' work is discussed in Olive Stevenson's Foreword.) Menzies suggested that by nursing sick people, nurses are symbolically repairing damaged figures in their internal world. This means that a sense of personal agency in the work and an element of success are vital for job satisfaction at a very profound level. The same must be true of social work.

However, contact with ill or damaged people arouses a lot of anxiety and this is increased when it is difficult to 'put things right', which is inevitable in clients whose difficulties arise from many sources, some outside our control. This situation is defended against by a variety of personal and institutional defences. These include fragmentation and depersonalisation of the contact with clients, the modern world of 'case management' and tick boxes at its worst. Denial of the extent of the difficulty, often reflected in unrealistic care plans or child protection plans or an over engagement in the fight for rights (this is discussed in Chapter 8). Finally there is an idealisation of the power of 'therapy' or counselling which is attributed to other people. 'We don't do that sort of work.'

These defences, while affording some short-term relief, are damaging in the longer term. As Menzies points out they deny workers the satisfaction of real emotional contact and the sense of personal responsibility for seeing things through, and making realistic changes. Unrealistic expectations can lead to despair or burn out. Many cases will need more than one worker or agency, however even when a social worker is in a co-ordinating role this is only likely to be successful if they have a personal relationship with the client, even if this is a difficult one.

How do these relationships contribute to change? In Chapter 1 I suggest that one of the values of theory is that it allows us to understand and process the experiences we have with our clients. Understanding is not only vital for workers; the experience for a client of being on the receiving end of this type of reflective response is in itself therapeutic. This is why there are often improvements even during an assessment. In the hurly burly of the work it is easy to lose sight of small but, for the client, significant changes that even brief encounters can bring about. For example in Chapter 9 Freedman suggests that a mother's ability to sit through a painful court case was one of the constructive outcomes of the assessment. Colleagues in services which do indepth assessments for the court have expressed surprise that parents have valued their service even if a decision is taken to remove the child. Parents in this situation are rarely offered adequate services for themselves and this may be the most sustained attention they are likely to receive.

The concept of cumulative trauma is easy to understand in our clients. However as Olive Stevenson points out in her Foreword, the concept of an inner world means that good experiences can be retained and built on. A helpful encounter, however brief, can facilitate a client using another worker or service. Social workers sometimes worry about clients becoming 'too attached'. There is a difference between unhelpful dependence and a good attachment. Psychoanalytic theory reminds us that for the client a relationship may be felt to be helpful even if it full of hostility and conflict if the worker is felt to be trying to tolerate and understand this. The end of this type of worker–client relationship can cause sadness and guilt for both worker and client. If the worker can tolerate this and help the client face it, they are helping the client take an important developmental step.

As workers we need moments of meaning and success to support our sense of professional worth. Understanding psychoanalytic theory increases our capacity to create and recognise such moments and supports our tolerance of the limitations of what can be achieved.

Key themes in the book

This section describes the themes in each chapter and how these can link with social work practice. It also indicates which chapters can be usefully read together. The book is divided into four sections. The first section 'A framework for practice' looks at theories, research and how change takes place. Chapter 1 is a summary of some of the psychoanalytic ideas in the book and should be read first. Chapter 2 by Briggs, looks at a number of different ways in which psychoanalytic research can be conducted, and what can be learned from these different approaches. It also looks at some existing research and its value for social work. Chapter 3 is a detailed account of some individual psychotherapy of a white patient by an Asian psychotherapist. It shows how the patient uses racist thinking as a refuge from knowledge and painful states of mind. It offers a theoretical model to understand this and also shows how the relationship with the therapist brings about a change in this defence.

Understanding and working with children and young people

Chapter 4

This chapter emphasises the importance of carefully examining what we see as part of the assessment process. Youell points out that words like 'settled well', 'good attachment' and 'self contained' may mask a very different reality. Social workers are usually excellent observers but often fail to give full weight to what they see. I think that this is partly the absence of an adequate child development theory which gives meaning to observations. However as Freedman points out in Chapter 9 the denial of reality is a very strong feature in child protection cases and this can get into the workers. Clear descriptions of what has *actually* been seen is a powerful professional tool. Courts are staffed by human beings who are as likely to be convinced by a careful description of behaviours and emotional states as the rest of us.

Chapter 5

This chapter looks at two very difficult aspects of work with children. Firstly, the anxieties about damage aroused in work with children who have been damaged not only in their original family but also by the care system itself. It also discusses the difficulties of establishing the feelings of children torn by conflicting loyalties. Daniel discusses the importance of theory, in this case systemic theory, in helping a worker find a helpful position, open-minded and aware of how they fit into the wider network.

It may seem surprising to find a systemic chapter in this book. However as well as its value in itself I wanted to show that there are considerable overlaps between systemic and psychoanalytic thinking. As Daniel points out there is increasing emphasis in systemic practice on the relationship with the therapist. In psychoanalytic practice there is an increasing interest in work with families and networks (see Chapters 12 and 13).

Chapter 6

This chapter describes clinical research with sexually abused girls. It demonstrates the importance of combining psychotherapy with social work support for parents and carers. Both this chapter and Chapter 7 make it clear that therapy can never be a substitute for adequate care. However the most surprising finding from this research is the discovery that *for the girls* the most urgent issue was the loss of early maternal care and containment, either through actual loss of the mother or her emotional unavailability. The first step in recovery was the internalisation of the therapists containing function (in the sense described by Bion), which allowed the girls to begin to process their experiences of abuse.

These findings have important implications for understanding children and adults who have suffered abuse or trauma (see also Chapter 14). Where there has been no early experience of containment the child not only suffers from the trauma but has no way of processing it. It also makes it clear that attempts to work with the experience of trauma before some containment is established can be felt as re-traumatisation. This is a more technical version of the old social work principle of 'starting where the client is at'.

Chapter 7

This chapter describes psychotherapy with an African Caribbean boy whose foster placement has broken down. Martin is underachieving in school and is making violent attacks on vulnerable children. This is one of the most important chapters in this book as it provides an in depth account of the pain and the difficulty of making psychological changes which bring us into contact with painful emotional realities. In Martin's case this includes the loss of his father and the death of his mother, as well as changes of placement.

Williams describes a combination of external deprivation combined with a psychological defence that denies both dependency and the need for help, these emotions are projected onto others. Martin is proud of having 'no feelings'. These defences may allow a child to survive major losses and upheavals, but in the longer run prevent their needs being met or even recognised. Not only may this produce a sort of secondary deprivation, but as Williams suggests can contribute to placement breakdown because of its impact on carers who are left feeling devalued or useless. Understanding these processes should be an important part of the training of foster parents.

Williams also illustrates very vividly some of the unconscious processes which underlie the formation of personal identity and racist behaviour. Martin identifies with *his version* of his dead mother, cold, hard and narcissistic. The Pakistanis who he attacks and despises represent the despised vulnerable aspects of himself. (At the time this chapter was written Pakistanis were relatively recent immigrants to Britain and may also represent some of his experiences or feelings about being a black child in a white foster family.) This chapter should be read in conjunction with Chapter 3. It illustrates how psychoanalytic theory not only contributes to the understanding of racism, but can actually be used to change it.

Chapter 8

Simpson discusses some of the powerful unconscious responses to disability which he suggests are universal, although expressed differently in different cultures. These include hostility, fear and disgust. (Attitudes of this sort may underlie the high prevalence of abuse of the disabled.) He discusses the impact of a learning disabled child on the parents and their marriage.

One of the very important messages of this chapter is that parental difficulties in facing the reality of their child's disability, which may involve idealisation or stress on what the child can do, can be additionally disabling for the child, as it may leave the child feeling that no one can face what they are really like. Simpson makes it clear that a very important task for those working with children with disabilities is to help parents mourn the child they did not have. He makes it clear that this is not an alternative to advocacy and the fight for resources, but that these tasks should not become a refuge from facing the pain.

I think feelings like this are also a factor in workers who care for children with disabilities. When I worked with a school for children with severe disabilities I noticed that when a child died, the staff not only felt the pain of loss, but pain of guilt about half conscious feelings that some of the children 'would be better off dead'.

Parent, families and professional networks

Chapter 9

This chapter describes an approach to the assessment of the capacity of parents to care for their child, which is used by a specialist service, the Portman clinic. However in my view the principles which underlie this approach can and should be part of all social work assessments where there are child protection concerns.

Firstly, this is the assessment of parents not only as individuals but as a couple. Freedman shows how for some couples mutual projective identification can be used to avoid aspects of themselves and the reality of their attitudes toward their children. She describes a couple who have created a shared myth that the problem is the father's 'anger management'. This masked the mother's hostility towards her children. The effect of this defence is to create a 'dangerous couple' where the mother subtly colludes with the father's abuse. This *denial of emotional reality* had got into the social services department who requested the assessment, as they already had evidence of serious injuries while the children were in their mother's care. Professional gender stereotypes can feed into these defensive systems.

Secondly, Freedman describes a psychological position from which an assessment needs to be made. Drawing on Britton's concept of a 'third position' she suggests that the assessor's role is to *understand* how the parents function and what their capacity is to face reality and use help to make changes. The importance of this position is that it is nonjudgemental and avoids a see-saw of blame by examining the couple as a system.

Chapters 10 and 11

These chapters look at borderline personality disorder and drug and alcohol problems from the perspective of adult services. They provide a perspective on the psychological understanding and treatment of these difficulties which will be of interest to those who work in both adult and child and adolescent services. For those who work in child and family services, adults with these types of difficulties are seen as 'parents' and the seriousness of their difficulties and the type of help they need to change can easily be ignored. Those who work in adult services can ignore the fact that their clients may also be parents and what this might mean for their children. Both Weegman and Mishan examine the emotional impact on children of a parent who is addicted to drugs and alcohol or has a personality disorder, and consider how this affects them when they become parents themselves.

Both Weegman and Mishan also look at the powerful impact on the worker of these types of difficulties, in particular the projection of guilt, inadequacy or omnipotence. These projections feel 'real' and are therefore a real hazard in the work.

Chapter 12

This chapter discusses the difficulties of working with families where there is chronic abuse or neglect, often occurring across several generations. It shows how the concept of pathological defensive organisations, developed in work with individuals, can be extended to understand family functioning.

The idea of the 'Mafia' a cruel and ruthless organisation which offers 'protection' to the vulnerable and demands total loyalty is used to understand families which function like a gang. These families regard professional intervention as the problem, as it threatens their abusive system of 'care' which functions as a defence against catastrophic anxiety and breakdown in individual members. Professionals who challenge the family's view of themselves will be subject to subtle or serious threats of violence. I suggest this lies behind some of the apparently inexplicable professional failures to recognise gross abuse.

Further examples of these defences operating at an individual level can be found in Chapters 3, 7 and 11.

Chapter 13

This chapter opens up the thinking about work with individuals and families into a discussion of the functioning of professional networks. Britton describes a phenomenon which is familiar, the way in which professional networks can come to mirror the families with whom they are working. He suggests that what may appear as professional activity is actually maintaining the family status quo, the cast changes but the plot remains the same. This may appear as professional inertia or precipitate action. Often increasing numbers of professionals are added without there being any change in the problem.

Britton examines in detail the anxieties and psychological processes which underlie these problems. He also advocates the need for facing the limitations of what can be achieved and taking 'small but necessary steps'. Both this chapter and the previous one show how psychoanalytic theories can help our thinking about families and professional systems and form a bridge between psychoanalytic and systems thinking.

Professional stresses and supports

Chapter 14

This chapter describes two intensely stressful aspects of working with refugees. Firstly, the terrible experiences of loss, violence and abuse they have experienced, this can be particularly poignant in working with unaccompanied minors. Initially there may be no way of mentally processing these experiences and unbearable emotional states may be projected into those around them. Fox discusses the type of support workers need to contain distress of this intensity. This chapter also raises the difficulty of facing the pain of limited resources available to those who really need them. This may be particularly acute for social services departments and social workers who face the limitations on the type of housing and care available. Part of the difficulty may be how different individuals and institutions cope with guilt.

Inexperienced or unsupported workers may be exposed to a double burden of pain both from the client, and the sense of guilt about not being able to provide the necessary material resources. As Fox points out, the role of supervision is both to help the worker process the emotional experience as well as tolerate the limitations of what can be provided.

Chapter 15

This chapter also examines an intensely stressful area of work, with victims of sexual abuse. Agass describes how disturbing experiences are not only projected, but the worker may be nudged into enactments in which they may be cast in the role of abuser or abused. Agass suggests that there is a crucial need for workers to process their countertransference, and provides a fresh perspective on Bion's concept of containment which runs the risk of becoming a psychoanalytic cliché. Drawing on a paper by Carpy, Agass suggests that an important aspect of containment is that the worker *must be affected* by what is projected and engage in a struggle to manage it. It is the observation of the worker's response to what is projected and their struggle to manage which is therapeutic for the client. (If the worker seems unaffected the client may project with increasing intensity.)

The difficulty of this task cannot be overemphasised, particularly as there has been a loss of the type of casework supervision so clearly described by Agass. However it is important not to simply bemoan this loss. Social workers need to fight for this type of support, and the organisations in Appendix 1 can offer help in this task. Agass also makes the point so rarely made in social work that personal therapy can both protect and enhance a worker's personal resources. Not everyone may want or be able to afford this, but details of reduced fee schemes are also in Appendix 1. We need to be active and resourceful not only on behalf of our clients, but of ourselves.

Acknowledgements

Chapter 4. An earlier version of this chapter was published in *Surviving Space: Paper on Infant Observation*. Edited by Andrew Briggs. (Karnac, London, 2002).

Chapter 6. An earlier version of this paper was published in 'Psychoanalytic Psychotherapy' 15(1). (2001).

Chapter 7. This chapter was originally published in *Internal Landscapes Foreign Bodies* by Graeme Williams. (Duckworth, London, 1997).

Chapter 9. The chapter was originally published in *Brief Encounters with Couples: some Analytical Perspective*. Edited by Frances Grier (Karnac, London, 2001).

Chapter 13. This chapter was originally published in *Psychotherapy with Families: An Analytic Approach*. Edited by Sally Box et al (Routledge, London, 1981).

Chapter 14. An earlier version of this paper was published in 'The Journal of Social Work Practice' 16(2). (2002).

Chapter 15. This paper draws on two previously published papers: 'Containment, supervision and abuse' in *Psychodynamic Perspectives on Abuse: The Cost of Fear* edited by Una McCluskey and Carol-Ann Hooper (Jessica Kingsley Publishers, London 2000); and 'Countertransference, supervision and the reflection process' in *Journal of Social Work Practice* 16(2). (2002).

I would like to thank my social work colleagues at the Tavistock Clinic for their encouragement and support for this project. Particularly Dr Stephen Briggs and Professor Andrew Cooper.

I would also like to thank colleagues and students from the Royal Holloway PQ in childcare who made me aware that interest in psychoanalytic thinking was still alive in social work.

The painting on the cover 'Meravigliare il Rosso' is used with kind permission from the artist Irma Irsara.

Finally, I would like to express my gratitude to my family: my husband Steve and my sons, Jacob and Bruno.

This book is dedicated to the memory of my parents Sanny and Yetta Peterson.

Marion Bower

Part 1
A framework for practice

1 Psychoanalytic theories for social work practice

Marion Bower

This is the first British book for nearly thirty years to be exclusively devoted to the use of psychoanalytic theories in social work practice. After thirty years of neglect or hostility why does social work need psychoanalysis now?

One of the uniquely valuable aspects of social work is the balance it holds between understanding and working with the internal and external realities of client's lives. This balance of course is an ideal and in reality workers may move between internal and external considerations, and between action and reflection. However on the larger scale the profession has undergone two major swings in the last fifty years. Initially there was a move towards psychoanalytic theory; however these ideas were never given time to be adequately integrated with the complexities of social work practice. From the 1970s onwards social work has been dominated by a sociological perspective which has stressed external factors, poverty, deprivation, trauma and racism coupled with a stress on the values of the profession. Unfortunately this has not been balanced with a psychological model which takes into account the internal world and the interaction of external and internal realities.

Currently it seems to me that there is a hole in the middle of social work where a comprehensive, coherent model of human personality and emotional development should be. The introduction of attachment theory has been helpful, particularly in childcare social work, and as a research tool. However as its name suggests it covers a very specific area of human experience. Psychoanalysis covers a wider area of human experience; it also has well-researched interventions in the areas of human behaviour which concern social work. Psychoanalytic theory provides a model of how external adversity impacts on the individual or family and becomes part of their internal world. These of course are rational reasons for adopting psychoanalytic theory which I shall return to below. However it is in the area of emotion and irrationality that the loss of psychoanalytic theory has been particularly damaging to social work.

Although emotional disturbance and the power of the unconscious internal world have been pushed to the edges of social work training, they are central aspects of our client's lives and make their presence powerfully felt in the relationships between clients and workers. Some clients are grateful for our help; however many are hostile, suspicious, critical or unco-operative. Most social workers have known clients who reject or spoil potentially helpful interventions or services, or who repeatedly put themselves in damaging or dangerous positions despite attempts to stop them or offer alternatives. This sort of behaviour is often rationalised although the rationalisations are rarely entirely convincing. Clients bring us into even closer contact with their internal world through their emotional impact on the worker. This can be gross and overt, or subtle and insidious. Workers may feel confused, fragmented, inadequate, despairing or enraged. The impact on the worker may go beyond feelings, and workers may find themselves behaving in ways which are not typical of them, for example being punitive or indulgent.

These experiences are taken for granted yet they are part of what we mean when we talk about being 'bombarded' by the work. One of the most satisfying aspects of teaching psychoanalytic theory to experienced social workers is the interest and excitement that workers feel when they discover that there is a theory which explains these emotional experiences and shows how they can be harnessed as a professional tool. I have written elsewhere (Bower 2003) on the importance of a theory which is congruent with the realities of practice to enable social workers to process their experiences with clients. I think that the absence of theory which makes sense of disturbing aspects of the work is a major contributor to stress in social work.

The loss of psychoanalytic theory from social work has opened up a gulf between what is taught and the realities of encounters with clients. However, if psychoanalytic theory is to be reintegrated into social work it has to take account of the realities of current social work practice. Therapeutic social work will remain a specialist option, but all contact with clients has therapeutic potential. Many workers will have a series of brief encounters with clients as part of an assessment or case management role; others will have opportunities for longer-term work. Whatever the situation there will be a need to understand the relationship with the client and what aspects of the relationship can help bring about change or even help a client make use of a service.

It is important to emphasise that the reintegration of a psychoanalytic perspective into social work is not a superior alternative to a sociological/structural perspective. Psychoanalytic theory provides additional evidence of the importance of external and environmental factors in peoples' lives. It is not possible to explore or work with the inner world without a proper structure for the work. The first priority for a homeless refugee is housing; therapy is not a substitute for adequate parental care. Holding two different perspectives is professionally stressful. Social work prides itself on working with and respecting difference, if these different views can be held together in a creative balance internally it will strengthen us professionally.

Anyone who is interested in using psychoanalytic theory in their practice will also need to make the time and effort to really get to know it properly. In my experience a great deal of the teaching of psychoanalytic theory in social work is inaccurate, distorted or out of date. During the thirty years in which psychoanalysis and social work have been estranged there has been an explosive development in theory and practice applications. An increasing number of very disturbed patients seen in private and public psychoanalytic and psychotherapy practice have led to new developments in theory. Psychoanalytically informed workers in the public sector are now working with many of the same client groups as social workers. This includes adult and child victims of abuse, children in the care system, refugees, and clients with personality disorders, drug and alcohol problems. Some of this work is on an individual basis, but there is a growing development of work with families, groups and the sort of complex interventions we use in social work practice. Psychoanalytic theory is also being used to understand racism, attacks on welfare and other policy issues. There is a growing body of research on the effectiveness of psychotherapy and psychoanalytically informed interventions (see Chapter 2).

Some of this work is represented in the *Journal of Social Work Practice*; however the majority of it is in journals or texts not readily available or well known to social workers. One of the purposes of this book is to make some of this work available to social workers. More than half the chapters are written by social workers and all the authors work closely with mainstream social services. Some of the work will translate very directly into social work practice; other chapters provide a framework of understanding which will need to be adapted to the social work task. The chapter on using this book suggests possible applications of some of the ideas and practices discussed in the chapters.

The rest of this chapter summarises areas of Freud's thinking which remain fundamental to the psychoanalytic approach. It also introduces key ideas and recent developments in modern British psychoanalytic thinking which are particularly relevant to social work. These ideas are developed further in other chapters in the book. I think that it is easier to understand ideas if they are placed in a context and something is known of how and why they developed so I shall start off with a bit of psychoanalytic family history.

Those who are familiar with modern British psychoanalytic theory will be aware that there is a concentration on the work of Melanie Klein and her followers and less on the modern Freudians, Winnicott and the Independent group. There are a number of reasons for this. Firstly, these are the ideas which I personally know best and find particularly helpful as a social worker. Secondly, by concentrating on a core set of ideas which reappear in each chapter, readers will gain a clearer understanding of the ideas and how they are used. Finally, I believe that there is a limit on how many theories or techniques of intervention anyone can really absorb. I think that professional development in social work involves an increasing depth of knowledge and understanding in key areas of knowledge, this forms a secure base from which further knowledge can be added.

Psychoanalytic theory, some history and context

For many people psychoanalysis means the ideas developed by Freud. This is true to the extent that psychoanalysis retains many of Freud's key concepts, however the theory has developed rapidly. Freud himself was a constant innovator always willing to discard an idea if it did not fit with new evidence and experience. As a result he made some radical changes in his own theory and laid down the seeds for further new developments. From the beginning Freud was keen on practical applications of psychoanalysis outside the consulting room, from the earliest years of its development psychoanalysts worked with disturbed children, in psychiatric hospitals and provided the forerunner of modern child guidance clinics.

In this book I am mostly concentrating on the developments of Freud's ideas by a group of very talented and innovatory psychoanalysts living in Britain since the Second World War. Some of the earliest members of the group, like Freud and his daughter Anna were refugees from Nazi persecution. However, Melanie Klein, who was the catalyst for a great deal of new development, came to England in 1927 as she found the British Psychoanalytic Society more receptive to some of the radical new ideas she was developing about children.

The Second World War provided a huge impetus to the practical application of psychoanalytic understanding. Wilfred Bion and other analysts worked with traumatised soldiers developing groupwork techniques and a therapeutic community to restore self respect. Anna Freud ran nurseries establishing the principle of family groups and key workers. A range of services was developed to meet the needs of children affected by evacuation, displacement and other disturbances. After the war psychoanalysts continued to be involved in innovatory practice with direct relevance to social work. James Robertson who started his career working for Anna Freud trained as a social worker and a psychoanalyst, and went on to make the films of young children which had a radical impact on how young children are cared for in hospitals and nurseries. He and his wife pioneered the use of foster care.

It is not widely known that John Bowlby, the founder of attachment theory, was a psychoanalyst whose work was supervised by Melanie Klein. Clearly Bowlby and Klein had major differences of opinion, however it is interesting that the modern version of attachment theory with its concepts of internal schemas and working models bears a considerable similarity to Klein's concept of internal object relations. Clare and Donald Winnicott are psychoanalysts whose influence on childcare practice is well known; both were closely associated with Klein and introduced some of her ideas and others of their own into social work practice.

After the war British psychoanalysts increasingly worked with patients who were psychotic or suffered from borderline personality disorder. This work was stimulated and aided by Klein's theoretical developments (described below). Experiences with this group of very disturbed patients also stimulated the development of new theories and techniques. Understanding this group of patients is very significant for social workers. Personality disorder is frequently linked to past histories of abuse and a large number of clients have these problems even if there is no formal diagnosis. Changes in psychiatric practice mean that many more patients with psychotic illness are caring for their children and understanding psychotic states of mind is a crucial professional tool. The Climbie case is an extreme and tragic example of the failure to recognise severe psychological disturbance in a parent or carer.

Freud

The development of psychoanalytic theory and practice was driven by two goals. One was to understand why and how people developed psychological symptoms and the other was how to help them become free of them. Freud's goal was to help his patients fulfil their potential and become free to 'love and to work'. Freud's earliest work was done with hysterical patients who had dramatic and often crippling physical symptoms without there being any physical cause. Both Freud and his colleague Breuer discovered that by allowing their patients to talk freely the symptoms rapidly improved. Freud suggested that these symptoms were symbolic expressions of unconscious thoughts or feelings. These were unconscious because they contained unacceptable sexual or aggressive wishes or feelings linked to significant people in their lives. Bringing these feelings into the open removed the need for the symptom.

This process introduces a fundamental aspect of the psychoanalytic approach. The aim is not a 'cure' by the expert, but to give patients insight into aspects of themselves and what is going on in their mind, understanding the truth about ourselves is potentially liberating and allows us more control of aspects of our lives. Not surprisingly Freud found that his patients were not keen to know or believe unpleasant things about themselves and improvement was often slowed down by resistance. However

Freud noticed that over time his patients developed a relationship to him which was clearly very similar to significant figures in their lives, particularly parents. These early relationships were 'transferred' onto the therapist. Initially he saw this as an irritating obstacle, later he realised that this was a powerful tool which enabled the patient's past relationships to be explored in the current relationship with the therapist. Transference is one area where Freud's ideas were developed by Klein. Freud thought that transference only happened in the context of an analysis, Klein discovered that it pervades all aspects of our ordinary lives, and this includes our relationships with clients.

Freud's experiences with his patients led him to realise the importance of sexuality in early emotional development. This infantile sexuality is different to adult sexuality and becomes transformed in the course of emotional development. This ordinary developmental process can become disrupted. Initially Freud thought that this was caused by a sexual seduction of the child, later he came to believe that these stories of seduction were fantasies. Unfortunately, Freud threw the baby out with the bathwater and we now know that many children are sexually abused. However, awareness of childhood sexuality casts a new light on one of the disturbing aspects of abuse. Something which normally remains a fantasy for the child becomes a disturbing reality. One consequence of abuse can be extreme states of confusion and it is common when talking to victims of abuse to feel very uncertain about what is true and what is not.

From his own self-analysis Freud discovered the 'Oedipus complex'. This is the child's wish to possess or 'marry' the parent of the opposite sex and get rid of the rival of the same sex. For some reason this particular theory of Freud's is dismissed as old fashioned or Eurocentric, although it is readily visible and often expressed by small children from many cultures. 'Love triangles' are a staple of stories and myths from many cultures. Criticisms of the Oedipus complex are often based on a rather literal misunderstanding. Freud suggested that young children have an innate knowledge of the 'facts of life'. In all societies a sperm from a man and an egg from a woman have to come together to form a baby, an event from which by definition we are excluded. The experience of having to share the attention of someone who is deeply important to us is a narcissistic blow which different individuals and cultures manage in different ways. Defences against the awareness of Oedipal reality can involve the denial or distortion of the facts of life, including the differences between the generations, and this is inevitably an important aspect of the thinking of a child abuser.

Freud believed that the child's fear of retribution for forbidden Oedipal wishes led to the resolution of the Oedipal complex by the internalisation of the parents and it is these internal figures who form the core of the 'superego' or conscience. The superego is not necessarily a mirror of the real parents. Freud noticed that people who seemed to have benign parents might have a harsh superego, suggesting that the external world is transformed in the process of internalisation. The concept of internal objects was taken much further by Klein. The word 'object' is used to describe an internal figure because it is the 'object' of an instinct. Freud's model stresses the importance of instinctual drives in human behaviour. Klein followed Freud in this but stressed the object of the instinct, and suggested that from the beginning of life the baby is seeking relationships.

In the years following the First World War Freud, rather understandably, became preoccupied by human aggression and self-destructiveness. This was also prompted by experiences with patients who seemed to cling to illness and suffering, and tended to regress whenever there was any progress in their treatment or their life. There was also the problem of the 'repetition compulsion' the tendency for certain patients to seek out and repeat traumatic experiences over and over again. (We often see this in victims of sexual abuse.) Freud suggested that the re-enactment of trauma served as a way of by-passing its emotional component, what cannot be remembered becomes repeated. It is also a way of trying to gain control of the original experience. From this point of view the repetition compulsion is a form of psychological defence, but one which could be very damaging.

The accumulation of clinical experience no longer fitted Freud's original model of a conflict between the sexual and self-preservative instincts. In 1920 in *'Beyond the Pleasure Principle'* Freud discarded his original model and put forward a new model of a conflict between the life and death instincts. He now saw sexuality as a component of the life instinct. The death instinct derived from the biological trajectory for all life to return to its prior organic state. Psychologically this can be expressed as a longing for oblivion or nirvana, which is a common motive for suicide. Freud suggested that the death instinct is rarely allowed to operate freely as it would present a serious threat to the life of the person. It can be turned outwards in aggression, this process can be observed when murder is followed by suicide. Using his new theory Freud was now able to explain sadism and masochism as fusions of the death and sexual instincts, allowing pleasure to be gained from suffering. The concept of the death instinct was controversial in Freud's lifetime and has remained so. However Klein and many of her followers have demonstrated its clinical usefulness and I will return to this later.

Work with children

Although Freud's discoveries placed enormous emphasis on the formative influence of childhood experience, most of his work was based on a retrospective reconstruction of childhood experience and there had been very few attempts to work with children directly. Freud's daughter Anna was an earlier pioneer of work with children, but she did not believe that children formed a transference to the therapist as the relationship to the parents was still dominant. She initially developed an approach which involved developing an educational alliance, and only worked with older children. Freud, himself an acute observer of children, made a series of observations of the play of an 18-month-old boy. He suggested the little boy's game of throwing a cotton reel and pulling it back over and over again was his way of working through symbolically his mother leaving him and returning. This idea of play as a means both of communication and symbolic working through difficult emotional experiences was taken further by Melanie Klein.

Melanie Klein

Melanie Klein was born in Vienna in 1882. An early marriage and three children put paid to her plans to study medicine. In 1910 she moved to Budapest and had her first encounter with Freud's ideas. This led her to start an analysis with one of Freud's followers, Ferenczi, who encouraged her to begin work with children. By 1922 she had divorced and moved to Berlin to begin an analysis with Karl Abraham. By this point in time it was expected that anyone wanting to work as an analyst should have an analysis themselves, an acceptance that analysts were no different to their patients and needed to know about themselves to be able to tackle the problems of their patients. Although Abraham was a follower of Freud he was already beginning to modify some of Freud's ideas, for example he placed more emphasis on the importance of the mother. Unlike Freud, Abraham was also a psychiatrist and was not afraid to tackle the analysis of psychotic patients, he was able to support Klein as her work with young children led her into disturbing areas of the mind.

Unlike other analysts Klein was interested and willing to work with very young children from 2 or 3 years old. However small children cannot lie on a couch and free associate. Klein's genius was to discover that play is a small child's natural means of communication. Not only does it allow them to explore and master the internal world, but it gives expression to an unconscious inner world of phantasies. Far from not forming a transference to the adult, Klein found that the dependence of young children leads to a very intense transference which could be worked with through the child's play. Klein used very small toys which were 'neutral', little figures of men and women, wild and domestic animals, pencils, paper, string and plasticene. The child could express what was on his or her mind and go at their own pace. Initially Klein was quite shocked by her discoveries, particularly the extent of aggression and anxiety, however, encouraged by Abraham, she found that interpreting this to the child led to a diminishing of anxieties and a reduction of the child's symptoms.

Klein discovered that the internal world of small children was dominated by fantastical figures who were either very good or very bad and cruel. She was particularly struck by the repeated emergence of a very harsh and cruel figure which she suggested was an early form of the superego. Ultimately this led her to a different view to Freud on the development and resolution of the Oedipus complex. Klein believed the Oedipus complex develops earlier and is resolved through the child's love rather than fear of the parents. Understanding this very severe early superego has considerable use for social work which I will return to below.

The unconscious inner world of 'internal objects' is based on the child's relationship to the parents, viewed through the lens of the child's love and hate. The internal objects are not static but change over time as the child's capacity to relate to the world and perceive external reality develops. Klein discovered two distinct patterns of relating to the world, each of which has very considerable implications for future development.

The paranoid schizoid and depressive positions

The baby is dominated by intense feelings of love and hate. It also suffers from acute anxieties of a life and death quality. (This is something which anyone who looks after a small baby is aware of and one of the reasons it is so exhausting.) The baby wants to internalise and keep inside it good experiences and feelings and get rid of bad ones. The baby splits its experiences of the mother into a very good object and a very bad one. Klein also observed that the baby splits off bad, unwanted feelings and projects these into the mother, who is then experienced as the bad aspects of the self. Klein called this phenomenon 'projective identification'. The consequences of this process include a distortion perception of the mother and this 'bad' version is also internalised as a 'bad object'. (Good feelings can also be projected and these intensify feelings of love and the internalisation of a good object.) This combination of anxieties about the survival of the self and the defences of splitting and projection are what Klein referred to as the paranoid schizoid position.

As the baby develops it becomes aware of the mother as a whole person who is both good and bad. This important step towards awareness of external reality brings very painful feelings in its wake. The baby becomes aware that the good, loved mother is the same person as the bad, hated mother, who the baby has attacked and destroyed in phantasy. At this point the leading anxiety is not the survival of the self but the survival of the mother. The combination of guilt and pain and the wish to make 'reparation' to the loved but attacked object are what Klein referred to as the 'depressive position'. It is clear that at this point in development it is deeply important that the mother does survive and that a mother who is in reality in a bad way is a source of unbearable anxiety to the child who is likely to feel responsible for this.

Klein called these two states of mind 'positions' because she found through her work with older children and adults that we tend to oscillate between these states of mind throughout life. The paranoid schizoid position, although an earlier development, is an essential step, because it allows the infant to make the first distinctions between good and bad. Reaching the depressive position involves the baby becoming aware of the mother as a separate person, which also involves becoming aware that she has relationships with other people. The depressive position therefore faces us with the pains of jealousy as well as guilt. Not surprisingly Klein identified a particular defence against depressive pain which she called the 'manic defence'. This defence is an attempt to reverse the experience of dependency. It involves feelings of omnipotence, control and contempt, and a phantasy of triumphing over the parents, and a denial that anyone matters. Feelings of excitement and power derived from many sources, including drugs and alcohol, can be harnessed in the service of this defence. This inflating of the self is different from the strength derived from the internalisation of an object who is genuinely strong and supportive. (This phenomenon is discussed further in Chapters 7 and 12.)

Envy

Klein built on Freud's theory of the death instinct to identify an aspect of human destructiveness which is expressed as a hatred or hostility to anyone who has something which we do not. Like many psychoanalytic ideas this is recognised in ordinary life as the person 'who bites the hand that feeds them'. For a baby this may be expressed in feeding difficulties, for an adult it can be a spoiling of attempts to help. Klein believed that envy was innate, but varied in different people, she also believed that it could be increased by external adversity or deprivation, this can tragically lead to a double deprivation. (A phenomenon explored further in Chapter 7.)

Projective identification

Klein only mentioned this concept quite briefly, however the concept has proved enormously valuable both clinically and theoretically. I will mention a couple of examples here before describing a further development by Bion.

By the 1950s there was a new emphasis on 'countertransference'. This is the emotional response of the analyst to the patient, like transference it was initially considered a nuisance, and a sign that the analyst needed more personal analysis. However in a key paper Paula Heimann observed that the use of the analyst's personal response combined with other information provided an important clue about what might be going on. For example, the patient might describe something in a calm manner while the analyst felt very anxious. This could be understood as the patient's projection of their anxiety into the analyst. In this way the mechanism of projective identification can be used as a way of understanding forms of unconscious communication as well as a way of ridding the self of unwanted experiences.

Bion

Wilfred Bion was a tank commander in the First World War and an army psychiatrist in the Second World War. His first wife died in childbirth leaving him to bring up their baby daughter. These personal and professional experiences of trauma provide an important background to his development of a model of how human beings deal with extreme emotions which may arise from internal or external sources.

Bion developed a theory which explored a particular aspect of the mother's care which helps the baby begin to process powerful and potentially overwhelming emotional experiences. Drawing on Klein's theory of projective identification Bion suggested that the baby projects raw emotions into the mother who processes them in her own mind and returns them to the baby in more digestible states. He called this capacity in the mother the capacity for 'containment'. Over time the baby comes to internalise this aspect of the mother's care and is able to give meaning to emotional states. If a mother is unable to be emotionally available to her baby in this way there is no modification of these terrifying states of mind, which become what Bion described as a state of 'nameless dread'. This type of deprivation can ultimately lead to psychosis. In social work we often encounter clients where a primary absence of containment is coupled with external trauma. Clinical research with sexually abused girls, described in Chapter 6, showed that it was the absence of a containing mother coupled with the external trauma of abuse which was so damaging. It was significant that the girls could not begin to process the abuse until they had some experience of a containing therapist.

Bion's theory of containment is immensely valuable in providing not only a model of the development of the capacity to manage emotional states, but a way of understanding how a thoughtful and emotionally receptive stance to clients can have therapeutic value without anything fancy being done. This theory is easy to understand and it can be used in a way which sounds very slick, 'I contained his feelings'. This does not take account of the fact that for containment to work the parent or worker must really feel the emotional impact of the projection. Bion found that people who have been deprived of emotional containment as a child project with great intensity when the opportunity is offered. Writing of his experiences as a tank commander Bion commented that tank commanders did not need to be very clever but they did need to be able to 'think under fire'. This experience of disturbance and bombardment is inevitable if we are to be emotionally receptive to disturbed or deprived clients, and is I think part of the essence of social work. (Hence the title of this book.)

Another aspect of Bion's work which I shall only touch on here was his theories about psychosis. As well as examining the roots of psychosis he explored in detail the nature of psychotic states of mind. Following Freud he suggested that in psychosis one part of the mind remains sane, but is dominated by the psychotic part, which claims to be sane, but is cruel and merciless and has its own version of reality. This I think accounts for certain types of abusers who are convinced that what they are offering is right for the child and professionals are the abusers. The power of the psychotic parts of the personality cannot be overestimated and I think this is reflected in professional failures to recognise quite gross abuse, where professionals can get caught up or taken in by the psychotic part of the client (Lucas 1992).

Borderline states

During the last twenty years there has been a growing body of theory, clinical work and clinical research with a group of patients suffering from borderline personality disorder. Conventional psychiatry has viewed this group of patients as untreatable. However developments of psychoanalytic theory and technique have proved helpful clinically. Underlying these states is a 'pathological defence organisation', which is a highly organised system of defences of a manic nature, as the underlying defence is against vulnerability and dependency. Rosenfeld described this type of psychological organisation as 'the mafia'. This organisation functions as a sort of retreat from the fragmentation and persecution of the paranoid schizoid position, as well as the guilt and pain of the depressive position. It therefore is a real obstacle to emotional development. The implications of these pathological defence organisations for understanding individuals, families and racist thinking are discussed in Chapters 3, 7 and 11.

Here I would like to mention two aspects of pathological defence organisations which have considerable implications for social work understanding. Firstly, a key aspect of these defences is powerful and rigid projective identification, keeping unwanted feelings and states of mind at bay. This is in contrast to more flexible depressive projective identification which is the basis of empathy. For example one mother described her three-year-old son as 'the destructive one'. Following a year of attending a therapeutic group for mothers and children she described this little boy as 'my most affectionate child'. As this woman was more able to re-own her aggressive feelings she was able to perceive her son's jealousy of his baby sister as an aspect of his love for her. This is, of course, a simplified account and powerful projections are never easily reversed.

Another aspect of pathological organisations is usually the presence of a cruel and sadistic superego, usually formed by a mixture of projected aggression and the actual aggression of the objects. This type of superego makes it exceedingly difficult to face guilt and responsibility. Feelings of guilt are often evaded by nursing a grievance or masochistic behaviour which replaces the pains of guilt with eroticised suffering. It is important to recognise that our clients do usually have highly justified grievances, but it is the nursing of grievance as a shield from any feelings of guilt and facing our own share in difficulties which I am talking about. Awareness of these issues can give us a more realistic perspective on what we can expect from our clients and the difficulties of facing change.

Using psychoanalytic theories in social work practice

Theories, values and interventions

When we think about how to use psychoanalytic theory (or any other psychological theory) in social work it is important not to confuse these three things. A theory is a model of human behaviour which will have implications for the type of intervention we make. There are a range of interventions which are based on psychoanalytic theory. There are interventions such as cognitive behavioural therapy which use more than one theoretical model. Social work values, such as antidiscriminatory practice, empowerment and working with difference are ethical ways of working. They are not theories of human nature nor are they models of intervention. Psychoanalysis provides a helpful theoretical model to put these values into practice. When we try to empower a client are we helping them to develop or get in touch with inner sources of strength, or are we colluding with manic omnipotence or denial of need? Is working with difference facing a reality or are we emphasising difference to escape uncomfortable similarities between our clients and ourselves? In other words when are we using our values developmentally and when are they used to defend our clients or ourselves from painful realities?

Setting: Work in a hostile climate

Psychoanalytic theory stresses the importance of a clear setting in which work can take place. There are two aspects of setting. One is the internal setting which a clear theoretical model can provide and the other is the external setting connected to the job we are trying to do.

It is very difficult to work without a framework which is clear both in our own minds and externally. At work there is the fundamental framework of role and task. There is the need to arrange a physical setting such as time and place and who sees who. In the nature of social work there will always be turbulence and attacks on the setting, with clients these can often be reduced by providing predictability, particularly for people whose lives have been out of control. It is striking that many families show improvements when a core assessment is taking place. Thoughtful explorations in a clear setting can have a therapeutic value.

Unfortunately much of the turbulence in social work today comes from the organisational settings of the work. There are constant policy changes, and structural reorganisations, target and tick box driven work and high staff turnover. Little time is allowed for workers to form attachments to their colleagues which would support them in their contacts with clients. The work is often structured so that contacts with clients are brief and there is an emphasis on referring clients on to other services when anything 'therapeutic' is required. The loss of contact with clients can create a vicious circle as workers lose their confidence in this work. I think that it is significant in social work that local authority management structures means that the most experienced workers have little or no face-to-face contact with clients. This is in contrast to health settings where skills in face-to-face work have high pay and status. Many professions in the health service now have consultant-level jobs.

In this climate social workers who want to work differently have to create their own external and internal support systems. Finding supportive colleagues and supervisors, and going on courses are essential. Personal therapy is rarely recognised or encouraged as a resource in social work. In my experience psychoanalytic understanding is an immensely powerful internal resource, however getting to know psychoanalytic theory in depth is also disturbing. While editing this book I was tempted to sanitise aspects of some of the chapters which were demanding, disturbing or provocative. I decided that readers will need to decide for themselves whether these ideas are true or helpful which is the ultimate test of a theory.

Further development

In Appendix 1 I have given a list of useful further reading and professional organisations which offer training and support. I also describe how to access high-quality psychoanalytic psychotherapy.

References

Bower M (2003) Broken and twisted. *Journal of Social Work Practice* **17**(2).
Lucas R (1992) The psychotic personality: A psychoanalytic theory and its application in clinical practice. *Psychoanalytic Psychotherapy* **6**(1).

2 Psychoanalytic research in the era of evidence-based practice

Stephen Briggs

This chapter aims to explore how research from a psychoanalytic perspective can be applied to social work research and practice, and the contribution that this can make to the social work profession. This will mean entering into a discussion in which there are many positions, differences and debates.

These debates – often arousing fierce passions – are to be found within both social work and psychoanalysis. To focus the discussion, it is important to briefly summarise the current position of social work research, particularly the precariousness of research within professional practice, and the attempts that have been made to strengthen research as an essential part of the professional activity. I shall then devote most of the chapter to the development of psychoanalytic research on the grounds that understanding the current debates and methods is a prerequisite for thinking about whether and how these can be adopted and adapted in social work. These discussions have to be placed in the current context in which the requirement for evidence-based practice (EBP) has brought about an intensification of differences about what research should be and what constitutes 'science'.

Psychoanalytically informed research has an essentially practice-based focus in which emotionality and relationships are central. It is an important approach in that it has a unique capacity to study complex interpersonal – face-to-face – relationships, and thus to generate understanding of relationships in practice settings. It has the capacity to generate knowledge about these interactions in specific contexts.

Social work research

Social work does have a very substantial research tradition. However, it is characterised by two fault lines: firstly, there are – perhaps more so than in other professions – splits between policymakers, practitioners and researchers. There is a lot of research generated by policy and very little by practice. Secondly, the active 'research mindedness' of social workers has been undermined by the successive waves of attack on the profession, and particularly the relationship-based paradigm which stems traditionally from the psychosocial and psychodynamic method of social casework (Howe 1998, Froggett 2002).

It is pertinent to compare social workers with other professions. Child psychotherapists, for example, cohere around a clear theoretical framework and agreed aims and objectives in terms of professional tasks. For sure they argue about some things – the relative importance of different theoretical perspectives – but, in context, these amount to no more than the narcissism of minor differences. Psychologists form a different case. Here the dominant model is methodological – positivistic, experimental, quantitative, behavioural – and the power of this model has been the subject of radical critique (Henriques et al 1984). Differences within the profession, in terms of theoretical preferences – psychoanalytic, systemic, social construction – are fought out over the methodological battleground. Social work differs from these two professions in that, relative to both, it is the theoretical basis for social work which has been weakened by successive onslaughts on the profession. It is also true that social work has experienced great difficulty in developing its own research and theoretical culture so that:

> 'in the absence of a credible culture of research and evaluation, sympathetic to its own priorities, social work and to some extent nursing have been subjected to models drawn from other disciplines that fulfil the criteria of those concerned with the governance of the profession, but not necessarily of practice values.'
>
> (Froggett 2002, page 170)

So, although social work does have a history of producing significant research, it is from a plurality of influences upon it that this tradition has been generated. Classic research texts are as diverse as Mayer and Timms (1970) 'The Client Speaks', the Dartington studies of children 'Lost in Care' (Millham et al 1986) in the 1980s, Mattinson and Sinclair's (1979) 'Mate and Stalemate' and the Robertsons' (1969) films of children in brief separation. These studies were undertaken by social work academics, sociologists, marital psychotherapists and psychoanalysts – which I think illustrates how social work has been a site for the research explorations of a wide range of disciplines. One concern has been about an inside/outside divide, in which a gap between research *on* social work and research *by* social workers has been lamented. Practitioner research programmes (Whitaker and Archer 1988, Fuller and Petch 1995) have attempted to devise models which, through programmes of training and support involve practitioners more actively with doing and using research in order to generate an 'insider' tradition of social work and to disseminate research mindedness, because:

> 'Concerns have been expressed that practitioners do not read, research, do not inform their practice with findings from research, do not influence decisions on what is researched, do not commission research and do not undertake research themselves'
>
> (Everitt 2002, page 109).

Currently the Social Care Institute for Excellence (SCIE) is actively taking up the aim of generating research from within social work. In assessing how social work research can be more effectively applied to practice, and has suggested three models:

- The research practitioner model (in which professional practice includes commitment to applying and keeping up to date with relevant research through continuous professional development).
- The embedded research model (in which policymakers and service delivery managers lead in ensuring that practice is research informed, including involvement with audit and evaluation).
- The organisational excellence model (in which the organisation develops a 'research-minded culture' including links with universities, adapting research to

local settings, encouraging continuous professional development within the organisation) (SCIE 2004).

The attempt here is to reprofessionalise social work, as these aims fit alongside the GSCC's aims for registration and post qualification continuous professional development. However, the SCIE knowledge review aims to 'develop and promote evidence-based knowledge about good practice in social care' (SCIE 2004, 1) and this – the evidence based practice movement – is contentious.

The practitioner researcher programme's emphasis on 'insider' research is desirable, but it is flawed because it does not recognise the importance of theory. Social work's theoretical base has become weak and fragmented (Bower 2003), but social work needs to draw on rigorous and robust theoretical frameworks for effective practice. Social work research underpinned by psychoanalytic thinking is the subject of this chapter. To assess how psychoanalytic thinking and research can underpin social work research, requires, now, an exploration of how psychoanalytic research is developing in the era of evidence-based practice.

Evidence-based practice

Contemporary practice in social work – as in other professions – is dominated by the demands for evidence based practice (EBP). Driven by a ruthless positivism and with highly political (and economic) implications, the movement for EBP is accompanied by a regulatory framework of audit and inspection, and tends to generate a quite persecutory environment, as well as provoking changes to working practice. Barker et al (2002) usefully point out that in the socio-political context, evaluation is always accompanied by a threat, and they list these as:

'• An oppressive sense of being continually scrutinized . . .
• Resentment at taking time to provide the data for evaluation . . .
• Fear that the results of evaluation will provide ammunition for managers . . . to attack the quality or quantity of work being done.
• Annoyance that the criteria used in evaluation do not capture the important aspects of a service's work.'(page 202)

EBP privileges certain research methodologies (especially randomised controlled trials (RCTs)) for measuring outcome of interventions. As this approach appeared to favour behaviourally oriented therapeutic approaches (especially cognitive behaviour therapy (CBT)) the initial response to EBP from those favouring psychoanalytically informed interventions was to critique the methodology and the politics of this approach to research. The EBP model, especially as promoted by government-supported bodies, such as the National Institute for Clinical Excellence (NICE), applies a rigid hierarchical approach to evidence[1], and thus:

---

1 NICE apply a hierarchical grading scheme, in which randomised controlled trials obtains the top grade, 'A'. 'Well conducted' clinical studies (meaning controlled, quasi-experimental, and correlative studies) get a 'B'. Expert committee reports score a 'C'. Clinical experience is notated as GPP (recommended good practice).

'imposes a paradigm for what counts as legitimate evidence that is external to the practices and ways of knowing of the many professionals who are now required to evaluate their interventions'.

(Hollway 2001, page 21)

In other words, it is antiprofessional and seeks to drive a wedge between professional experience and research. The hammer which drives home this wedge is a methodological one, so that aligned on one side, representing EBP are quantitative, positivistic, experimental and quasi-experimental, whilst on the other side are qualitative, observational, naturalistic methods. Thus the EBP movement has tended to nullify research which is extremely important to social work, and which aims to connect quantitative and qualitative, validation and discovery, comparison and in-depth understanding. One particular casualty is the extremely productive and generative psycho-social research method which stemmed from Brown and Harris' life events approach and their seminal work, the 'Social Origins of Depression' (Brown and Harris 1978, Bifulco 2004).

The EBP movement, to mix the metaphor, has also had the qualities of a juggernaut. It has been impossible to ignore, such is the sound and fury that it has created in its wake. As Wendy Hollway wrote

'Evidence-based practice – the phrase – has crept up on me from all round (academic discussions, the newspapers, politicians on the radio) so that it gradually accrued meanings in that intuitive way that ideas do before you look at them full face and pin them down with conscious thought and language'.

(Hollway 2001, page 15)

Certainly, in addition to loathing, the initial impact of EBP was to create fear in those who worked psychoanalytically. It was feared that psychoanalytic approaches would not survive in such a culture and climate. The demise of psychodynamic work in the Probation service was one example of persuasive evidence that this fear might be realistic[2]. Fear brings defensiveness and/or compliance. It is hard to engage thoughtfully with a juggernaut, that is, an overbearing authority. Defensiveness included disinterest, criticism and a sense of superiority. Compliance – turning psychoanalytic research into a kind of behavioural, outcome-oriented method – evokes Will's (1986) critique of Bowlby, that he was in 'epistemological identification with the aggressor', that is, with the dominant behavioural empiricism of the time.

EBP has created catastrophic change, to use Bion's (1963) term. Some, like Alessandra Lemma (2003), in an overview of contemporary psychoanalytic thinking and practice, have argued that it has been a matter of rising to the challenge rather than hiding behind defensive conservatism. Echoing Holmes' (1998) comments on the demise of 'self serving professionalism', she writes that, 'the tidal wave of interest in evidence based practice has now shaken the cosy cocoon of psychoanalytic practice' (Lemma 2003, page 63). The current world of outcome measurement, value for money and choices between different therapeutic approaches has transformed

---

2   Indeed, the demise of the psycho-social tradition in Probation (now National Offender Management Service) as competencies, outcome-driven targets, behaviour-oriented treatments and CBT took over, led to the loss of this service to social work altogether.

therapeutic practice. Although these external 'market' factors might not be welcome in themselves, there is perhaps something to be gained. For example, there are reasons for optimism in that recent outcome studies show that psychoanalytic therapies do work. People with neurotic and psychosomatic conditions benefit, patients offered more intensive and longer treatments have better outcomes, especially for those with more severe difficulties (Fonagy 1999). A recent systematic review of the evidence for the effectiveness of psychoanalytic child psychotherapy concludes that:

> 'There is evidence to support the effectiveness of psychoanalytic psychotherapy for children/young people with a range of psychological disorders. Beneficial effects are shown with treatment on a variety of outcome measures and many studies showed that improvements were sustained or even enhanced at long term follow up. While short term treatment is shown to be effective, particularly where the level of clinical disturbance is not severe, there is evidence to support the view that greater benefits accrue with longer more frequent treatment.'
>
> (Kennedy 2004, page 42).

This amounts to a sea-change in the relationship between psychoanalytic practitioners and the EBP movement. Far from being swept away by the more easily evidenced behavioural therapies, there is evidence that long-term treatments are more effective – with consequent implications that resources to support these interventions should be made available. Engagement with EBP has put psychoanalytic psychotherapies in a stronger position in the modern order (Richardson and Hobson 2003). Some RCTs have produced innovative work which assesses the value of psychoanalytic therapy for certain patient and client groups. Judith Trowell and Gillian Miles (see Chapter 6) have shown that for children who have been sexually abused, psychoanalytic psychotherapy leads to positive outcomes (Trowell and Kolvin 2002, Trowell et al 2003). Studies showing the effectiveness of psychoanalytic psychotherapy for borderline personality (Bateman and Fonagy 2001) and for self harm (Guthrie et al 2001) show that both intensive and brief interventions can be effective.

The emerging success in engaging with the EBP movement has at least limited the fear of annihilation for psychoanalytic therapeutic practice. Better than this, it has provided a legitimised base for promoting the efficacy and effectiveness of these practices. There are advantages, of course, to take from these developments. However, this does not, and should not, mean that the EBP principles are adopted uncritically and that critical appraisal of the EBP objectives should be dropped.

On the whole, the RCT method does not easily apply to assessing effectiveness in psycho-social interventions, which are of necessity complex and operating in an ambiguous social field. Indeed it can be argued that these kinds of research intervention, in social work, are highly inappropriate since they reduce the field of change beyond an acceptable level. The 'gold standard' of an outcome finding using an RCT has its uses, politically, though it is extremely expensive and cumbersome. The enormity of the undertaking can be gauged from the example of NICE's estimation of the size of a research study measuring treatments for self harm:

> 'to be able to demonstrate adequately the effectiveness of an intervention for people who have self-harmed, in terms of reducing the proportion of later

suicides, an RCT would need a sample size of over 40,000 people divided between intervention and control groups.'

(NICE 2004, page 159)

Clearly this is not a realistic undertaking! RCT is most useful when a simple, single-outcome measure is being compared between, usually, two treatments or a treatment and no treatment. Most social work interventions simply do not operate in these conditions, and the kind of information required by research is often of a more complex nature. Similarly, the cheaper methods of audit and evaluation are highly subject to the political purposes of the studies, and 'methods of evaluation should foster – or at the very least do no damage to – the capacity for ethical, reflective practice' (Froggett 2002, page 170). Generating the reflective space is thus the central task in working with EBP.

We can identify two contrasting states of mind in these circumstances. Firstly, a sense of persecution and paranoia, in which reflexivity and curiosity cannot function. Secondly, bearing the anxiety of scrutiny, a more benign state of mind may prevail. Here, critical self appraisal is felt to be essential to being able to practice. The practitioner focuses on the (inevitable) gap between what is desired and what is actually happening (Healy 1998). In this more benign state of mind, research mindedness and reflective practice are possible.

The effects on research of EBP have been radical, particularly methodologically. Whilst one essential division – between qualitative and quantitative approaches – represents a very long argument, which now continues in a different form, the costs of EBD are profound. That the tradition of psycho-social research has been ruptured by these developments has already been mentioned. Alongside this, the split, or divide between two traditions and approaches has been made more distinct, and these lead to divisions between practitioners and researchers within professions. The chasm between the current positions of both traditions is a hard one to bridge – and I must at this point confess to a perhaps unusual position of seeing something of merit on both sides, and that making attempts to cross the divide is worthwhile – indeed essential.

I shall now look at the current state of both positions from a methodological perspective and consider how each has something to offer social work research.

'Emergence' and the ethnographic tradition

As an intellectual tradition, psychoanalysis has a particular research culture based on the single case study. Some of these – particularly Freud's but not only these – are classics and make extremely vivid reading. The aphorism – you can't generalise from one case, generalise from two – is an ironic acknowledgement of the lack of 'scientific' merit of this method, something that caused Freud himself some anguish and led to the castigations of psychoanalysis as a pseudo-science by Eysenck and others[3].

Psychoanalysis, perhaps ironically, finds a much more natural home in sociology and anthropology departments than in psychology, which, as I have said, has since

---

3   It was the alleged unfalsifiability of psychoanalytic theory which aroused this opposition as much as the single case study. This claim – the unscientific nature of psychoanalysis – has recently been overthrown, not just by the evidence that it works but also by innovative research which shows that psychoanalytic judgements can be objective. I will discuss this below.

the 1920s been dominated by experimentalism and behaviourism. It is interesting to hear how Elizabeth Bott Spillius related to Klein's work:

> 'I found the clinical material of early papers about children absolutely compelling. These papers were among the first things I read in psychoanalysis, and certainly the first that seemed real. Rita, Trude, Peter, Ruth, Fritz, Felix all became persons in a new but somehow familiar world . . . each of the early clinical papers seemed to me like a good anthropological monograph – social anthropology being my profession at this time and my first intellectual love. There were vivid data, just enough theory to make sense of the data, sudden jumps of imagination and theoretical understanding that led on to the next paper'
>
> (Bott Spillius 1994, page 324)

The anthropological analogy of psychoanalytic research is echoed by Rustin's (1989) discussion of infant observation, which he compares with ethnography and participant observation, drawing on Bick's own description of the observer's role:

> 'it was felt to be important that the observer should feel himself [sic] sufficiently inside the family to experience the emotional impact, but not committed to act out any roles thrust upon him, such as offering advice or registering disapproval. This would not seem to exclude him from being helpful as a particular situation arose – by holding the baby or bringing it an occasional gift. In other words, he would be a privileged and, therefore, grateful participant observer'
>
> (Bick 1964, reprinted in Bick 2002, page 38)

Of course, this mirrors the psychoanalytic position of the analyst, who is both participant and observer, using free-floating attention to move between experiencing and observing.

The anthropological analogy is not universally shared by psychoanalytic practitioners, who see the 'science' of psychoanalysis in different ways. It does though provide a way of conceptualising the quality of psychoanalytic 'data', which is rich in texture, providing depth and detail about specific cases and situations. It also illustrates the strength and limitations of the method. The problem that arises from this is that psychoanalysis can be marginalised, and, as we have seen, when under the pressure of EBP has experienced the urgent need to come out and engage with the mainstream – or perish. This has led to attempts to relate psychoanalytic work to 'science'. Three paths have been taken.

- Firstly, an objectivist route, in which outcome studies feature strongly but also there have been research projects which aim to demonstrate the 'objectivity' of psychoanalysis and thus focus on the validity of psychoanalysis. Hobson et al (1998) provide the seminal text for this approach, and this is discussed further below. This follows in Bowlby's footsteps, and attachment theory has been central in objectivist approaches, perhaps most closely identified currently with the work of Fonagy (e.g. 2001).
- Secondly, there have been approaches which, based on a critique of positivism, aim to show that validity can be obtained from alternative approaches to science. For example, it has been argued that observations show us the effects of

underlying, 'deep' structures. 'Science ... is the systematic attempt to express in thought the structures and ways of acting of things that exist and act independently of thought' (Bhaskar 1978, page 250). This view of reality suits psychoanalytic inquiry which theorises the deep structure of the unconscious. We can't see the unconscious, but we can recognise it by the effects which are observed – slips of the tongue, symptoms and dreams and transference. This position is best articulated by Rustin (1992).

- Thirdly, and perhaps more radically, the notion of 'objectivity' is strongly critiqued and it is argued that by drawing attention, through in-depth research, to the subjective, lived experience provides a more convincing social science than the statistically driven view of the dominant quantitative method. In this genre, Hollway and Jefferson (2000) propose a holistic qualitative methodology based on a free associative interview and method of data analysis. Chamberlayne et al (2002) explore the emergent methods of biographical interviewing, and the narrative form is praised for its own sake (Froggett 2002).

These three positions are usually represented as being incompatible with each other, and indeed adherents to one of the above approaches often engage in intense arguments with proponents of the others! There are philosophical, epistemological and methodological differences which are often seen to be unbridgeable. For example, it is often proposed that 'hard' science is always quantitative and that the 'soft' approach of qualitative methods are lower down the hierarchy, providing a means of undertaking initial, exploratory work which is validated by quantitative methods yielding statistically significant findings. This hierarchical approach has been severely critiqued in recent years (Fuller and Petch 1995), so that it is now possible to see the dichotomy of quantitative and qualitative methods as false. Thus quantitative studies can lead on to qualitative methods, when the aim is to understand further, or in more depth, the meaning of a quantitative finding. It is also false to uphold a dichotomy between objective and subjective. As Britton (1998) has shown, there is a need for exploration of the relationship between subjectivity and objectivity in the course of seeking truths[4]. From the qualitative perspective, the recent emphasis on reflexivity has shown that a subjective element is always present in research – both quantitative and qualitative – and these should be made 'more open to view, more transparently a part of the research activity.' (Wren 2004).

Contemporary objectivist approaches

The identifying features of contemporary objectivist approaches are, firstly, that a data source is analysed in a standardised format, usually quantitatively, with categories that are precoded and, secondly, that reliability between raters is a require-

---

4 Britton's thinking about the relationship between subjectivity and objectivity is illuminating of the process underpinning the issue. He wrote: 'I am using the terms "subjective" and "objective" *ontologically*, that is, to mean the first person point of view when I say subjective and the third person point of view when I say objective. So "I feel stupid" is subjective and "he is stupid" is objective. In this usage subjective does not necessarily imply prejudiced and objective does not mean unprejudiced.' (Britton 1998 page 43).

ment. Thus raters are 'trained' to code similar evidence in the same way. The claim for objectivity arises from rater agreement. Thus, Hobson et al (1998) showed that raters who had been trained as psychoanalytic psychotherapists agreed (with statistical significance) with regard to the characteristics of two distinct kinds of patient (borderline and depressed personalities) after viewing videos of clinical sessions. The rating instrument in this study, ingeniously, consists of a list of statements which each capture an aspect of Klein's paranoid schizoid and depressive positions, the Personal Relatedness Profile (PRP). Each rater was asked to make judgements on the rating scale. Since the raters did agree about which patient belonged in which category, it could be concluded that psychoanalytic theory effectively enabled these distinctions to be made and, secondly, generalising from this, that psychoanalytic judgements have an objective quality. Thus psychoanalytic practitioners can be relied upon to come to the same conclusions about cases.

This use of the term 'objective' is partly methodological and partly an application of Britton's definition of objective as constituting a 'third person'. This study situates the raters as therapists judging a therapeutic session, recognising their professional capacity. This is a validation of the view that psychoanalytic practitioners work within a context of normal science. The key is that the raters are trained to make sense of observations in particular ways.

Contemporary attachment theory uses similar features. It is built upon obtaining data from a semistructured narrative interview[5] and the data analysis is systematised, following a manualised and precoded schema. Training is required in order to undertake the data analysis and satisfactory inter-rater reliability is required. Since the rapprochement between attachment theory and psychoanalysis (Fonagy 2001) there is a 'mapping' of attachment narratives on to psychoanalytic theory. The attachment narratives are themselves very important in the application of attachment theory, especially the insecure narratives. These distinguish, basically, between anxiety and avoidance. Anxious insecure attachment generates narratives in which there is worry, and an absence of prioritisation of worry. Separation from others and the fear of the unavailability of others to make decisions is a central source of worry. The subject is overwhelmed by experiences, and maybe has weak boundaries between self and other. The stories which are produced often lack coherence.

Avoidant insecure attachment generates a different kind of narrative. In this narrative pattern emotionality and relatedness are underplayed and understated; emotional meaning is negated or denied. At the extreme the aim is to get rid of emotionally. The subject produces rigid stories which are clung on to. These schema of attachment narratives describe contrasting ways in which subjects defend against emotionality – are what Hollway and Jefferson term 'defended subjects' (Hollway and Jefferson 2000). In attachment research, an intensely qualitative approach – a narrative interview looking at the quality of relatedness and emotionality – is categorised and coded quantitatively, and this coding is organised around a central principle, relating to the 'deep structure' of anxious or avoidant attachment. The application of this method to a psycho-social problem can be illustrated from a project I am involved with (Wright et al 2005), and which is on-going.

---

5   The method for children, adolescents and adults is a semistructured interview. For infants the method is an experiment, the 'strange situation' (Ainsworth 1978).

Adolescents at risk of suicide and self harm present clinically as a widely diverse group. Some are depressed, preoccupied with suicidality and talk about it with great anxiety. Others seem to not know themselves they are at risk, and fail to communicate about their difficulties and suicidality. These adolescents have different effects on the therapists (countertransference). The first group get the therapists very anxious, particularly at points of separation. The second group tend to generate an emotional under reaction. We interviewed a sample of adolescents at risk of suicide/self harm and a matched group who were not suicidal, but had other mental health difficulties and a third group who were controls (no mental health difficulties). The interview is an attachment narrative interview, the Adolescent Separation Anxiety Interview (ASAI) (Richard et al 1998)[6]. We found that the suicidal adolescents were more likely to be insecurely attached than the other two groups and that they were evenly distributed between the two insecure categories, entangled/preoccupied (anxious) and dismissing (avoidant). This provided a framework for looking more closely at the narrative interviews. We could see then that suicidality was expressed in terms of defending against painful or unbearable emotionality and that, consistent with the views of attachment theory the subjects in each of the insecure categories defended differently against the pain, and engaged differently in relationships with others. The preoccupied (anxious) group tended to involve the other in anxious interactions and the dismissing (avoidant) group aimed to get rid of or eliminate emotionality. This finding has significance for practice, since, often, the most worrying cases are those where suicidality is understated and the worker is induced to under react or underestimate the risks.

This example, which is in the tradition of psycho-social research, involves a combination of quantitative and qualitative aspects, and the quantitative findings serve as providing a framework for further exploration. There is thus interaction between qualitative and quantitative elements rather than a hierarchical distinction between them. The end product of this research may be an ideal typical case study, or a series of them, as well as a summary of findings obtained through comparing cases.

Emergent methods

The alternative to the objectivist approach can be thought of as consisting of 'emergent methods'. Essentially the relationship between the narrative and the data analysis is reversed from that discussed in the previous example. These methods cohere around activities that have been developed in the training of social workers and other professionals in the Tavistock Clinic, and by academics working within a similar paradigm. The best way of illustrating the method is to describe the activities which include supervised clinical or therapeutic work, work discussion (a discussion of a case or work situation), infant and child observation, and institutional observation. From a more academic base, biographical methods have been developed which rely on a similar set of research activities.

---

6   The ASAI is a semistructured interview which includes photographs of adolescents in separation situations. The subjects are asked what would they think and feel if they were the young person in the photograph, what would their parents think and feel and what would they think their parents would think they were thinking and feeling.

All these methods have in common a number of features, namely:

- The worker/observer undertakes clinical interviews/observations in a set time and place (usually for 1 hour or just under). Usually there is a series of observations/interviews at regular intervals, usually weekly, over a substantial period of time. Biographical interviews are different in that one or two detailed interviews take place.
- A detailed verbatim written account is made of the interview/observation, emphasising detail and description (interpretation in these accounts is eschewed).
- A one-to-one or group discussion takes place, usually with a senior clinician in which the recording is read and then discussed. The aim of the discussion is to understand what is going on in the session (interview or observation), with the help of relevant theoretical formulations. The aim is to develop tentative 'hypotheses', usually focusing on understanding patterns of relatedness, which will be corroborated by further observations/interviews.
- In the course of these discussions, there will be a process of reflection on the part played by the worker/observer, to establish how these may have influenced both the interaction and way these are recorded. These discussions will include taking account of social factors, such as race, gender, age, class, and also the emotional impact of the observation on the observer.

These features, or activities, which have been developed in training contexts, can be articulated in research methodological terms.

- Firstly, a narrative source of data is generated which can be scrutinised and analysed.
- Secondly, analysis of the data is undertaken by seminar discussion, in which different points of view or 'takes' on the data are possible.
- Thirdly, the seminar leader/supervisor provides an 'expert' viewpoint, bringing theory and experience to bear on the data. Thus the data analysis is theory driven. Part of the creativity of the process is the search for an application of a relevant aspect of theory, which is applied in a grounded way to the data.
- Fourthly, the observer/interviewer is able to provide a reflective and self-reflective account of the experience of the interview/observation.

These methods are 'emergent' because something of the lived experience is captured in the engagement of worker/observer/biographer and the subject, and that the meaning of these engagements 'emerge' as do the methods of data analysis. However, as a caveat, I add that there is nothing mysterious about these analytic processes when the idea that the theory and professional driven focus is kept in mind. As I have put it, the 'expert rater' is the mind of the supervisor/seminar leader applying a honed theoretical framework to the material. The analytic process involves the constant interaction between theory and data: Hollway and Jefferson (2000) point out that 'the categories were part of our analysis, not prior to it: they emerged out of a grounded theory approach where theory and data informed each other at every stage' (page 108). From this process of generating emerging categories, problems of systematisation arise. As an illustration I can refer to my own study of infants at potential risk (Briggs 1997).

The method for this study was infant observation, in which each of five infants was observed for 1 hour each week for two years. I wrote a detailed account after each observation and discussed these in a small seminar group. This generated a very rich account of the development of each infant in her/his family context. The vicissitudes of the impact of 'risk' on the infants' development was followed chronologically in each case. However, it was also important to find ways of facilitating comparison across this small sample of five infants and their families. Through the process of constantly relating data to theory and vice versa, categories were developed. Particularly fruitful were the grounded categories which derived from the dynamics of the container-contained relationship (Bion 1962). Three categories were high-lighted: concave, flat and convex container 'shape'. Judgements could be made about the strength of each of these shapes in each observation, and about the way these interacted with infant development. Through using multiple raters, a study could be designed to compare different raters' scores (Rhode 2004).

One problem which emergent methods has had to face is how to justify the method of data analysis according to scientific criteria. This is a complex discussion, involving epistemological as well as methodological issues (see Rustin 1992 for a detailed discussion). The point is whether it is safe to make generalisations from cases. The practical need has been to try to find a way of making systematic comparisons between cases. The psychoanalytic method is very strong in providing in-depth, detailed descriptions of individual cases, in a way which illuminates and makes sense what is going on within the case. When making comparisons between cases, methods from social science have to be adopted, and adapted. Generating categories which are articulated as grounded, situated categories, through the oscillating process of moving between data and theory and using these to form the basis for comparison has become the most usual way of proceeding (Hollway and Jefferson 2000 page 105). It is through the generation of these emergent categories that comparisons can be made within and across cases. Specifically, these categories can be formulated so that it is possible to address key areas of concern for psychoanalytic inquiry, including emotionality, shifts between different states of mind and the impact of these on subjectivity and development. In other words the data source (usually a narrative text) is studied from a perspective in which the primary preoccupation is the impact of emotionality, including anxieties, defences and patterns of object relatedness. The approach of generating grounded categories enables comparisons to be made within and across cases, and thus provide a framework for studying samples as well as individual cases.

Areas of application of psychoanalytic research to social work

Psychoanalytic research provides a way of studying an often excluded or margin-alised aspect of social work practice, namely, the focus on emotionality and the processes of relationships. This emphasis is derived from the fundamental tenets of psychoanalytic theory and practice, where depth – the role of the unconscious, and relationships, including unconscious intersubjectivity, is placed at the very heart of the enterprise. A different perspective on practice and policy can thus be generated.

Two fields of inquiry are most appropriately the subject for this kind of research. Firstly, it has a role to play in the reprofessionalisation of social work, in which the organisational context of social work is critiqued and evaluated from the perspective of understanding the emotional impact of the work on the worker and the implications this has for organisational behaviour and service delivery. Thus supervisory, team, management and interagency practices are explored from the perspective of the unconscious processes which impact upon the organisation at all levels. This aims to illustrate and evaluate social worker's stressful experiences, supervision relationships and the impact of reflective space for undertaking relationship-based work.

The second field of inquiry relates to specific issues of social policy application in social work practice. This was the generating factor behind Hollway and Jefferson's study of the fear of crime. They proposed an alternative to the mainstream view of fear of crime, namely that fear would relate to intrapsychic and intersubjective factors and would differ therefore between individuals. There are, of course, a multitude of research subjects in which the focus of exploration and examination of the emotional and relational factors provide a different perspective on social policy and practice.

The application to social work of these methods is particularly well suited to a practitioner research model. Whether as students undertaking post qualification programmes and researching and writing a masters or doctoral level dissertation, or as a practitioner in collaboration perhaps with other colleagues, the methods of work discussion, observation, and biographical interviewing are all applicable to small-scale research. The work discussion model is particularly tuned to the needs of busy practitioners since it provides opportunity for reflection on work undertaken in role, and this, in itself, provides a reflective space for thinking.

Conclusion

What is perhaps most striking from this discussion is that psychoanalytic research has diversified in the era of EBP. We have seen that, perhaps surprisingly, psychoanalytic therapy has begun to find ways of measuring its effectiveness in the terms of the dominant methodology – positivism. This has provided a potential springboard for psychoanalytic therapy to gain respectability in the mainstream. It also means that psychoanalytic approaches continue to be able to obtain contracts in the NHS! Whilst engaging with the demands of EBP, the sometimes furious debates about methodology and epistemology have led to vigorous defences of the traditional, core qualitative psychoanalytic, method. Alongside this, the widening application of psychoanalytic approaches to research has generated interest in and assessment of the validity of psychoanalytic thinking about research data. This particularly applies to the application of psychoanalytic thinking to the gathering and analysis of observation, practice interactions ('work discussion') and biographical interviews. In an emerging field a lot of innovation is taking place and the current diversity has the potential to enable research from this perspective to have justification for the in-depth study of a small number of cases, or subjects, and also the tools through which comparisons of cases can be made.

A consistent feature of psychoanalytic research is the central role given to the gathering of narrative sources of data. This is axiomatic in the clinical psychoanalytic setting, where through recalling the detailed interactions of a session, the internal world of the patient and the quality of interaction between the patient and therapist (transference and countertransference) can be understood. The diversification of the psychoanalytic method into observation, work discussion and biographical interviews maintains the importance of this process. Though there are different views about how the narratives should be understood, I have proposed that movement to and fro between the objective and subjective, provides the potential for integration. I have also shown that, for all approaches, there is a narrative, qualitative core to the research activity, and the challenge is to find ways of systematically representing that process in research findings.

The effect of psychoanalytic research is to enrich the reflective psycho-social space in which social work takes place through bringing another perspective, focus and method. Social workers may wish to engage with this emerging new tradition either through including it in their thinking – to increase 'research mindedness' – or through participation in research projects, including practitioner research.

References

Ainsworth M (1978) *Patterns of Attachment*. Hillsdale NJ, Erlbaum.

Barker C, Pistrang N, Elliott R (2002) *Research Methods in Clinical Psychology: An Introduction for Students and Practitioners*. London and New York, John Wiley and Sons.

Bateman A, Fonagy P (2001) Treatment of borderline personality disorder with psychoanalytically oriented partial hospitalization: An 18-month follow-up. *American Journal of Psychiatry* **158**(1): 36–42.

Bhaskar R (1978) *A Realist Theory of Science*. Brighton, Harvester.

Bick E (1964) Notes on infant observation in psychoanalytic training. *International Journal of Psychoanalysis*, 45: 484–488, reprinted in Briggs A (2002) *Surviving Space: Papers on Infant Observation*. London, Karnac.

Bifulco A (2004) Personal communication.

Bion W (1962) *Learning from Experience*. London, Heinemann.

Bion W (1963) *Elements of Psychoanalysis*. London, Heinemann.

Bott Spillius E (1994) Developments in Kleinian thought: Overview and personal view. *Psychoanalytic Inquiry* **14**(3): 324–364.

Bower M (2003) Broken and Twisted. *Journal of Social Work Practice* **17**(2): 143–151.

Briggs S (1997) *Growth and Risk in Infancy*. London, Jessica Kingsley.

Britton R (1998) *Belief and Imagination: Explorations in Psychoanalysis*. London, Routledge.

Brown G, Harris T (1978) *The Social Origins of Depression. A Study of Psychiatric Disorder in Women*. London, Tavistock.

Chamberlayne P, Rustin M, Wengraf T (eds) (2002) *Biography and Social Exclusion in Europe; Experience and Life Journeys*. Bristol, The Policy Press.

Everitt A (2002) Research and development in social work. In: Adams R, Dominelli L, Payne M (eds) *Social Work: Themes, Issues and Critical Debates*. Basingstoke, Palgrave, in association with Open University Press.

Fonagy P (ed.) (1999) *An Open Door Review of Outcome Studies in Psychoanalysis*. London University College/International Psychoanalytic Association.

Fonagy P (2001) *Attachment Theory and Psychoanalysis*. New York, Other Books.

Froggett L (2002) *Love, Hate and Welfare: Psychosocial Approaches to Policy and Practice*. Bristol, The Policy Press.

Fuller R, Petch A (1995) *Practitioner Research: The Reflexive Social Worker*. Milton Keynes, Open University Press.

Guthrie E et al. (2001) Randomised control trial of brief psychological intervention after deliberate self poisoning. *British Medical Journal* **323**(7305): 135–138.

Healy K (1998) Clinical audit and conflict. In: Davenhill R, Patrick M (eds) *Rethinking Clinical Audit. The Case of Psychotherapy Services in the NHS*. London, Routledge.

Henriques J, Hollway W, Urwin C, Venn C, Walkerdine V (1998) *Changing the Subject: Psychology, Social Regulation and Subjectivity,* 2nd edn. London, Routledge.

Hobson P, Patrick M, Valentine J (1998) Objectivity in psychoanalytic judgements. *British Journal of Psychiatry* **173**: 172–177.

Hollway W (2001) The psycho-social subject in evidence based practice. *Journal of Social Work Practice* **15**(1): 9–22.

Hollway W, Jefferson T (2000) *Doing Qualitative Research Differently: Free Association, Narrative and the Interview Method*. London, Sage.

Holmes J (1998) The changing aims of psychoanalytic psychotherapy: an integrative perspective. *International Journal of Psychoanalysis* **79**: 227–240.

Howe D (1998) Relationship-based thinking and practice in social work. *Journal of Social Work Practice* **12**(1): 43–55.

Kennedy E (2004) *Child and Adolescent Psychotherapy: A Systemic Review of Psychoanalytic Approaches*. London, North Central London Strategic Health Authority.

Lemma A (2003) *An Introduction to the Practice of Psychoanalytic Psychotherapy*. London, Wiley.

Mattinson J, Sinclair I (1979) *Mate and Stalemate. Working with Marital Problems in a Social Services Department*. Oxford, Blackwell.

Mayer J, Timms N (1970) *The Client Speaks*. London, Routledge and Kegan Paul.

Millham S, Bullock R, Hosie K, Haak M (1986) *Lost in Care: the Problems of Maintaining Links between Children in Care and their Families*. Aldershot, Gower.

National Institute for Clinical Excellence (2004) Self-harm: The short-term physical and psychological management and secondary prevention of self-harm in primary and secondary care. *NICE Clinical Guidelines* www.nice.org.uk/.

Rhode M (2004) Infant observation as research: cross-disciplinary links. *Journal of Social Work Practice* **18**(3): 283–298.

Richard M H, Fonagy P, Smith PK, et al. (1998) *The Adolescent Separation Anxiety Interview.* Unpublished interview protocol, Goldsmiths College, University of London.

Richardson P, Hobson P (2003) In defence of NHS psychotherapy. In: McPherson S, Richardson P, Leroux P (eds) *Clinical Effectiveness in Psychotherapy and Mental Health: Strategies and Resources for Effective Clinical Governance*. London, Karnac.

Robertson J, Robertson J (1969) *Young Children in Brief Separation*. Ipswich, Concord Films.

Rustin M (1989) Reflections on method. In Miller L, Rustin M, Rustin M, Shuttleworth J (eds) *Closely Observed Infants*. London, Duckworth.

Rustin M (1992) *The Good Society and the Inner World*. London, Verso.

Social Care Institute for Excellence (2004) Improving the use of research in social care practice. *SCIE Knowledge Review 6 www.scie.org.uk/*.

Trowell J, et al. (2003) Sexually abused girls: patterns of psychopathology and exploration of risk factors. *European Child & Adolescent Psychiatry* **12**(5): 221–230.

Trowell J, Kolvin I (2002) Psychotherapy for sexually abused girls: psychopathological outcome findings and patterns of change. *British Journal of Psychiatry* **180**: 234–247.

Whitaker S D, Archer L (1988) *Research Partnership*. Central Council for Education and Training in Social Work, Study 9.

Will D (1986) Psychoanalysis and the new philosophy of science. *International Review of Psychoanalysis* **13**: 163–173.

Wren B (2004) Editorial Clinical Child Psychology and Psychiatry. **9**(4): 475–478.

Wright J, Briggs S, Behringer J (2005) *Attachment and the Body in Suicidal Adolescents* **10**(4): (in press).

3   Racist states of mind: an attack on thinking and curiosity

Narendra Keval

In psychoanalysis, the acquisition of knowledge has a special significance, in the sense that our capacity to comprehend and relate to reality is thought to be intimately connected with our emotional development. This means that we are often preoccupied with understanding the kinds of anxieties and quality of thinking in particular states of mind that obstruct the desire to learn and acquire knowledge about ourselves in relation to others in the world.

The aim of this chapter is to explore how this discovery is obstructed by a retreat into racist thinking as part of a pathological organisation of the mind whose aim is to put the brakes on psychic growth and development. One of the main functions of such an organisation is thought to be a defence against the experience of separateness.

This means all manner of differences and therefore potential conflicts in the self are felt to be threatening. Minor but salient differences such as the colour of the therapist's skin can also be seized upon and targeted for attack because it triggers underlying anxieties to do with the prospect of change and development.

Pathological organisations of the personality (e.g. O'Shaunessy 1981a) have also been referred to as 'psychic retreats' (Steiner 1993) which offer shelter from both persecutory and depressive anxieties that the experience of separateness can bring to the fore.

They are brought into play when the individual is unable to cope with anxieties of a paranoid-schizoid nature such as fragmentation and chaos or the pain of mourning such as guilt that the depressive position can give rise to (Klein 1946).

All manner of differences and potential conflicts in the self are hated because movements in either direction represent potential changes in the self. One way in which this is dealt with is to obliterate the object representing these differences and potential threats to the self by a retreat into racist thinking. In this way it gives expression to the inner workings of a pathological organisation whilst providing the military arsenal to defend it.

Despite the suffering, the retreat offers relative security and comfort from the illusion of permanence which can override the anxiety of coming out of the retreat as represented by emotional contact with the therapist. Freud (1937) was preoccupied with this problem in 'Analysis Terminable and Interminable' when he tried to understand why his patients preferred their own versions of reality in the face of understanding even when this was at the cost of an impoverished and crippled life.

Our experiences in the consulting room would confirm this picture when we witness our patients' struggle to keep things the same at considerable cost to the self. Where violence and destructiveness play a major role, these highly organised defences have come to be known as narcissistic object relations in which recognition of dependency and separateness is viciously attacked (Rosenfeld 1971).

We can often sense a menacing atmosphere in the patient's internal world in the way they describe feeling gripped and seduced by parts of themselves which can only be described as a 'corrupt gang' offering easy painless solutions to their life difficulties. This shortcut is aimed at keeping everything same and familiar versus the inevitable pain of mourning that conflict, change and growth involve. It is often voiced in terms of a predicament between risking the feelings of shame, embarrassment and humiliation of being exposed versus the relief offered by remaining in the retreat at the cost of much pain, frustration and despair.

Racist thinking and feeling appears to be underpinned by a specific phantasy of fusion with an object and can come into play by a hostile attempt to control the object in such a way that you are not allowed to be yourself as a separate person with an identity (Kovel 1970, Fanon 1986, Davids 1992, Tan 1993).

The level of brutality can emerge in both overt and covert ways which may or may not accompany physical violence. When it is done covertly there is often the experience of being at the receiving end of something awful being done to you without being able to pinpoint the experience in any tangible way except that there is often a sense of outrage after the event.

I have suggested elsewhere that a minor difference such as skin colour as a visible sign of difference can upset an inner equilibrium by triggering unconscious anxieties to do with the recognition of dependency on and separation from the maternal object in the first instance, widening out to include the paternal object in a triangular or oedipal situation. This upset could be described as a narcissistic rage that emanates from what is perceived as an injury or insult to the self (Keval 2001).

Whilst Freud (1917) thought that the effects of such a 'narcissism of minor differences' was relatively harmless he underestimated the power of the destructive forces that could be unleashed when the narcissistic phantasy is punctured.

Quite why a minor difference should unleash such destructiveness is not clear but it is thought that feelings of shame, humiliation and embarrassment may play a critical role (Steiner 2001). Perhaps these are the intervening factors which culminate in an insult that drives the rage and destructiveness. The following quote from Hitler's (1939) 'Mein Kampf' illustrates his blueprint for creating a world of sameness, an attempt to keep a narcissistic phantasy and the integrity of a pathological organisation intact with chilling consequences:

> 'the systematic concentration of pure blood, together with the expulsion of all that is foreign or undesirable is the only way to succeed in eliminating impurities in the body of the nation. The body of the nation must be purified. The German people must become a single body in order to be able to unite with mother earth'.

The pure/impure split keeps internal anxieties manageable at the expense of considerable distortion of reality that racist thinking gives rise to. This distortion has the effect of creating misery and suffering in those at the receiving end who are deemed 'impure' and has profound consequences on the way mental space is structured which will affect the development of the mind of the individual or group who habitually use this form of defence to cope with anxiety.

Racism as a defence against thinking and curiosity

In order to keep the integrity of a pathological organisation intact certain types of knowledge or 'facts of life' (Money-Kyrl 1968) or in the case of the above, undesirable or foreign knowledge has to be kept out of awareness. Minor differences which are attacked in racism are part of a defence against the recognition of major differences such as the sexual differences and the differences of generations.

This means that the discovery and recognition of mother as a separate person on whom one is dependent would be the first rumblings of curiosity in the unconscious, paving the path out of the psychic retreat and one step away from a further recognition that she has an independent mind and life of her own, particularly a relationship with her partner, introducing parental sexuality and the Oedipus complex.

In this way contemporary analysts have been interested in exploring and elaborating the link between the 'epistomophilic drive' (Klein 1946), the in-built desire to explore the mother's body and the discovery of the parental intercourse (Britton 1989, Feldman 1989).

Working through of the depressive position which recognises the separateness of mother also parallels the working through of the Oedipus complex with all the oedipal anxieties of exclusion, envy and jealousy that this situation can bring to the fore. This discovery or its obstruction has profound consequences for the way mental space is structured affecting the capacity to comprehend and relate to reality (Britton 1989).

The triangular situation introduces new anxiety-provoking challenges to the child's mind. If the anxieties of feeling excluded from the parental relation are manageable it introduces different possibilities, that of being an observer of the parental relation and allowing oneself to be observed in relation to another. This capacity is dependent on whether the individual can 'play' with different configuration of links between objects in the mind, i.e. become curious about these links and what it gives rise to. This in turn determines whether mental space will expand with curiosity or contract if the anxiety that links give rise to is too intolerable.

In this way a link can be made between the quality of thinking and the degree of recognition of separateness. The prevalent anxieties dominating the individual at any given moment are likely to determine whether thinking changes from two to three dimensional. Thus the capacity for symbolic thinking is thought to be a continuous process which enables the differentiation of inside and outside spaces, subject from object, mindlessness and mindfulness and the bringing together and integration of past and present experiences including the comprehension of time, space and ultimately one's mortality.

The difficulty in creating a space for thinking thoughts (Bion 1962) is borne out in our clinical observations when we see some patients who are unable to think with us as if the anxiety of exploring or letting their mind wander is too catastrophic. They seem unable to play with ideas to act as symbols bridging into the possibility of a space in which they could potentially observe themselves and others in relation to one another. In other words degree of separateness and symbol formation are intimately connected (Segal 1957). The difference seems to be whether the symbol *is* the mother's body in which case we witness a concrete thinking and relative inpenetrability in our patient that characterises paranoid-schizoid functioning or whether the symbol *represents* the mother, characteristic of the depressive mode of functioning where mourning has led to a possibility for both curiosity and creativity to proceed.

In a similar way I would like to suggest that the racist imagination or state of mind captures the struggle to avoid this dual recognition in the service of achieving a fusion with the maternal object.

Meltzer (1992) argues what is often masquerading as curiosity is actually an attempt to get inside, possess and control the maternal object and space. Put another way the masquerade is one way in which discovery and knowledge of the parental intercourse is denied which affects the capacity to form links in thought processes that determine how curiosity, learning and creativity will proceed.

If we look at some of the contents of racist imagery one cannot help but notice that it echoes anxieties that centre on the coming together of two objects in a productive intercourse that is life enhancing, be it the relationship between mouth and nipple or penis and vagina. In the racist imagination these links are attacked (Bion 1959) in various guises. For example, there is often a curiosity about the size of a black man's penis attributing him with a possession of unbridled sexual potency contrasted with how this object of imagined potency is violently intruded and robbed by portraying him as a little boy and treated with a paternalistic attitude as if he was stupid. Similarly, the black woman is often perceived as an object of unbridled eroticism and the 'mama' with bountiful breasts treated with a mixture of idealisation and contempt in various ways. They all contain a lethal mixture of curiosity, excitement, threat and violence to the potency of both the mother–infant and parental relations. This envious castration has been amply observed in colonial history (Baldwin 1952, Wolfenstein 1988) which points to an observation often overlooked. The object of racism is of enormous significance in the psyche, important enough to be eventually attacked.

Racism appears to be a story of how knowledge about 'facts of life' is distorted through an internal attack on the links in object relationships. This means that just as objects are not allowed to come together in the mind so do thoughts representing these objects. The result is a sterility in thinking aimed at putting the psychic brakes on growth and development.

Thinking and curiosity are felt to be dangerous because they imply links to be made between objects paving the path towards the discovery of not only dependency and separation from the maternal object but also the parental intercourse leading to a central conflict in the human psyche, the Oedipus complex and recognition of one's place in the world.

Case material

In this case study I hope to show how the patient oscillated between spaces in her mind represented by the paranoid-schizoid and depressive positions with racist thinking that seizes the most salient differences between us, namely the colour of our skin (white female patient–Indian male therapist) to bring into play the workings of a pathological organisation in order to put the brakes on further growth and development. I have mentioned only those aspects of the patient's material that are relevant to the main themes of this chapter.

Ms. A

Ms. A was a doctor in her late thirties who came into treatment because she was stuck in her life. I came to learn that this applied to almost everything she did. This included her job which she disliked but 'stuck it out' for the security it offered, her unfinished research papers, and a relationship with a man which was going nowhere, sexually or otherwise. I later came to learn that she was terrified of being penetrated by him. I got the impression she was going through the motions of living her life but was not plugged into anything real which was in sharp contrast to something I found rather hopeful. This was a certain desperation in her voice when she spoke of life passing her by but feeling unable to do much about it.

Ms. A had the outward impression of managing well but gave me the impression of being phobic in almost every aspect of her life. During her adolescence I learnt that she was petrified when she had her first period and dreaded both her physical bodily changes and the emergence of sexual feelings within herself that made her feel terribly out of control. In appearance she wore clothes that kept her shape hidden, an apt metaphor for her life. Similarly, on the couch she often appeared stiff and terrified that I might say things which could touch her emotionally and catch her 'off guard' or say things that she had not thought of herself.

The opening gambit is her first meeting with me when she remarked on the dark colour of my carpet in the consulting room as a 'most unwelcoming colour' and said she preferred 'lighter colours'.

She brought a dream the following session in which she was sitting behind the couch whilst I was sitting at the bottom of the couch with my shirt off and having a conversation with her. She said she could not recall the content of the conversation but knew that I was married to a woman with blonde hair (the patient has blonde hair) and had a baby who also had blonde hair.

The session I am describing in some detail was following a summer break and about two years into her three times weekly treatment.

Ms. A started by telling me she had an uncomfortable thought that was usually expressed by some of her white friends. She said she did not take kindly to the grass being replaced by hard wooden decking in my garden and thought it must be related to Asians not wanting to take the time and trouble to spend cultivating nice gardens opting instead for an easy, bland and unimaginative solution. She quickly tried to reassure me that she was aware it was a ridiculous thought and went on to speak of her fondness for the green countryside. She recalled an early memory of travelling alone to her aunt's house in the summer break and watching the uninterrupted countryside rush pass her in the fast train, a trip that she resented because she did not want to be separated from her parents.

In our break she tried to complete her research in the library but felt too intimidated by the prospect of approaching the staff to ask for help. She also felt intimidated by others in the library who looked like they were working hard and then the thought of 'labouring' over her paper with little satisfaction put the final nail in the coffin when she left the library to go home.

At one point in the session she said she had also gone shopping in an area of London with a large population of people from the ethnic community. She said she felt frustrated and resented the language and food which was so unfamiliar to her and felt invaded by 'all this foreign stuff'. However, much to her surprise she liked the way the Asian greengrocers talked to the old ladies and then later in the session she imagined that I had invited people for a party in my garden during the summer break.

Discussion

At the beginning of treatment I understood her dream to be telling me about how she imagined the treatment would pan out. I was to be under no illusions about who was going to be the vulnerable and exposed patient in treatment. She was going to keep me at arms length by remaining in control behind the couch and keep me at the other end of the couch. Whilst ostensibly having a conversation together it was empty (she could not recall the content). One of the first things that struck me about the dream was the colour of the baby's hair which had no trace of my colour or presence. This pointed to a particular version of her oedipal phantasy which left no trace of the 'unwelcome colour' and presence of the father.

It was supposed to look like we had made a baby together but no intercourse would have taken place, it would be fake, the same course I thought she intended her treatment to take to ensure that she remained stuck in her life.

This material was consistent with the way her sessions were full of associations and dream material but I was sometimes left with the feeling of being dissatisfied, like a sterile marriage devoid of any real emotional intimacy or contact.

I came to learn that as a baby, Ms. A experienced considerable difficulties in being breast fed. Her mother told her that as a baby she behaved as if she lacked an appetite and had difficulties latching on to the nipple. She brought an association which she imagined was an actual experience of choking whilst being breast fed and imagined this to be her mother forcing the nipple down her mouth.

Her next association to this memory was that she found the idea of a penis and giving oral sex quite abhorrent.

I wondered about this early situation she described and its possible link with the way she frequently interacted with me in the session. She would often pre-empt what I was going to say by trying to complete my sentence. I felt she snatched what I said and completed the sentence on her own. It gave the impression that she knew what I was going to say as if both of us were working in harmony but it was designed to be a seamless transition that robbed my train of thoughts.

I felt her frustration out of waiting became so intolerable that she wanted to hurry me along as if to say 'yes, yes I know, get a move on'. This did not square with somebody who lacked an appetite.

Initially, I found myself either slowing down or hurrying what I spoke, thinking that I could fend off her predatory behaviour but of course I was clumsily trying to establish my own space to think. I am reminded of an instance, not in this session, when she physically choked as she was telling me about a colleague who had managed to get their research published which she said she was unable to read because it would make her feel useless.

She experienced similar difficulties with me when she was unable to listen to my interpretations because she felt that it emphasised just how inadequate she was in her thinking compared to my capacity to think. She felt that she should have been able to come up with the same interpretation herself without having to rely on me.

Instead of mulling over the content of my comments or interpretations she was more preoccupied with my motive which she felt was to dazzle her for the purpose of making her painfully aware of something she lacked.

I thought in Ms. A's mind, my thinking appeared to both choke and make her feel small and helpless like an infant. I think her predatory behaviour was an attempt to both intrude and disrupt my thinking in order to make it her own. In this way she violated our separateness and ensured that she kept the illusion of her self sufficiency intact whilst remaining inside her psychic retreat at the cost of watching her life go by but giving the impression that she was working with me; like in the dream she brought her intention was to keep me at arms length.

This becomes racialised in the material about changes that have occurred in my garden in the summer break without her permission. The changes represented by contrasting hard and soft textures in the garden represent the struggles that Ms. A was experiencing between an internal parental couple. At one level, it seems to represent an unwelcome presence of a hard texture similar to the unwelcome colour of the oedipal father but in my view it had deeper origins linked to the dark colour and texture of the mother's nipple in contrast to the soft and lighter shade of her breasts.

Perhaps the persecutory experience of choking at the breast associated with the dark nipple was transferred to the penis so that both milk and semen were now equated in her mind with something toxic. Toxic because it made her feel utterly small, helpless and dependent not only in the feeding relationship but also in relation to the parental couple from which she felt excluded.

This internal scenario was being re-enacted with me but despite her determination to remain stuck there was a secret desire and hunger to be reached hence the desperation in her voice that she was going to miss out on life.

She found contrasting relations (mother/father, male/female, hard/soft, dark/light, etc.) not only too conflicting, unfamiliar and bewildering but also potentially exciting and rewarding as she could see that despite their differences, the greengrocer/therapist and the old lady could have affectionate, rewarding conversations together, something she missed having with me because of our summer break.

I thought this was hopeful because she was not content with looking through the window of her psychic retreat and had started to become curious, dipping her foot out of the retreat which suggested that some mourning had taken place from our separation in the summer break and prompted her to look for me symbolically amongst the people from the ethnic community which she unconsciously associated with me.

This journey, however, that her curiosity was taking, was short-lived when she experienced a rich and different mix of languages and people from which she also felt terribly excluded. Hearing a foreign language with people talking in their 'mother tongues' must have also brought home to her our separation in the break. Her anger then escalated into a hostile racist response tantamount to running back into her mental retreat.

However, this was still a development if compared to the state of mind she displayed when we first met which suggested very little or no space for difference to exist between us. In fact the momentary awareness (colour of the carpet/me) was immediately expelled from her mind.

Her behaviour in the library showed how she managed to snub out the fires of her curiosity but this time it did not culminate in a racist response. Witnessing others engaged in productive work in the library and drawing on the help from staff to 'labour' over ideas for her research meant having to tolerate the experience of being in a feeding relationship and allowing a feeding relationship to flourish in her mind as represented by the 'labour' of thoughts and feelings. She had convinced herself that the fruits of her labour would amount to nothing.

Yet she clearly found the experience of the greengrocer and the old lady pleasurable if only for a moment before her narcissistic defences in the form of a racist assault began to unfold to help her recover from the injury. She could see that in fact something quite the opposite of bland, unimaginative and easy had taken place in our relationship before the break. Indeed it was her need for me as a separate human being which had been cultivated that created the problem for her. She wanted to have the pleasurable conversation with me, the greengrocer/therapist rather than the old lady or as she had imagined my party guests.

These painful feelings of loss, exclusion and narcissistic injury are expressed in the conflict between the old and new/same and different. Here the wish to cling to the old and familiar was also a wish to have things back to the way they were before my summer break, particular the phantasy of only me and her in a cosy retreat which excluded everything and everybody, idealised in the form of the retreat into uninterrupted green pastures of the countryside. Perhaps this served to comfort her from the grief and anger when she experienced the separation from her parents and from me in the break. In her mind she wanted to keep time frozen and believe that a separation had not taken place, much like she imagined the 'uninterrupted' green pastures to cope with her feelings of grief.

This must have been suddenly punctured when she saw my garden on her return from the break. Her anger was to do with the sudden traumatic recognition that the new garden triggered, namely that she and I were separate and that I also had a life independent of her. This is expressed in her grievance about Asians who exercised their independence of mind in choosing to speak their language but made her feel small and helpless and excluded. She wanted me to take the time and trouble making her the centre of my preoccupation.

This difficulty in both being and allowing others to be separate pervaded her attempts to experience pleasure in her life. What I referred to as her phobic response seemed to be about not wanting to be touched or penetrated by anything that would put her in touch with either joy or pain. Instead she poisoned her mind with a grievance that attacked all potent links in her mind which she could have drawn on to become more resourceful and creative in her work. This is illustrated in a dream she brought.

She brought this dream following a session that I rescheduled for her so she could attend an important meeting at her work. In the dream, she reported going to a place with her friends who had been very helpful to her. She noticed that her mother was not present but she still managed to enjoy this experience, however this was only short lived as she started to feel resentful towards her for letting her go with her friends. She felt her mother wanted to get rid of her so that she could do other things without the patient. This escalated into a deep resentment which turned into a vicious berating of her mother.

Having worked together towards rescheduling her time for her benefit she could only enjoy this for a moment before her grievance got the better of her. Her need for this grievance poisoned her capacity to enjoy her independence and use her talents to become more creative in her life. The stumbling block was that just as her grievance attacked the link between her internal parental couple so she was unable to link up with thoughts in her mind that would enable her to do her research and writing satisfactorily. Any thinking and potential creativity was therefore stifled.

Creating a mental space to play with curiosity in professional practice

Ms. A's difficulty in labouring over things in her mind and her life in general can help us to think more generally about issues to do with ethnicity and race that face social work thinking and practice.

Labouring over things can have at least two components. First, it requires taking risks in learning from experience (Bion 1962) which often involves much uncertainty, second it involves keeping linkages alive in the mind in order for a space to develop genuine collaboration which can pave the way for curiosity and ultimately creativity in thinking and practice.

As we know the general aim of a psychic retreat is to provide a shelter from anxieties to do with psychic growth and development. Specifically the aim is to avoid conflicts at any cost and thereby avoid any experience of and recognition of separateness or difference. Internally this means that links that lead to a recognition of the mother–infant relation and parental sexuality have to be severed or attacked in order to ensure retreat into a shelter which provides relative comfort and security from a sense of sameness and certainty even when this is quite deluded.

In a nutshell, Ms. A was unable to sustain a feeding relationship in her mind to be able to participate in a relationship, be an observer of it or be the object of observation, in a triangular situation. In the instance I have described she used racism as her defence against this acknowledgement which clearly affected not only her capacity to enjoy her own and others' fruits of labour but in her capacity to think and become more curious.

We know that professionals face pressures both from within and outside their organisations to create certainties in their work which may not always be possible. It is sometimes expressed in a culture of prescriptive thinking or a manual for thinking in place of discovery that can run into the danger of recreating a psychic retreat of sorts by avoiding the inevitable pain (and joy) of learning from experience and genuinely labouring over ideas.

Ms. A tried to snub out the fires of her hostility towards me by trying to reassure me that *she* was not being racist towards me, it was her white friends. In this way she was trying to protect herself from acknowledging hateful impulses towards me to keep things cosy and what she imagined would be the damage these impulses would do to me as well as her fear that I may retaliate. In essence, the fear was of 'labouring' through the morass of feelings in relation to me/her treatment and deepening her bond. Similarly, she tried to do a runner from both the anxieties of seeing people from the ethnic community and the racist impulse that was unleashed in her.

As professionals grappling with issues of ethnicity and race there is often a temptation to do what Ms. A had the habit of doing but it comes in various guises. For instance, taking a purely intellectual approach to the subject matter and draining it of any feeling so it becomes sanitised and 'safe' to work with. This is particularly the case with very contentious issues in social work practice.

Statutory regulations and procedures are facts of professional working life but once again the difference lies in whether their marriage to understanding is a happy productive one or sterile/hostile. The danger is to mimic the very simplicity and lack of depth or dimensionality that forms the very fabric of racist thinking.

Often the statutory function involves the social worker treading a fine line in their role which may involve an element of 'policing' on behalf of the state and being supportive or therapeutic to clients.

An example that comes to mind is one that was described to me in a seminar of social workers who were grappling with thorny issues to do with ethnicity and race in their daily work.

A black social worker who visited an elderly client in her home was faced with a barrage of racist remarks and phoned for assistance as the client needed to be taken into hospital for medical reasons. However, when her white colleagues arrived and witnessed the racist abuse, they refused to take the client to hospital and left the scene. According to their understanding of the 'antiracist' policy and procedures they did not have to assist the client who was being abusive, however, their 'antiracist' action left their black colleague alone having to deal with this vulnerable and hostile client. Had the ambulance staff and their black colleague been able to recover a space to link up and work together collaboratively they may have been able to rescue themselves from being drawn into the client's splitting that was getting re-enacted.

This elderly client seems to have projected her infantile anxieties of uncertainty and helplessness triggered by the thought of going into the hospital into the colour of the social worker's black skin. On this occasion the 'policing' functions of statutory regulation put a strangle-hold on thinking and colluded with the very splitting that is characteristic of racist thinking. Instead of a productive 'marriage' between the professionals thinking, the antiracist action resulted in an unwitting 'divorce', an attack on linking and thinking.

Ms. A was also 'policing' her psyche when she told me that it was her white friend, not her, that engaged in racist thinking. She too tried to 'escape the scene' just as the ambulance staff had left their black colleague.

This issue of 'escaping the scene' is a critical one for the way we think about how best to facilitate curiosity and learning about race and ethnicity for social work professionals. In my experience of running seminars for social workers I am initially experienced as the 'expert' with an expectation that I will give answers to questions that preoccupy them. I think this reflects a wish to escape their own minds and project the capacity to think into me. More often than not this means I am idealised in an unhelpful way because lurking in the shadows is a constant experience of me as a persecutory object on whom is projected the cloak of 'political correctness' or 'antiracism'. The issue then becomes the right and wrong way to think, inhibiting their own curiosity and learning. My task is to turn this around so that they will learn to use themselves as a potential resource for arriving at an answer that has undergone their own 'labour' of thought and feeling. To my mind this involves moving them from a dyadic space (them and me) to a triangular space in which they can start to observe their own thinking and feeling which involves not escape but engagement with often very difficult issues. When this state of mind starts to prevail in a group, the atmosphere is palpably different in the sense that it feels like a breath of fresh air.

There is literally more space to breathe and think more imaginatively and fluidly but the residue of depression in the group is not to be underestimated and is to be expected as the difficulties of truly engaging with issues of race and ethnicity without quick solutions start to become more real.

Much of racist thinking is aimed at keeping the world a flat place where there is little room for conflict, ambiguity, uncertainty or change. This is why racial stereotypes often have this painful but comical simplicity aimed at dissipating internal anxiety quickly. In the session I described it was the lack of depth or dimensionality that Ms. A was accusing me of being when she thought that I like all Asians was bland and lacked imagination. She obviously let the cat out of the bag because it was she who could not afford to become curious in her life because of the dangers involved in where her curiosity and imagination might take her.

If she started to become curious about me, which she showed some signs of becoming, this put her in touch with painful feelings of loss introducing her to a recognition of her dependency, with feelings of frustration and envy. It would also mean a recognition that I did not belong to her and was part of a couple (e.g. the imagined conversations I was having with my party guests) from which she felt excluded. The difficulty in acknowledging these links first of a dyadic then a triangular nature meant that thoughts representing these links were not allowed to come together in her mind.

She managed to become seduced into opting for an apparently easier solution by giving up asking for help in the library and labouring over her thesis. The first example she brought suggested that she had indeed managed to keep the link with me alive and symbolically translated this into an unconscious search for me in her curiosity about people from the ethnic community but this was cut short by her intolerable anxiety, which she reacted to by retreating into her racist thinking. Her second example was also an attempt to come out of her retreat and begin to unconsciously 'play' with her internal parents represented in her wish to play with ideas in her thesis. Having got to the library, this was as far as she could go before running away again. She could not stand the 'busyness' of the people in the library whom she imagined were being productive in their work.

An area of work that remains contentious is the issue of matching patients to therapists on grounds of race/culture. Again I think there is a question to be asked here about whether the solution proposed is an escape or engagement and I expect that this will also have some bearing on issues to do with matching parents on grounds of race/culture to children in fostering and adoption cases which I am less familiar with.

One of the arguments put forward by those who support the idea of matching therapists and patients on grounds of racial and/or cultural similarity is that it facilitates the positive transference or the 'therapeutic alliance', a partnership in the service of understanding the patient's difficulties. I imagine that by 'matching' it is also assumed that the experience of strangeness and alienation is minimised on the part of the patient, facilitating trust and empathy.

First, there is the obvious need for having a common language between patient and therapist that both can share, therefore matching on these grounds seems pretty straightforward but what about the situation of matching on other differences such as assumed racial/cultural similarity? It is not too difficult to see how this argument could be used where, for example, a patient has been racially abused in such a brutal way by say a white person that he is completely dominated by concrete thinking characteristic of the paranoid-schizoid mode of functioning as a result of the trauma.

He may have temporarily lost the faculty to discriminate between the white racist and white people in general, a faculty that needs a capacity for symbolic thinking which is the first casualty in a traumatic incident. He may therefore insist on being seen only by a therapist from what he deems to be his own racial/cultural background if only to feel temporarily safe, which is understandable from the point of view of his psychic state.

However, it is also a matter for the individual therapist and/or institution to decide whether to comply with this request and use the opportunity to explore the patient's thinking and reasoning behind his choice or not to go along with this request if it was felt to be colluding with the patient's difficulties and deemed unhelpful.

Whatever decision one arrives at, it is still an interesting issue to unpack and explore. For example, what is it that one is being matched for when it is race or culture? Is it really possible to do something called 'matching' on such an amorphous and diverse concept without reducing it to concrete categories like skin colour or which part of the world one comes from? We know that race or culture is not something one puts in the pocket to carry around but it gets spoken and even thought about often in that way and I wonder what it is that we have got drawn into when we do this.

I am quite aware of the argument often used that matching also ensures that the therapist chosen is aware of certain issues of sensitivity that might apply to a particular ethnic group, be it religious beliefs or, say, the experience of racism which a white therapist if aware of may not regard it as important enough to explore or grapple with in the transference. There is some mileage in this when one sees how often the issues of difference, particularly race or racism get overlooked in the thinking of clinical cases in many institutions. However, there is also the opposite problem of placing too much emphasis on external events and not enough on their connection with internal factors or dynamics.

The real difficulty seems to be centred on keeping the linkage between the internal and external alive long enough to allow some curiosity to flourish before it becomes hijacked by a rush into certainty. This would be equivalent to my patient running away from the brown faces she saw on the streets of London or the ambulance staff who escaped the heat of the moment.

There is an argument that it is precisely when confronted with difference that the real 'grit' of therapy emerges, i.e. issues that really matter can emerge in the transference to be worked through rather than remain hidden behind a phantasy of sameness.

The real challenge is to be able to create a proper space in oneself or the organisation (if that is not too omnipotent) to be able to think and take different positions to arrive at a conclusion. The opposite would be the two-dimensional thinking that often pervades these discussions driven more by a wish to tidy everything up and reduce ambiguity in order to soothe the skin, something that is human and understandable but not necessarily helpful.

References

Baldwin J (1952) *Going to Meet the Man*. London: Penguin Books.
Britton RS (1989) *The Missing Link: Parental Sexuality in The Oedipus Complex Today*. R.S. Britton, M. Feldman and E. O'Shaughnessy (eds). London: Karnac Books.

Bion W (1959) Attacks on linking. *International Journal of Psychoanalysis* 40: 308–315; reprinted in *Second thoughts*. London: Heinemann (1962) 93–109.

Bion W (1962) *Learning from Experience*. London: Heinemann.

Davids MF (1992) The cutting edge of racism: an object relations view. *Bulletin of the British Psychoanalytic Society* 28(11).

Fanon (1986) *Black Skin, White Masks*. London, Pluto Press.

Feldman M (1989) The Oedipus Complex: manifestations in the inner world and the therapeutic situation. In: R.S. Britton, M. Feldman and E. O' Shaughnessy (eds) *The Oedipus Complex Today*. London, Karnac Books.

Freud S (1917) The Taboo of Virginity. Standard Edition of the Complete Psychological Works of Sigmund Freud, London: Hogarth Press.

Freud S (1921) Group psychology and the analysis of the Ego. Standard Edition of the Complete Psychological Works of Sigmund Freud, London: Hogarth Press.

Freud S (1937) Analysis terminable and interminable. Standard Edition of the Complete Psychological Works of Sigmund Freud, London: Hogarth Press.

Hitler A (1939) *Mein Kampf*. London, Hurst and Brackett Ltd.

Keval N (2001) Understanding the trauma of racial violence in a black patient. *British Journal of Psychotherapy* 18(1), 34–51.

Klein M (1946) Notes on some schizoid mechanism. *International Journal of Psychoanalysis* 27, 1–24, reprinted in *The Writings of Melanie Klein*, Vol 3, 1–4. London, Hogarth Press (1975).

Kovel J (1970) *White Racism: A Psychohistory*. New York, Pantheon Press.

Meltzer D (1992) *The Claustrum: An Investigation of Claustrophobic Phenomena*. London, The Roland Harris Education Trust.

Money-Kyrle R (1968) Cognitive development. *International Journal of Psychoanalysis* 49: 691–698; reprinted in *The Collected Papers of Roger Money-Kyrle*. Perthshire: Clunie Press (1978), 416–433.

O'Shaunessy E (1981a) A clinical study of a defensive organisation. International Journal of Psychoanalysis 62: 359–369.

Rosenfeld H (1971) A clinical approach to the psychoanalytic theory of the life and death instincts: an investigation into the aggressive aspects of narcissism. *International Journal of Psychoanalysis* 52: 169–178.

Segal H (1957) Notes on symbol formation. *International Journal of Psychoanalysis* 38: 391–397; reprinted in the *The Work of Hanna Segal*. New York, Jason Aronson (1981), 49–65.

Steiner J (1993) *Psychic Retreats: Pathological Organisations in Psychotic, Neurotic and Borderline Patients*. London, Routledge.

Steiner J (2001) *Prejudice, Judgement, and the Narcissism of Minor Differences: notes stimulated by articles by Isaiah Berlin and Michael Ignatief*. The Melanie Klein Trust, London.

Tan R (1993) Racism and similarity: paranoid-schizoid structures. *British Journal of Psychotherapy* 10(1) 33–43.

Wolfenstein EV (1988) *The Victims of Democracy: Malcolm X and The Black Revolution*. Berkeley, University of California Press.

Part 2

Understanding and working with children and young people

4   Observation in social work practice

Biddy Youell

Observation is part of the day-to-day work of most social work practitioners. They are required to take careful note of what they see and hear in their interactions with clients in the office, on home visits, in contact centres, etc. They have to summarise what they observe as accurately as possible, in their files. In the current climate of accountability, they are trained to strive after 'objective' evidence.

Much of this kind of observation is directly linked to assessment. As such, it is anxiety provoking and potentially persecuting for both observer and observed. If workers feel confident that observations and judgements check out against measurable criteria, they are reassured that the assessment is fair and just. In this chapter I will argue that this approach to observation can leave out a vital element, which can be crucial in making sense of what are often troubling and confusing experiences.

The approach I am advocating is what is loosely called 'psychoanalytic observation'. It is a method, a skill, a way of looking, seeing and thinking, which is at the very root of clinical practice in psychoanalysis and psychoanalytic psychotherapy. It is also at the root of courses run at the Tavistock Clinic and elsewhere for allied professionals, such as teachers, social workers and nurses. The way in which it is taught within training programmes and post-qualification courses is as follows. Students spend an hour each week (for a prearranged period of anything from ten weeks to two years) observing an infant or young child in their home setting or sometimes, at nursery. They are asked not to take notes during the observational hour but to write up as much as they can recall after the event. These written accounts are taken to a weekly seminar where the group, with an experienced seminar leader, think together about the development of the child and about the meaning of specific incidents and interactions. The impact of the experience on the observer is part of the discussion. The observational material is explored against a framework of psychoanalytic concepts; aspects of unconscious communication such as projection, splitting, transference and countertransference. Students are dissuaded from premature theoretical formulation; rather they are encouraged to bear the frustration of not having answers, to tolerate 'not knowing' and to wait and see how situations develop.

It is the opportunity to reflect on one's feelings, which marks this method out from other training experiences. 'Subjective' responses are seen as valuable 'evidence' when explored in a rigorous way, with the help of the seminar group. The discussion is likely to put the student in touch with his or her own preoccupations, prejudices and established patterns of thought. It may also shed light on what can be understood about the child's experience, about the child's internal world. Without the seminar forum or some opportunity to discuss observational material with a supervisor or peer group, it is difficult to make sense of the feelings, which are evoked. If you allow yourself to be open to 'feeling' as well as to watching and listening, how can you tell what is your own response and what belongs to the child or parent? The complexity of unravelling what belongs to whom is one of the reasons why supervised observation is central to psychoanalytic training and why it has been so vigorously promoted as a valuable component in courses for social workers and others (Trowell and Miles 1991, Briggs 1992, Trowell and Rustin 1992).

Many courses, which have an observational component, also have a module called 'work discussion'. This grew out of the infant observation method and work well when taken alongside an observation seminar. There are, however, many courses in which students take part in work discussion without having the luxury of undertaking an infant and child observation and they still find that it has a remarkable impact on their working lives. Students write up as much detail as they can remember of a period of time at work, in role and in interaction with others. They are expected to take note of their thoughts and feelings in just the same way as in infant observation. The purpose of the discussion in the seminar is to enhance the worker's understanding of their client but also to support the worker in thinking about aspects of their own emotional experience, and reflecting on their professional practice.

Students are often anxious about being asked to do something which they feel to be outside their normal practice. They worry about exposing their mistakes or admitting to their hostile and intolerant feelings about the people they are trying to help. They see their negative responses as failings, rather than as potentially valuable information. They feel embarrassed about having felt upset or disturbed by their work, believing that part of being a professional is being able to avoid any emotional involvement. My purpose here is to illustrate the fact that to engage with one's feelings in the psychoanalytic sense is not to become over-emotional and over-involved but to be able to keep thinking about difficult things when under pressure. It does depend on the observer/worker being prepared to be open to noticing and describing feelings, which are stirred up in him- or herself. In psychoanalytic theory this phenomenon is what is termed 'countertransference'. The opportunity to grapple with this notion is immensely valuable and is the first step towards establishing what has become known as the psychoanalytic 'observational stance'. Many students say that it is the work discussion seminar, which helps them to understand the purpose of the infant or young child observation. The method suddenly becomes relevant to their professional lives and they begin to incorporate it into their way of thinking.

I hope now to illustrate some of the ways in which psychoanalytic observation can enrich social work practice. I shall focus on the observation of very young children and their parents with particular reference to understanding children's play and the role of observation in making assessments of children's emotional development.

Observing young children

Infant and young child observation in family or community settings tells us that, on the whole, very young children are not persecuted by being watched. They want and need to feel that they can interest the adults, most importantly their primary carers, and they like to show off their skills and achievements. Indeed, it is through being attended to that a child has the experience of being thought about. Most children, in nursery settings for example, will actively seek adult attention. If there is a limited amount available, they will compete for it. At this early stage, it is often possible, through observation, to pick out those who fight for attention and those who give up and turn away. Amongst those who fight, will be some who do so with an edge of ruthlessness, without concern for the needs of others. Others will be more aware of their peers and better able to share the attention. Of those who turn away, some will find ways of occupying themselves, while others will seem more cut-off or aimless.

In ordinary 'good enough' (Winnicott 1960) circumstances, what these toddlers are seeking is the kind of affirmation they are used to receiving from their mother or primary caregivers. Many are having to adjust to a new degree of separation from mother and home and are seeking reassurance from other adults, or they are demonstrating that they don't know how to do so. For some, the early experiences may have been less positive and their ruthless demands may be a desperate bid for compensatory experience. Similarly, lack of protest, where protest might be appropriate, may be learned 'good behaviour' or may be an indicator of depression, of a child who has given up hope of being noticed as special or important.

I want to suggest here that the observational stance we promote is something akin to the kind of attention offered by a thoughtful parent. That may sound idealised or a little sentimental. It is not intended to be so. In fact, observation of this kind is rigorous, robust and challenging. It is a way of watching oneself and others with questions in mind. 'What is going on here? How can I understand more about it?'

My examples are drawn from the experience of working as part of a multidisciplinary team in a family assessment centre. Our task was to make assessments for the family courts in cases where there was concern about serious neglect and abuse. Because of the nature of the work, the examples are somewhat extreme and the point needs to be made that the assessments were very thorough and children were observed by a number of different people in a variety of settings. The context of any particular observation was always taken into account. Families attended for several whole days and were seen in a variety of combinations in a variety of clinical settings as well as informally around the centre as they took breaks, ate their lunch and interacted with other families. In addition to these observations, home visits were always made (to family homes and/or foster homes) and children were sometimes seen in their nursery or school setting. They were given the opportunity to make relationships with staff members as well as being observed with their foster carers and with members of their birth families. The multidisciplinary team took on a similar role to the seminar in that observations would be discussed in detail over several weeks before any conclusions would be reached about the children's best interests.

Trowell and Miles (1991) draw attention to a statement made by Lord Blom Cooper in his report on the circumstances surrounding the death of Maria Caldwell (1985). He comments on the failure of the key fieldworker to *see* the child's predicament. Her focus was the parents. Almost twenty years later, Lord Laming's report (2003) on the death of Victoria Climbie tracks similar failures on the part of multiple professionals. Margaret Rustin (unpublished papers) draws attention to the fact that interactions with Victoria's aunt and her partner were so difficult that nobody attended fully to the child. Observations of Victoria herself were scattered and sketchy and were never brought together for proper consideration. There is no doubt but that the adults were intimidating, but there is still something puzzling as to why Victoria became so 'invisible'; unable to attract the adults' attention and interest.

My argument in this chapter is that we still have some distance to go in being able to focus effectively on the children in complex family situations but that psychoanalytic observational skills can help social workers and others to face some of the painful realities of children's experiences. I have written (2002a, 2002b) about the usefulness of psychoanalytically informed observation in thinking about the development of babies and very young children and about the parenting capacities of mothers and fathers when there are child protection concerns. My main purpose has been to draw attention to three ideas. Firstly, that a quiet and uncomplaining baby is not necessarily a healthy and contented one. Secondly, that children's play can be misleading. Thirdly, that some parenting 'skills' can be learned, but that parenting demands more; it demands a capacity to think about and understand the child's emotional experience and to manage anxiety.

The quiet baby

In spite of an ever-increasing body of knowledge about the cognitive and emotional development of very young babies there is still a tendency in society at large to hold onto an idea that all an infant really needs are warmth, food and plenty of sleep. There is a tendency to assume that an uncomfortable or unhappy baby cries a lot and does not sleep. The idea that a baby who sleeps a lot and who rarely cries might equally give cause for concern is a difficult one to grasp. Infant observation has provided a body of knowledge about the complexities of infant development; the intricacies of the match or mismatch between mother and baby and the huge variety of ways in which babies manage physical discomfort, anxiety and disappointment. It is now an accepted fact that some babies 'shut-down' in the face of maternal depression. Others seem able to put enormous energy and determination into their efforts to engage their mother's interest. In the face of neglect, emotional deprivation or active abuse, many babies find ways to cut off from the world. They either learn to stay quiet so as to avoid the hostility shown to them when they protest, or they demand little because they have simply given up hope of being able to evoke a satisfying response.

Case example: Kylie

Seven-month-old Kylie was an extreme example of this phenomenon. She was brought to the family centre by her foster carer who handed her over on the threshold like a parcel, together with a large bag of nappies, bottles and clean clothes. She left without speaking to the baby, telling the workers she would return at the end of the afternoon. This was an experienced carer who was said to be offering good quality care to Kylie who was lying asleep in a cosy carrycot, dressed in a pretty frock and bootees. Staff only became concerned when she continued to sleep for several hours, despite the noisy activity of other children in the centre. When she did wake up, she made no sound and although she accepted the teat of her bottle and began to take the milk, she did so without any enthusiasm and made no eye contact with the worker who was feeding her. The following is an extract from an observation written by a worker who was trying actively to engage with her in a playful way.

I placed Kylie on her tummy on a blanket on the floor and got down so as to be alongside her and within her view. She made one attempt to lift her head and there was a slight twist in her torso such that I thought she might be trying to turn over. I made encouraging sounds but she soon flopped her head onto the floor and remained very still, showing no response to my voice. I turned her over onto her back and she seemed more comfortable. However she did not meet my gaze as I spoke to her and her head remained in the mid-line regardless of what was going on to either side of her. She showed no response to sound or to movement. When I put a toy into her hand, she held it for a moment, but it quickly slipped from her grasp. I concentrated on trying to make some contact and talked to her in a lively way, moving my hands and taking hold of her hands to clap them together as I sang to her softly. Eventually, we made eye contact and I felt hugely rewarded and redoubled my efforts to maintain contact with her. I tickled her tummy gently and her mouth moved in what I thought was the beginning of a smile or a giggle. I put the toy in her hand again and she shook it and made faint gurgling noises. At this moment I was interrupted for a few seconds by somebody at the door and when I turned back to Kylie it was as if she had switched off. She was staring blankly ahead and made no response when I spoke to her and took her hands again.

The idea that babies or toddlers might be so damaged as to fall into states of despair at a very young age is deeply abhorrent, particularly to social workers who feel impotent in the face of shortage of resources or the absence of sufficient evidence to take action under child protection legislation. Hindle and Easton (1999) make the point that field workers are often in a very lonely position and protect themselves against the full impact of what they see in order not to be overwhelmed. When babies are removed from abusive homes and are placed in foster care, the relief is enormous and it then requires a huge effort of will to keep up the momentum in planning for permanency. Once safe, and living with experienced carers, babies are often assumed to be developing normally. Observations of very young children with their carers, or at contact sessions with birth parents often focus on aspects of physical care; feeding, nappy changing and so on. The notes usually focus on the parent or carer rather than on the baby and are often overly positive. The emotional development of the infant is frequently neglected when professionals so earnestly want to believe that parents are capable of change.

Case example: Mrs B and Steven

The following example is of a baby boy who was observed with his mother as part of an assessment as to whether or not the mother could manage to care adequately for this baby, having previously lost five children to the care system. She genuinely believed her life had been transformed by the arrival of the baby and was committed to proving it. She was seeing her baby for several hours each day at the foster carer's house and the carer's heart had gone out to this woman, whose life had been so full of abuse and trauma. The carer was hoping that we would find a way to let Mrs B keep this baby. A newly appointed social worker was similarly overwhelmed by Mrs B's life story and became an advocate for Mrs B's right to be given another chance. After all, she had separated from her abusive partner and was trying to make a fresh

start on her own. The social worker was keen that we should know details such as
how clean and tidy her flat was and how she took great care not to smoke near her
baby. It was difficult, but vital, to set all this aside and to concentrate on observing
the baby and the mother–baby interaction.

> Mrs B told me that she was intending to bond well with this baby and that noth-
> ing else mattered. She began to unpack the bag of supplies which the foster carer
> had prepared, explaining that Steven was now on 'hungry baby formula' because
> he was such a greedy boy. Steven took the bottle willingly but I had the impres-
> sion that he was not very hungry and the milk soon began to flood out of the side
> of his mouth. I drew his mother's attention to this and she withdrew the bottle
> for a moment before pushing it back into Steven's mouth. The spillage continued.
> Mrs B alternated between talking to me about her current life situation and plans
> for Steven and talking to Steven about how much she loved him and how sorry
> she was for all that she had put him through. Her voice was thick and tears began
> to fall down her face and onto the baby's head.
>
> She stopped half way through the bottle and winded Steven very carefully,
> stroking his back and talking to him all the time. As she turned him around and
> picked up the bottle again, she buried her face in her baby's face, rubbing noses
> and Steven regurgitated some of the formula. Mrs B laughed and mopped it up
> before resuming the feed. Steven tried to twist away and avoid the teat and then
> arched his back and let out a loud cry. Mrs B said she could take a hint and put
> the bottle down before standing up and walking back and forth, jiggling Steven
> up and down and singing. Steven brought up some more milk. His mother
> laughed and this time made no move to clean him up but kissed his face and
> pinched his nose vigorously. Steven cried in real distress and began to sound quite
> breathless.
>
> Sitting down again, Mrs B held her baby very close and stroked the top of his
> head repeatedly. Steven had his eyes closed, his face screwed up and was arching
> away with his fists tightly closed. He had fallen silent. Mrs B was talking about
> her other children and about her determination not to let go of this one. I felt a
> desperate urge to wrest him from her arms but restrained myself and suggested
> that Steven might like to sit in his rocker for a while. Steven relaxed as soon as
> he was in the rocker and there was a sequence of interaction in which his mother
> talked to him from a distance and he rewarded her with a big smile. As I com-
> mented on this, his mother said that she knew her baby better than I did and in
> her view, Steven preferred to be held. She took him out of the chair and a look
> of alarm crossed Steven's face. He turned his face away from his mother's kisses.

The impact of spending time with Mrs B and Steven was dramatic. After about
twenty minutes of watching the mother's desperate efforts to stay in close touch with
Steven and Steven's increasingly desperate efforts to get away from the voice and the
stroking, I was overcome by a desire to shout at her to put the baby down, or even
to grab the baby out of her arms. I felt that Mrs B's extreme neediness and distress
was being 'fed' to the baby along with the unwanted milk. At the end of the session,
I got out of the room and raced into the garden, taking gulps of fresh air. This was
undoubtedly a very powerful response to having watched and 'felt' something of
Steven's experience of a claustrophobic contact with his mother.

Misleading presentation

The family centre team became increasingly aware of the need to observe the babies themselves, however young. This was partly the result of seeing a large number of toddlers who had met their developmental milestones in terms of walking and talking but who were severely delayed in terms of their emotional and social development. These children were often misleading in their presentation. Referrals and reports from other agencies often described them as 'robust', 'self-sufficient' or 'resilient'. Some went so far as to suggest that the children were 'contented' or 'easy going'. These descriptions seemed incongruous when set against what we knew of their traumatic life experiences and our observations often revealed a different picture.

I remember watching an introductory family session through a one-way screen. A small girl (20 months old) was busying herself while her parents and older brother (11 years) argued with my colleague in the room about the grounds for the interim care order. The toddler dragged toy boxes off the shelves, bustled around the playhouse and made loud noises with pots and pans. She went to the book corner and took one from the display, carrying it half way across the room towards the life-sized teddy before allowing it to slip from her fingers. She threw herself into the arms of the teddy, then got up and went back to the toy boxes, rifling through and dropping things to one side and the other without looking at them. Her brother caught her as she went passed and tickled her and she giggled obligingly. When he paused, distracted by the conversation between the therapist and his mother, she broke away and went back to the playhouse. Her mother suddenly screamed angrily at the worker and her brother stood up threateningly. I looked over at the toddler and was amazed to see no response. As mayhem broke out in the rest of the room, she returned to the toy boxes and took out more toys. I went into the room and explained I would look after the baby in the next room until they had all calmed down. Nobody acknowledged my arrival. The little girl did not react as I approached her but took my hand without hesitation and left the room with me without looking back.

In subsequent weeks we tried hard to make sustained contact with this little girl but achieved little. She would smile obligingly when we greeted her and held her arms up to adults to be picked up, but as soon as she was in somebody's arms or on their lap, she would wriggle free and wander off. She would go to her mother when she first arrived in the morning but made no protest when separated at the end of the day. She was a child who had slipped out of her mother's mind as easily as she had slipped off her lap and our observations indicated that she had developed ways of protecting herself against the impact of these sudden breaks in connectedness.

Misleading play

The capacity to play is an absolute essential in healthy development. Through play activities children learn, they master skills, they experiment with roles, and they explore fantasies. Playing with other children, they learn to co-operate, to share and to compete. If they have experience of key adults being interested in them, they will be keen to share their ideas and will look to adults for approval.

However, children's play can be deeply misleading. Much of what passes as play in damaged or deprived children is an impoverished version, devoid of vitality, playfulness or imagination. Many children in the centre played in the way described above, constantly on the move and picking up and dropping toys almost at random. Some of these children were described in contact reports, and even sometimes by their carers or birth parents as 'happy to play alone' as if this were a positive characteristic. Children who never look to an adult to share their play or who actively move away from adult attention are a cause for concern.

Equally worrying are children who 'perform' for the adults, maintaining a bright, smiling persona which belies the emptiness beneath. Many children attending the centre would gravitate towards the dressing-up box, the percussion instruments and the glitter. They would make glittery cards for their mothers, dress up and dance around with noisy, exaggerated and unconvincing pleasure. Unwelcome thoughts or feelings would be blocked out by frenetic activity. Returning to Victoria Climbie, there is an account in the report of her dressing up and dancing on the hospital ward. Whether this was a manic defence or a genuine expression of relief and pleasure at being with benign adults, we cannot now know. What we have to accept is that this kind of presentation was part of what misled professionals into thinking she was a secure and happy child.

Similarly, while imitation is an important aspect of play it is a cause for concern if imitative play becomes repetitive and lifeless. One three-year-old at the centre became completely stuck in play which involved delivering 'cup of tea' to all the adults in the room. She journeyed back and forth to the playhouse for an hour at a time and nothing could distract her. Another three-year-old, a boy, became completely obsessed with the vacuum cleaner and paid no attention to anything or anybody else, throwing tantrums if his mother tried to take it away. It is very common for children to go through phases in which they are passionately attached to 'Teletubbies' or 'Bob the Builder'. However, if the obsession goes on for a very long time and is accompanied by high levels of anxiety, the indications are that it is antidevelopmental. I was once treated to a complete rendering of the script of 'Who wants to be a Millionaire?' complete with applause. At first I was amused and impressed by the accuracy of this five-year-old's imitation of the compere, Chris Tarrant but as the session wore on, I began to feel acutely anxious.

Case example: Paul

Paul, at five years old, was on the verge of being given a diagnosis of Asperger's syndrome or autistic spectrum disorder. His overwhelming enthusiasm for trains had at first been seen as age-appropriate and rather endearing. When adults found they could not distract him from his play, could not get him to make sustained eye contact and could not engage him in any joint activity, they began to wonder about autism. Trying to separate him from his 'Thomas the Tank Engine' book resulted in tearful collapse. The following is an extract from an observation of him in an individual assessment session.

> Paul left his siblings and came with me without any hesitation, clutching his 'Thomas' book and asking me whether I liked trains. He did not seem to expect an answer but raced straight over to the toys. He kept up a constant chatter whilst he searched through the toy box and I noticed his commentary left no space for any comment from me. It was peppered with references to things being

'broken' and 'needing mending' and to the animals and vehicles 'leaving'. He commented sadly that there were no trains. He picked out the toy phone and made a quick pretend call to an unidentified person, saying quickly that the 'little ones' were OK. I felt that he was imitating somebody reporting on the welfare of his brothers and began to say something to him about his family. However, at this moment, noisy children poured into the adjoining playground. Paul froze and then said in a very feeble voice that he wanted to go out because he liked playgrounds. He made no move towards the door but began to make very loud noises, as if trying to blot out any awareness of the noise outside the window. He turned to the dolls house and said he was going to play with it but became very agitated when he found that the roof lifted off to allow access to the upper floors. He said it was broken and grabbed at the glue stick and the sticky-tape, trying to open one and find the end of the other, whilst stating that he was going to fix it and glancing anxiously at the window as if he expected the noisy children to burst through it.

Paul suddenly dropped to his knees and reached for his 'Thomas' book, turning the pages and 'reading' the story. I tried to talk to him about what I thought he was feeling but I could not make my voice heard and was left feeling anxious and filled with a sense of helplessness. A few minutes later, Paul seemed to register my presence and asked me to draw a train. I did so and he put it on the floor and then ran it back and forth along the carpet making train noises and asked for a second one.

At the end of the session, Paul did not want to leave. When he realised that he had to go, he grabbed the toy taxi and a handful of toy animals as well as his 'Thomas' book and tried to push past me at the door. When I insisted that he leave the toys, he dropped them to the floor, 'became' a train and shunted past me, making steam engine noises and miming the movement of the piston bars with his arms. He went straight out into the garden and raced around in this fashion for the next twenty minutes. Nobody could persuade him to stop.

It was clear from this encounter that Paul's use of trains was deeply defensive. He was capable of some symbolic play and he demonstrated the fact that his head was full of ideas about his own situation and that of his brothers. He was preoccupied with things being broken and needing to be mended. However, he showed in his attempt to use glue and tape to mend the doll's house that he believed he had to do it all himself. He had no idea that the adult in the room with him, might be able to help. He also showed that he needed to defend himself against what he experienced as the threat from the children outside without reference to me. He retreated into repetitive play with trains when he was overwhelmed by anxiety. For some minutes, there was no attempt to engage me in the play; rather it seemed designed to keep me and any other imagined threat at a safe distance. Even when he became aware of me again and asked me to draw a train, my feeling was that I was being placated, being given something to keep me busy so that I would not do anything unexpected.

Paul's mother had mild learning difficulties and a chronic addiction to drugs and alcohol. She was also agoraphobic and had been shut in her flat with the children for many months. The father of her younger boys was a frequent visitor to the flat and the couple were known to have violent fights. When they came to a meeting at the centre to talk about the assessment and the possibility of treatment, they sat hunched up and silent. When asked what they thought about our suggestions, they admitted that all they could think about was getting back home. It was almost unbearable to think about the tragedy of this young couple's lives and even more painful to dwell on what must have been the children's' experience of living in the flat with them. It made sense of what I had observed of Paul's preoccupation with things being broken, his hypervigilance and his belief that he had to manage alone.

In cases such as this one, there is sometimes a tendency in the professional network to look for organic explanations for children's difficulties. I mentioned that questions were being raised about autistic spectrum disorder in Paul. We were able to say with confidence that his difficulties were not consistent with such a diagnosis. A few weeks later, however, we were asked to comment on the possibility of ADHD.

Soon after our assessment, Paul and his siblings were moved to a long-term carer who was determined to promote the children's development in every possible way. I had the opportunity to visit this foster home six months later. The carer talked about the progress Paul had made and I could see that he was both much calmer and much more aware of the adults in his life. He glowed at their praise and was keen to show me some of his achievements. When asked to show me a book, he selected not 'Thomas the Tank Engine' but a book about zoo animals. A main railway line happened to run along the back of the house, just beyond the garden hedge, but Paul showed no interest in the trains as they passed by. The progress I saw at this visit was such that we felt able to continue to hold out against any formal diagnosis, persuading the network to wait and see how things developed over a longer period of time.

In the case of Kylie we were much less confident. During the assessment period we had become increasingly worried about the likelihood of organic damage and had recommended immediate neurological investigation. We also recommended a change of foster placement. Seven months later, I made a visit to the second placement with some trepidation; fearful that there would be no development and that the battery of hospital tests would have shown up serious organic damage. In the event, what I saw was a bright-eyed little girl who was less mobile than an average 14-month-old but who was beginning to crawl and who showed a lively, smiling response to her devoted foster carer. Her carer approached her with playfulness and I was again reminded that the development of play in the real sense is dependent on an experience of playful interaction within a caring relationship.

Symbolic play and re-enactment

In imaginative, symbolic play, ideas emerge and storylines develop. It is sometimes then a difficult task to tease out what is imitative from what is imaginative; to tell the difference between re-enactment and symbolic play. This is a serious issue in cases where judgements have to be made as to whether or not children are communicating actual abuse. My argument here is that psychoanalytically informed observation can help social workers and others to reflect on more than just the content of the play, to examine the impact on them as observers and to use this as evidence in thinking about what may have been the child's experience.

In child protection cases, there is a strong temptation to look for evidence from children's play in the form of re-enactment. If a child accurately simulates sexual intercourse in play it can make everyone feel more confident about concluding that sexual abuse has occurred, or at least that the child has been exposed to inappropriate sexual activity. It is much more difficult to be sure of one's ground in an assessment if a child does not engage in obvious play and does not disclose.

Children do sometimes re-enact events in a way which is utterly convincing. One toddler, Mickey, whose baby brother had died in his sleep with no apparent cause, re-enacted a scene in which a baby doll was suffocated with a pillow. The therapist in the room with him was left in no doubt that this was something he had witnessed. The emotional impact was such that she felt convinced that he was re-living an actual trauma and not playing out some phantasy or some story that he had heard people tell. The suffocation was staged with a tremendous sense of urgency, punctuated by anxious glances at the closed door. The baby had actually died when this little boy was only one year old and so it was a traumatic experience, which happened before he had words (and sufficient ego function) with which to try to understand it. The re-enactment was silent but suffused with terror, which was communicated very effectively to the attentive observer.

In contrast to the above example, another two-and-a-half-year-old, Natalie, whose baby brother had received serious, unexplained head injuries, was observed to pummel a baby doll's stomach and then hit the doll's head against the floor. This took place at home shortly after the baby brother had been rehabilitated into the family after a six-month absence. The observer felt that it was not re-enactment, but was a response to having the baby back in the house . . . an expression of feeling about a particularly acute and complicated experience of sibling rivalry.

In normal circumstances, children use symbolic play to explore and work through all kinds of ideas and experiences. Adults are sometimes taken aback by the kinds of preoccupations which show through in children's play. Free play is often characterised by expressions of hatred as well as of love. There is likely to be rivalry, competitiveness, trickery, cruelty and triumph. It is important to recognise that this is usually born from unconscious phantasy and not from reality. The difference is in the affect. When children are playing out their ordinary developmental preoccupations, observers do not feel the kind of terror, which was so much a feature of the observation of Mickey. The difference in 'ordinary' imaginative play is that children know that they are playing. They may be temporarily caught up in a fantasy but they can quickly be brought back in touch with reality, which they know to be different.

Summary

The examples I have used in this chapter are extreme and were selected to illustrate my main arguments; namely that it is vitally important to focus on children, however young, and that psychoanalytic observation skills provide the social worker with a perspective on the meaning of children's behaviour and play which is potentially very informative. I have suggested that observations should be checked out against a theoretical framework (psychoanalytic concepts and child development research) and I have sought to stress that observing in this way can be demanding as well as rewarding. However experienced they may be, workers need the opportunity to discuss their observations with a peer group, supervisor or seminar group. It is through these discussions that the worker is able to bear the frustration of 'not knowing' long enough for possible meanings to emerge.

References

Briggs S (1992) Child observation and social work training. *Journal of Social Work Practice* 6(1) 49–61.

Hindle D, Easton J (1999) The use of observation of supervised contact in child care cases. *The International Journal of Infant Observation and its Applications* 2(2) 33–51.

Laming, Lord (2003) The Victoria Climbie Inquiry. Report of an Inquiry by Lord Laming. London: DH Publications.

Trowell J, Miles G (1991) The contribution of observation training to professional development in social work. *Journal of Social Work Practice* 5(1) 51–60.

Trowell J, Rustin M (1991) Developing the internal observer in professionals in training. *Infant Mental Health Journal.* 12(3) 233–245.

Winnicott D (1960) True and False Self. In: Sutherland JD (ed.) *The Maturational Process and the Facilitating Environment.* (1990): London, Karnac.

Youell B (2002a) The relevance of infant and young child observation in multi-disciplinary assessments for the family courts. In: Briggs A (ed.) *Surviving Space: Infant Observation and Other Papers: Essays on Mrs Bick's Centenary.* London, Karnac.

Youell B (2002b) The child psychotherapist and multi-disciplinary assessments for the family courts. *Journal of Child Psychotherapy* 28(2) 201–215.

5 'Thinking in and out of the frame'; applying systemic ideas to social work with children

Gwyn Daniel

In this chapter I will discuss ways in which the systemic approach can help social workers identify constraints on their thinking and describe how it provides creative ways to avoid stuckness and impasse and discover more maneuvrability. I will use as an example how systemic thinking can help social workers when they are making decisions about children at risk. These decisions are especially anxiety provoking because of the responsibilities they involve and the feelings they evoke. Social workers so often feel caught between the rock of systems and persons that have failed children and the hard place of inadequate resources and limited opportunities to make anything better. In this context, I will discuss the constraints that our own feelings about children who have been constantly let down may create for us and how the frame that we bring to our thinking about children influences the way we talk with children to elicit their point of view. The risks professionals can run if we do not require ourselves to think outside our own frame will be discussed and examples given.

Systems thinking probably has a longer history within social work than in any other professional discipline. Social workers have paid attention to the family context as well as the wider social system since the end of the nineteenth century (Leupnitz 1988) and general systems theory has been taught on training courses for at least the last thirty years, largely as a means of helping social workers to plan at what level of system they should aim their interventions. The systemic approach to psychotherapy (Jones 1993, Gorell Barnes 1998, Dallos and Draper 2000, Vetere and Dallos 2003) has also been increasingly influential in the past forty years both as a therapeutic method and as a conceptual framework for enhancing professional practice.

During the 1980s there was a key shift in systemic therapy in moving from the more mechanistic or modernist view of systems, exemplified within earlier texts used by social workers (Pincus and Minahan 1973) and family therapists (Watzlawick et al 1967, Minuchin 1974). In these writings, systems were conceptualised as objective entities whose intrinsic properties can be uncovered, understood and altered by 'experts'. Within this paradigm there was less space for discourses of subjectivity, emotion or self-reflexivity, although of course these features were rarely quite as absent in practice as subsequent theorists might choose to argue.

The paradigm shift involved a key understanding that the observer of any system is inevitably part of the system because the act of defining it in one way rather than another is a product of the observers view as much as it is a systemic property. Reality is thus understood as socially constructed and systems and structures are as much products of the discourses of the time and social context as they are descriptions of the phenomena themselves. This means that it is crucial to understand the position of the observer (therapist or practitioner) to the system, a position which is always contingent on the contexts of time, professional or personal values, class, gender and culture.

Within this paradigm, we are required to constantly reflect on what we ourselves bring to our professional interactions. This is, of course, key to all self-reflective practice whether informed by psychoanalytic or person-centred theories. However, systemic practitioners place greater emphasis on the contexts within which these transactions take place and the feedback processes that they create. The core of systemic practice is thus a constant movement between pragmatic engagement and epistemological reflection. Put simply this involves a reflexive relationship between doing and thinking, thinking and doing. It means taking a step back to observe oneself as an actor and questioning the premises (and, frequently, the certainties) from which our actions are propelled. This stance is difficult to achieve, especially under the fire of the daily demands on social workers, where positions of certainty are invited to justify contentious and/or contested actions. It is nonetheless essential if we are to maintain both ethical practice and our own 'creative edge'.

From a systemic perspective then, what are the most common barriers to thinking and how are systemic concepts and methods useful in overcoming them?

Four processes that I have identified both from my own practice and when I consult to social workers in training contexts are:

- Being too certain of a specific outcome
- Feeling individually responsible for an outcome
- Feeling undervalued, helpless or hopeless
- Becoming blaming or pathologising.

Becoming too certain of an explanation or outcome

When we become certain in our explanation for something, we may feel much more secure about the course of action we should take, but we will have given up, even if temporarily, our curiosity about all the other possible explanations and courses of action. In systemic parlance, we will have developed a hypotheses which has now become rigidified into a truth. Of course when there is clear evidence that children are being abused, we need to act immediately and holding a position of certainty will underline this. However, the most insidious effects of certainty are that they blind us to other explanations or points of view which may help our thinking to become more complex. In a recent incident from my own practice, I and other professionals became convinced for a variety of reasons that a child should not go home from school because he was seriously at risk of harm from his mother. To act, it was necessary to take a strong position that did not allow for ambiguity. However, once the child was safe, it became extremely important to enter into much more complex thinking around the mothers response to this action and how free she might now be to act differently in relation to her son, rather than to stay with the certainty of her dangerousness which had buttressed the action of removal.

One of the most helpful systemic ideas is that of conceptualising uncertainty as a rigorous, intellectually robust and ethical position, rather than a sign of weakness or equivocation. The uncertainty principle, as outlined by Heisenberg (1962) in the natural sciences and adapted by Anderson, Mason and others in the systemic therapy field, stresses the fact that the means we bring to observe any phenomena will alter and influence those phenomena, so that we are always faced with the effect that our own input has on altering that which we observe. This invites us to take a position of curiosity about the effect that we are having, whether as therapists, practitioners or researchers. An obvious example of this is that parents who are the subjects of scrutiny by statutory agencies are likely to behave in ways that are as much influenced by that surveillance as by any intrinsic qualities they may have. Being evasive, untruthful or aggressive can all be understood in terms of the response to and the meaning given to interventions by a statutory agency. Any assessment that is ethical needs to take into account that there is no objective neutral space from which we can observe and assess others; we are always in the frame.

We all have to live with this level of 'not knowing' and, if we can think of it as an intrinsic and valued part of our practice, then we can be more curious about the times when we become rigidly certain. We can ask ourselves why it is that we can only think about a family or a child in a particular way, what stops us engaging with a different explanation, such as the one that a parent or another professional is offering, so that we can only see it as wrong or misguided. After all, to describe another person as 'lacking insight' is really only saying that they do not view the world in the way that we do!

Feeling that we alone are responsible for an outcome

The burden that social workers feel when having to make life-changing decisions on behalf of vulnerable members of society can be overwhelming. It is very easy to lose the sense of our position as a member of a system which is set up to protect or to feel disconnected from the others, whether parents, extended family members or other professionals who all share responsibility for the outcome. Family group conferences have been a very effective means of promoting just this sense of connection. We all have cases which keep us awake in the early hours of the morning wondering whether we have done enough to protect. For social workers probably more than any other profession there is the spectre of the case that goes wrong when we may be publicly vilified and exposed in the press and to our colleagues.

In my own experience, monitoring my feelings about responsibility can be a helpful guide to how well I am thinking about my position within the system as a whole. Signs that I am getting over-responsible might be that I start trying to persuade clients of a particular reality and lose interest in exploring the effects of their view of the world. I might start acting beyond my usual professional role, I might find myself expecting less of families or other professionals, as if I have given up on any contribution they can make. This can lead to a sense of isolated personal responsibility rather than relational responsibility (Gergen and McNamee 1999) in which new and creative ideas can emerge from a sense of connectedness.

Additionally it is helpful for all members in the helping professions to reflect on their individual and family stories about responsibility and helpfulness. Given that most members of the social work profession have some experience that creates a desire to ameliorate lives, whether this is because of personal experience of deprivation or perhaps of privilege that invites a wish for reparation, it is important to be aware of the particular 'edges' in our work. These may mean that we are at risk of becoming over-helpful or responsible in ways that can disempower others in the system or lead us to feel isolated or 'burnt out'.

Feeling undervalued, helpless or hopeless

Social workers are mostly engaged with clients who are among the most economically deprived and socially marginalised in the country. They include parents who have suffered abuse or neglect in childhood that makes it hard for them to parent their own children, ethnic minorities who have experienced racism and discrimination or asylum seekers with a background of trauma and persecution. In the context of a society where economic divisions are increasingly polarised and where our own professional status is undervalued, it is easy to give way to despair about our ability to make any difference, as the number of social workers who leave the profession testifies. Additionally the clients themselves, resenting or feeling humiliated by our intrusion in their lives or our failure to deliver the material help that they think would make a difference, may blame us for any subsequent failures or setbacks. The most frequently expressed dilemma by social workers in child protection is that they are damned if they do intervene and damned if they do not. Additionally, the lack of resources in fostering placements and the devastating effect of abuses in the care system undermine our confidence in being able to provide anything safer for children. All of this is productive of pessimism and despair and such feelings are hard to live and work with.

One of the ways we might close down our thinking, especially if we feel an excess of personal responsibility, is that we become less realistic about what we *can* do, and less alert to 'news of difference'(Bateson 1973) which might enable us to see strengths and resilience in our most seemingly 'hopeless' clients. It is very hard to live with feelings of helplessness or failure and one solution is to convince ourselves that the clients are inadequate or resistant or to use other such pathologising language.

Becoming blaming and pathologising

While there has been a much greater emphasis in the professional discourse of social work on the use of non-pathologising language and on the empowerment of service users, it is still very difficult in social work to avoid using a deficit model. In the context of decisions to remove children from parents or foster placements, an emphasis on all the negatives is understandable as these actions have to be justified. However the risk that labelling poses for our ability to think is that it ossifies into a unidimensional view of persons or systems and often sets up adversarial processes between us and our clients. The temptation to go to experts who will provide a diagnosis of a child for whom repeated foster placements have failed, may lead, for example, to that child being labelled as having attachment disorder but the lodging of the problem within the person of the child then makes us less curious about the relational and contextual factors at work and possibly less likely to be able to plan effectively for the next placement, taking into account all the other factors.

We can see how all these four constraints might act on and inform each other. Feeling over-responsible can lead to feelings of hopelessness or despair which can lead to pathologising or labelling clients, a process which, if the family then acts to confirm the label, can reinforce our certainties and constrain us from looking at other perspectives.

Systemic ideas that may be helpful

- Identifying patterns and being aware of context
- Identifying strengths, resources or 'logical' actions
- Placing our own belief systems alongside those of our clients.

Identifying patterns and being aware of context

One of the problems about the very high turnover of social work staff is that it becomes harder to gain an appreciation of the history of a family's connection with social services, one which may extend over several generations, and thus to find ways of identifying the patterns in relationship. Indeed we could argue that the families themselves have a much stronger sense of the patterns over time, as they hold the narrative of their relationship to social services much more than does an individual social worker. Families may be acutely aware that each new social worker starts from the same position as the previous one, with little sense of how an evolving narrative between the family and the agency can be addressed and understood. This can lead to a false sense of optimism on the part of a worker that a particular intervention will be helpful without exploring the pattern of response to such interventions. Or it may result in an overly pessimistic response without an understanding of how the family has had periods of managing stressful experiences without inviting professional involvement.

Therefore, it is often very helpful to spend some time tracking these relationships and exploring what has contributed to a good working relationship and what has been problematic. Looking through the file with an eye to pattern may create an interest in gaps when the family seemed to manage without outside help so that the worker can be curious about what was happening at these times. If a family has a fixed explanation that all would be well if it were not for social services' intrusions into their lives, it can be more helpful to explore patterns in terms of when social services have needed to do this most and when they have done it least, so that some ideas may emerge about possibilities for the future. Sometimes ideas will emerge about specific life cycle events or other transitions that have created crises where outside agencies have needed to be brought in. Another important aspect of looking for patterns is that it avoids the trap of fragmented thoughts and actions that can follow from simply following guidelines and procedures without thinking about the wider context. For example, a rule that placing a child with another family member is always preferable to being fostered by strangers, needs to be understood not just in terms of the suitability of that person on the usual criteria but also to take account of the nature of relationships within the extended family and whether such a placement could set up more conflict that would make it less likely to work.

Identifying strengths, resources or 'logical' actions

An appreciation of context is fundamental to systemic practice. Indeed when faced with baffling, infuriating or self-defeating behaviours which tempt us to blame or pathologise our clients, an essential question to put to ourselves is 'in what context could this behaviour make sense?

An example is of a mother whose older children had been removed from her and who was expected to conform to some rules regarding her younger children, one of which was receiving help from various voluntary agencies and attendance at a family centre. She was failing to do this and had become very aggressive towards the allocated social worker. We were asked to give an opinion as to whether the children should be removed. When we explored with the family and the social work team, from a stance of curiosity, why the mother might be jeopardising her position in this way, the following pattern emerged. The social workers believed that, in order to demonstrate good parenting, she needed to accept help. The more she refused help, the more this was seen as a sign that she was unfit. The social worker's response was to try harder to persuade the mother to conform. The mother, however, had an equally strong belief, which she had not articulated before and which came from a family tradition of managing things without outside help, that receiving help meant you were a bad parent. This, of course, opposed the social worker's view that accepting help was a sign of being a good parent. Articulating these differences not as rights or wrongs but as 'reasonably arrived at differences' proved helpful in moving the relationship between family and social services onto a more positive footing.

Finding oneself in a position of trying to persuade is usually a sign of having lost the ability to think outside the frame and is a signal to take a step back, think about the patterns that are developing in the relationship and the possible reasons for seemingly self-destructive behaviour. This does not of course mean abandoning a position of clarity about risks and responsibilities. We encountered a mother who described how, following a traumatic episode in her life, she had started abusing alcohol and this was putting her young children at risk. She told us that nothing had any effect and she only stopped drinking after the social worker said to her that she had to choose between her children and the bottle; she could not have both. While we have only the mother's version of this conversation, it sounded as if the social worker was able to take a position that implied both a respect for her ultimate right to choose either path and a clear delineation of the consequences.

Placing our own belief systems alongside those of our clients

Beliefs, as we have seen, arise in particular contexts. These are both the contexts in which children and families live and which influence their thinking and the contexts that influence professionals in the own thinking and indeed to the way childhood and family life are themselves constructed (see Lindsey 1993 for a helpful framework for understanding the links between practitioners' personal and professional stories). We may be used to reflecting on how our own values about children's up-bringing are seen very differently from different cultural perspectives and the social work profession has indeed been at the forefront of promoting antidiscriminatory practice. However, cultural stories may constitute a more readily accessible narrative of difference between majority and minority families and professionals. It is sometimes harder to access less evident beliefs which impinge upon the relationship between professionals and clients and which stand in the way of developing a collaborative relationship. These may be idiosyncratic family stories which can only be understood in the context of patterns or experiences from the past.

A mother who was showing what seemed like extremely rejecting and emotionally abusive responses to her children, behaviour that was hard for the professionals involved to bear witnessing, was told by the social worker to cuddle her children and tell them she loved them. She reacted very strongly to this, saying she did not go in for 'that emotional stuff that you people think I should show'. While it was, of course, very important in individual work to explore the meaning of this, it was also important to explore the contexts in which she could be engaged with the children because their needs were pressing and could not wait for the longer-term effect of individual therapy for their mother. One context was that of the mother's strong fear that, as black children, they were at risk of being let down by the education system. She found it less threatening to work on ways of raising the childrens' self-esteem in relation to their learning than on directly working on her relationship with them, although, of course, both were intimately connected.

Systemic practitioners and therapists find it very useful to use a consultation model with colleagues, so that when we are stuck or feeling that we are engaged in 'more of the same' behaviour which either makes no difference or makes things worse, we invite a colleague to interview us as an outsider to the system we and the family or client have evolved between us. Even if this happens briefly, it can be set up in a relatively formal way with an agreement that the conversation is not about the family but about the relationship between the worker and the family, with a view to helping him or her understand the patterns and beliefs that may be contributing to the stuckness.

Making decisions about children at risk; ascertaining childrens' views

Dilemmas arising for social workers when they are asked to elicit children's views include how to ascertain children's wishes without implying that they will get these needs met, how honest to be about the shortcomings of the family and how to explore children's feelings without causing them more pain and distress. Here I hope to illustrate how the systemic principles outlined above can be helpful in managing this delicate process. The model presented here is essentially a collaborative one for talking with children, many of whom may have chosen silence or extreme antisocial behaviour as their 'language'.

Changing contexts for thinking about childhood

Much recent thinking about children emphasises their position as actors in the social worlds rather than as passive recipients of welfare or protection (Smart et al 2001). Without in any way challenging the idea that the welfare and protection of children is central to the social work task, this does create a different framework for engaging with children and with their understanding of their familial and social worlds.

If we work on the basis of a developmental model of childhood, in which children are not expected to understand certain things until they have reached the relevant stage, we can become trapped in a self-fulfilling process. We may never ask children questions that would enable them to demonstrate their understanding. For example, children who have been exposed to violent or unpredictable behaviour from a very early age are likely to have become ultrasensitive to the minute changes in adults' body language as an essential skill for their own or their younger siblings' survival. Older children in less dangerous households may not have needed to learn these skills.

Failure to address context may also lead professionals to think that the process of ascertaining a child's wishes and views involves getting at what the child *really* thinks and feels, independently of their relational context and their understanding of the positions of significant others in the system. Addressing context means engaging with children to explore their wishes in the light of how they understand the positions of significant others in the system rather than assuming that it is possible to get beyond it. Wishes and feelings are inextricably linked with how a system has been understood and how relationships have been assessed and prioritised. Ten-year-old Ravi, who lived with his father and grandmother and was refusing to see his mother who had moved out of the family home, was convinced by his experience of conflict between the two women that they could not both be good parents to him. By choosing his closeness to his grandmother, he had to construct his mother as bad and neglectful and not allow himself to acknowledge any of her positive attributes. This 'accurate' reading of the family relational system meant that, as well as facing his sadness that his mother had left him and his brother, he had to refuse an engagement with her that might over time have helped alleviate these feelings.

Reflecting on our own beliefs and feelings

Conversations social workers have with children usually take place in a context where relationships have been conflictual and/or placements have broken down. All participants to the decision are likely to have powerful feelings about it in terms of what has gone before and in terms of desired outcome. The context will be one of relational dilemmas, loyalty conflicts, disagreements between parents, between parents and professionals or between professionals themselves. Here professionals' own beliefs and feelings are crucial. Social workers will talk to many children who have been persistently let down, firstly by their parents and then by the care system. Inadequate resources are likely to feature strongly. Social workers will have feelings of guilt, shame or anger about this, together with uncertainty about what can be delivered. In this context, the construction of children as innocent victims of failed parenting or a failed system, together with the fear that they will be failed again, can create a powerful constraint on exploring how children themselves make sense of their reality. While children are obviously not responsible for their parents' inability to parent them, a focus on victimhood creates many limitations in conversation. It may lead a professional to be overly protective and anxious to interpret the child's experience in particular ways, for example to reassure children that none of this is their fault, they have done nothing wrong. It may make us less alert to all the skills that children have learnt to manage such experiences or to learn from them how they have come to evaluate adults' behaviour.

Identifying strengths and resources

Systemic therapists, which while being fully cognizant of all the profoundly harmful effects of neglect or abuse, choose, in conversations, to highlight the positive or logical ways in which people have come to think or act in the way they have. This involves tracking carefully and respectfully how children have come to make sense of their relational world and acknowledging the thinking that has gone into its construction, however bizarre or misguided it may appear (Cooklin 2001). An approach which validates children's thinking also protects us from labelling or pathologising children, metaphorically as 'damaged goods'. A child who, for example, has behaved in such a way as to cause breakdown after breakdown of foster placement, may be labelled as having 'attachment disorder'. A systemic approach aims to go beyond this labelling to explore whether the child may be expressing a hidden loyalty to a 'failed' birth parent or has developed a style of attachment that professionals have not yet understood. Thinking of children as 'expert witnesses', as having expert knowledge on their own lives and their own chosen method of communication (which may of course include not talking) can be freeing to those interviewing children, provided that we can remain open to their thinking and avoid imposing our own meanings. Children who have experienced neglect or abuse or have had constant changes of carer, will have learnt a great deal about the dark side of adult behaviour, about being used in conflicts or ignored and about promises made and not kept. Some children may respond to this by feigned indifference, others by 'switching off' and becoming 'mindless' or by refusing to talk. Many children, however, have become active and expert at scrutinising the adult world and their conclusions can make uncomfortable listening.

Thinking about children as active social agents is especially important when we work with those who have suffered emotional or physical abuse. Children who have experienced powerlessness or a total lack of control need us to help them develop a sense of agency. However, workers may find this difficult with precisely this group of children. We may wish to restore their lost childhood, we may want to avoid hearing how they have constructed the adult world or we may want to rescue them by being the person who *really* understands, or by perpetuating a fantasy of the ideal placement. All of the above constraints come into play when we are asked to interview children in order to make a decision about their future. We may feel we are loading children with too much responsibility or are at risk of not being able to deliver what they ask for, either because we consider their option to be unsafe or not in their long-term interests. However it is essential to remember that asking for children's views is not the same as telling them that, if we know what their views are we can give them what they want. What children might really want, i.e. that their parents stayed together or were able to parent effectively is already unavailable to them. The most honest and productive conversations with children are those which foreground this constraint rather than act as if it will not have its effect on the conversation.

Maintaining uncertainty

Systemic approaches, by acknowledging the inevitability of uncertainty in human relationships and by embracing the complexity and diversity of positions within a system, will think of these dilemmas as a cue for opening up rather than closing down.

As we have seen, it is part of the approach to constantly question and challenge our own thinking, especially when we are very sure that we know what is right for others. Being aware of our own assumptions will hopefully make us more curious about the views of others, especially when they are very different to our own. This enables us to take a genuine position of 'not knowing' when we talk with children (Blow 1997) and an openness to being surprised and challenged by their views especially when they make us feel uncomfortable. It is, however, important to be clear with children that, while we want to know what they think, the responsibility for deciding will reside elsewhere. We are representing their views to the panel or to the judge and the more we can understand their point of view the better we can do this. We are therefore asking children to help us in our thinking because they have knowledge that we do not, even if they may decide not to share it with us.

We were asked to interview thirteen-year-old Winston, together with his siblings, to assist in the decision around whether a care order should be revoked. This had been imposed after the father had served a prison sentence for sexually abusing a neighbour's daughter. Although Winston and his brother had been accommodated for a time, the family had been re-united and the father was once again living at home. The whole family had a history of an extremely hostile and conflictual relationship with social services. Winston was prone to violent outbursts at school and was considered to be unable to express his feelings. We were warned by the father that if we asked Winston the wrong question he would lash out at us. In the interview, Winston's older brother expressed himself very forcefully on the subject of social workers and told us that he wanted the care order revoked, so that the family could get on with their lives in peace. Winston said virtually nothing except that he did not trust any professionals. He sat hunched in his chair with his anorak hood up. However, while he did not speak with us, he noticeably resisted joining his brother in his opinion that the care order should go. At the end of the session we congratulated Winston on how he had managed the session and how he had kept his temper under control, despite being asked some difficult questions. We wondered if not talking was perhaps a way of keeping his own opinions to himself, showing that he had a mind of his own or was treading a difficult path between what the rest of the family said they wanted and some different thoughts of his own which might not be popular with the others.

In subsequent sessions, Winston was able slowly and hesitantly to express his fear that, without the care order, his father would bully the rest of the family, especially his mother.

Conclusion

Traditionally, there has been a tension within social work between engaging with the macro social and economic context in which individual problems are conceptualised as resulting from inequality, discrimination and marginalisation and the micro level of individual or family difficulty or dysfunction. Some of these tensions continue to operate within social work, especially around the contribution that approaches derived from therapeutic models can make. I hope in this chapter to have shown some of the ways in which systemic thinking can address the macro level of context for families as well as attend to idiosyncratic family processes in ways that do not pathologise. Systemic approaches can be useful both as conceptual frameworks for addressing and understanding complexity but also provide helpful practical methods of intervening. One of the strengths of systemic ideas is that they encourage a stance of curiosity about patterns and processes. In my experience of working with and consulting to social work teams, finding a position from which to stay curious not only helps with finding new ways of understanding and acting within stuck situations but in itself makes the job seem more intriguing and interesting. This has the potential to protect workers from the stress and burnout that inevitably leads to such a high rate of staff turnover in a profession that is constantly 'under fire'.

References

Anderson H, Goolishian H (1986) Problem Determined Systems; towards transformations in family therapy. *Journal of Strategic and Systemic Therapies* 5: 1–13.

Anderson T (1987) The Reflecting Team: dialogue and metadialogue in clinical work. *Family Process* 26: 415–428.

Bateson G (1973) *Steps to an Ecology of Mind,* Paladin, London.

Blow K (1997) Using ideas from Systemic Family Therapy in the World of Education. *Educational and Child Psychology* 14(3): 57–63.

Cooklin A (2001) Eliciting children's thinking in families and family therapy. *Family Process* 40(3): 292–312.

Dallos R, Draper R (2000) *An Introduction to Family Therapy.* Open University Press, Buckingham, Philadelphia.

Gergen K, McNamee S (1999) *Relational Responsibility.* Sage, London, New Delhi.

Gorell Barnes G (1998) *Family Therapy in Changing Times.* MacMillan, Basingstoke, London.

Heisenberg W (1962) *Physics and Philosophy.* Harper and Row, New York.

Jones E (1993) *Family Systems Therapy.* Wiley, Chichester, New York.

Leupnitz D (1988) *The Family Interpreted.* Basic Books, New York.

Lindsey C (1993) Family systems reconstructed in the mind of the systemic therapist. *Human Systems* 4: 299–310.

Mason B (1993) Towards positions of safe uncertainty. *Human Systems* 4: 189–200.

Minuchin S (1974) *Families and Family Therapy.* Tavistock, London.

Pincus A, Minahan A (1973) *Social Work Practice, Model and Method.* Peacock, Itasca, Illinois.

Smart C, Neale B, Wade A (2001) *The Changing Experience of Childhood.* Polity Press, Cambridge.

Vetere A, Dallos R (2003) *Working Systemically with Families.* Karnac, London, New York.

Watzlawick P, Beavin J, Jackson D (1967) *Pragmatics of Human Communication.* Norton, New York, London.

6 Individual brief psychotherapy with sexually abused girls and parallel support work with parents and carers

Reflections from a clinical research study

Julie Long, Judith Trowell and Gillian Miles

Introduction

The material for this chapter arose from a psychotherapy outcome study with sexually abused girls, funded by the Department of Health and the Mental Health Foundation; it involved the Tavistock Clinic, the Maudsley Hospital, the Camberwell Child Guidance Clinic, the Royal Free Hospital, the Great Ormond Street Hospital and Guy's Hospital. The overall project has been described elsewhere (Trowell and Kolvin 1999).

The project offered up to thirty sessions of individual psychoanalytic psychotherapy, or up to eighteen sessions of psycho-educational group therapy to girls between six and fourteen years old, randomly allocated to each therapeutic intervention. All the girls had been the subject of contact abuse on the balance of probabilities. All were troubled and had symptoms, and predominantly came from very deprived backgrounds.

The individual therapists who worked with the girls were either qualified or trainee child psychotherapists, clinical specialist nurses or medical senior registrars. They were asked to keep detailed process notes of the individual therapy sessions, and a clinical analysis was carried out from these notes. The purpose of the clinical analysis was to identify, retrospectively, factors which emerged from the individual psychotherapy which could add to the understanding of the effectiveness of such treatment.

The analysis was particularly interested in the impact of the trauma of sexual abuse on personality development and on the children's internal worlds. It looked at the girls' predominant anxieties and preoccupations, their capacity to relate to others, and to tolerate frustration; their capacity for self-reflection and for symbolisation, and the nature of their unconscious thoughts and phantasies. The study also attempted to identify changes that had taken place over the treatment period, and whether there had been any lessening of their behavioural and emotional difficulties.

It is important to note that all parents and carers of the girls were offered parallel support and parent work (Rushton and Miles 2000) and this work will be described later.

Some relevant literature

Over the last decade research in the field of child sexual abuse has led to an increase in information and knowledge about the identification, nature and prevalence of child sexual abuse. Outcome studies focus on the short- and long-term effects of child sexual abuse on personality development (Russell 1983, Wyatt 1985, Finkelhor 1990, Trowell 1997) and symptomatology (Gnomes-Swartz et al 1990, Kendall-Tacket et al 1993) and long-term follow-up studies (Beitchman et al 1992). Cotgrove and Kolvin (1993), Brown and colleagues (1991) and Zanarini and colleagues (1989) suggest that children who have been sexually abused:

- are more likely to show evidence of psychological disturbance, including post-traumatic stress disorder, depression, eating disorders, anxiety and fear, low self-esteem, guilt, suicidal behaviours and ideas, and dissociative disorders
- are likely to develop some form of inappropriate relationships, sexual promiscuity or sexualized behaviour and re-victimisation
- are more likely to be involved in behaviours including self harm, drug use, prostitution and running away.

There is evidence to show a link between abuse in childhood and multiple personality disorder and personality disorders in adulthood.

Despite the recent advances of knowledge in the field of child sexual abuse, there has been little investigation of the effects of the abuse and the resultant symptoms on the child's unconscious thoughts, their feelings, and their perceptions of themselves and others, or of what changes can occur in their internal worlds during the treatment. This chapter is an attempt to address this deficit by identifying and understanding those factors which emerged in the individual psychotherapy of twenty girls on the project.

Structure of the psychotherapeutic work

The individual sessions were structured in such a way that the sequence and duration of sessions remained consistent for each child on the project. The sessions were fifty minutes long, at the same time each week, over a period of thirty weeks. A set box of toys suitable for child psychotherapy together with drawing materials were available for each child to use. The girls were aware that they were attending the project subsequent to a disclosure of child sexual abuse. Each girl was told in the initial meeting with her allocated therapist, that the sessions were for her to bring any issues which concerned her.

The therapists, as well as keeping standardised psychological checklists on child sexual abuse, were asked to keep detailed process notes of the therapy sessions. These notes, written after each session, included descriptions of how the child presented herself on arrival, her relationship to the therapist, her capacity to play or engage in meaningful dialogue, the content of the activity in the session, and the impact of these activities on the therapist's own emotional and thinking states (transference and countertransference communications). All therapists received regular supervision from senior child psychotherapists.

The clinical analysis

The analysis was conducted using the process notes of every fourth psychotherapy session, including the first and the last, for twenty girls who had completed thirty sessions of individual psychotherapy. A baseline was drawn from the written notes of the initial meeting between the therapist and patient, which included the therapist's initial impressions, the content of the session, and the impact the patient had had upon the therapist.

It was initially hypothesised that the girls who had remained at home within their family situation subsequent to the disclosure of sexual abuse were more likely to do better by the end of the therapy than the girls who had been accommodated by the local authority. However, what emerged from the clinical analysis was evidence that the girls' predominant preoccupation was not primarily with the sexual abuse they had experienced but more with disturbances and disruptions in their early experiences with a maternal figure. The nature of this earlier trauma, in all cases but to different degrees, was an experience of early maternal loss – a loss which preceded the trauma of sexual abuse and which did not directly relate to whether they were currently living with a birth parent, or in care.

From this analysis, based on a subjective review of the data, three distinct groups emerged, although this was seen as a continuum:

- The group who showed, through the therapeutic relationship and process, the capacity to retrieve a protective and attentive available relationship.
- The group who showed limited or poor capacity to retrieve or to experience an available and attentive relationship through the therapeutic relationship and process.
- A small group of girls who, despite the therapeutic process, exhibited a continuing experience of relating to a bizarre or fragmented maternal figure.

General findings

The narratives told by the girls on the project were twofold. The first and foremost narrative was one of an experience of early maternal loss, and the second narrative conveyed the subsequent experience of sexual abuse. The two stories, throughout the thirty sessions, were intimately and complexly entwined with one another.

With few exceptions, overall the girls did not use the sessions to talk about the sexual abuse, but brought material through their play, body language, drawing, and stories to communicate, unconsciously, their preoccupation with their experiences of early maternal loss. Even though the experience of sexual abuse had become linked with the experience of loss, it was the earlier loss which was conveyed both verbally and non-verbally to their therapists on a weekly basis, both in their communications and through the transference relationship with the therapist. It became evident to the therapists working with the girls that either a lack of emotional containment early in their lives, or a breakdown of this containment, had impacted severely upon the girls' internal worlds.

Within the first few psychotherapy sessions the girls presented quite marked emotional, cognitive and behavioural difficulties. Across the group, the therapists found that all the girls showed an impaired capacity to communicate and relate to them in a meaningful way, either due to withdrawal into a state of mindlessness and dissociation, or into a manic state with chaotic and sexualised behaviour. These two main ways of presenting themselves gave evidence of the girls' excessive use of psychological defences as a means of protecting themselves from experiencing repetitive distressing and frightening thoughts and feelings; this related especially to any further experiences of loss or abuse, which may have been stirred up within the therapeutic work. It was striking how extensive was the use of splitting and projective identification. The bad/feared experiences were often split off and projected either onto the therapist or, more seriously, out of awareness. There was also evidence of an extensive use of denial, as shown by complete or partial loss of memory of traumatic events; sometimes the girls remembered the facts about their experiences but not the emotions. In some cases dissociation, seen as a narcissistic withdrawal, was also evident.

As a result of these defensive mechanisms the following clinical issues emerged. There was

- an inability to mourn losses
- an impaired capacity for introjective processes
- an inability to manage premature sexual experiences
- an impaired capacity for symbolic representation (and hence limitations in thinking, learning and remembering)
- and, finally, a lack of reflective capacity (Fonagy et al 1991, 1997), which limited the use the girls could make of the therapeutic relationship to think about their past, or the impact of this for their future.

Psychodynamic inferences from the material of the process notes

An inability to mourn losses, particularly of the mother

From the moment of meeting their patients, the therapists noticed how the girls externalised their internal sense of deprivation. Even though many of the girls came from homes where their physical welfare was well provided for, they did not convey this provision. On the contrary, their physical appearance seemed to be an unconscious communication of a feeling of being internally impoverished. In nearly every case, therapists made reference to the girls' unkempt appearance. The way they looked seemed incongruent with their size and age, wearing clothes which didn't fit properly, or were dirty, torn, too small, or too big, or the child was described as thin, pale, small or too old looking.

One therapist wrote in her initial notes of an eleven year old child 'She was grubby, messy looking, with clothes that did not look like they fitted her properly'. Another therapist wrote that she thought her thirteen year old patient looked like a character out of a Dickens novel 'pale, unkempt and unhealthy . . . and her clothes seemed too small for her body'. Generally the girls were described as looking 'unkempt, withdrawn and rather lifeless'.

A small number of girls had experienced the death of their mothers, most before the age of four years. For most of the girls, though, their mothers remained present throughout their early lives, but had at some point become emotionally absent or remote from them. Case histories suggested that a number of mothers had experienced and continued to experience either physical or mental illness, turbulent relationships and depression, and that these mothers were preoccupied with their own past and present difficulties. The girls did not talk about their experience of maternal loss, but re-enacted their internal experiences through their external deprived appearance, or in their play and the stories they told, or in the way they related emotionally to their therapists. One small nine-year-old's play conveys the experience of loss so typical of the girls on the project. The therapist wrote:

> Today she focuses on the doll family, especially the mummy and baby doll. She struggles to place the baby doll in the mummy doll's arms, and the baby doll falls. She persists, but it does not matter how many times she repeatedly tries to get the mummy doll to hold the baby, the baby does not get held. It is painful for me to watch her in what became a despairing and futile activity. Eventually she discards the baby doll by putting it inside the ambulance, and the play between the other dolls becomes excited and sexualised.

This story, like so many stories and scenes enacted by the girls in their play, communicated a desperate wish to be attended to, nurtured and understood. Many of the drawings and stories told by the girls in these early sessions conveyed extreme states of pain, isolation and loneliness. The feeling of not having a parent who could 'hold them in mind' was a common theme throughout their play. Furthermore, it was not uncommon, when the wish to be 'psychically held' and 'emotionally contained' went unnoticed, that the child often turned towards excited, sexualised or chaotic activity, in what came to be understood as a defence against overwhelming pain and despair. The experience of loss of an available maternal relationship had also led to extreme states of isolation and loneliness for many of the girls.

An impaired capacity for introjective processes

What became interesting to note was the difference between the girls who persisted in their attempts to get their therapist to know about and understand their experience of loss and isolation compared to girls who became so overwhelmed by their needs that they became either more withdrawn, chaotic or dissociated, and so were unable to communicate their needs to their therapists in a meaningful way. It tended to be girls who persisted in their attempts to find an available and attentive maternal figure who could attend to the theme of loss, and who also conveyed a feeling that there was something worth persisting for, as though there was an awareness of someone who was available but temporarily distracted. These girls were repetitively able to communicate externally their internal feeling that there was someone or something missing in the therapeutic relationship. They did this by focusing their attention and that of the therapist upon losses which occurred in the moment-to-moment interactions between therapist and child. There were frequent cries of 'Where are the tissues, you forgot them?' or 'I can't find the pencil sharpener – it's gone!' or 'Where has the baby doll gone?'

At other times missed or late sessions, or a disrupted session, or moment within the session, could be experienced by the child as a feeling that the therapist's time and attention had been taken away from them. It was noted that the level of panic and distress which the girls expressed at these moments of loss came to be understood by the therapists as related to whether an object could actually be found and retrieved, and hence taken in to become internalised.

In contrast there was a group of girls who did not have the capacity to continue to search for a lost object, or whose distress or anger became overwhelming. There appeared to be a breakdown in the belief that something which was felt to be there and good (either a useful item in the box, or a quality of feeling between therapist and child) was now gone, and could not be found and retrieved. For these girls it really was a case of 'out of sight out of mind'.

At the extreme end of the scale there was a small group of girls whose internal psychological state seemed particularly bleak. These girls conveyed to their therapists an extreme state of withdrawal and dissociation, to the point of being described as mindless. One therapist wrote, after ten months work with a twelve-year-old:

> She continues to sit in her seat, with her head turned away from me, remaining silent. It is as though she does not want to see, hear, or know anything about the room or me. Her silences are long and heavy. I feel like I hardly exist to her. If I attempt to speak, my words are met with a stony silence. I am left in a void. It seems hopeless.

The girls who conveyed this extreme sense of emptiness and desolation impacted on their therapists most profoundly. Overwhelmingly, their therapists were to experience feelings of rage and frustration; feelings of desperation, sleepiness and despair in their work. Within the transference relationship, it was the therapist who had to experience what it was like to be in the room with someone who was completely 'withholding' and 'gone', where there was no possibility of contact or of taking anything in. Unlike the girls who were able to convey a feeling of 'something missing', highlighting the experience that there had once been someone there, this group of girls did not indicate any such awareness. It was this extreme group for whom it was felt that their early experiences had really been bereft of any good experiences of a warm and containing figure.

An inability to manage premature sexual experiences

From the initial sessions it was evident that the experience of being accepted for individual therapy had stirred up anxieties as to how and why the girls had been chosen by an adult for a particular experience, and what the nature of that experience might be. Some of the girls felt special, whilst others felt they were victims. One-nine-year old, in her third session, asked her therapist why she had been chosen for therapy and without waiting for an answer, said:

> I was the one at home who everyone hated and despised; they all told me lies, and that he (father) came to me because he hated me and didn't care what he did to me. One minute he would be there and the next he would be gone.

It was often noted that the girls' perception of the experience of 'being with someone' or of 'being together' might appear ordinary on the surface, but internally the girls tended to view relationships as being based on trickery and lies. They experienced relationships in which boundaries between adults and children, or between siblings, were blurred, and where ordinary rules of relating were broken. Often this resulted in a blurring of internal and external reality.

However, the therapists noted that for all the girls, there was little talk of the actual abuse, only a marked repetitive enactment of their internal state of feeling invaded and contaminated through external and concrete means, through their appearance, and their use of words and play. The girls often came to their sessions looking grubby, with ripped tights or skirts, ink spilled or dirt under the fingernails. Within the sessions paints would get spilt, or the colours would run into each other, glue getting everywhere and making things sticky, or the room would be left in a complete mess, and in some cases very smelly.

Other girls came in skimpy skirts, or low-cut blouses, appearing seductive. Some looked older than their years, others as though their development had ceased at an early age. Some girls conveyed a feeling of being special, or of having seductive powers over the therapist. Particular everyday words such as 'come', ' together' , ' us', 'excited, ' inside' would quite suddenly become concretely sexual in meaning, becoming seductive, perverse and exciting on the one hand, and on the other (as many therapists wrote in their notes) leaving them feeling invaded and dirtied by the girls. Furthermore, the need to talk repeatedly and graphically about sexual or self-abusive activities, or repeatedly ask the therapist questions, became a means to project their own disturbing experiences, which they were unable to bear. At other times, it was the therapist who felt her presence in the room or her interpretations were intrusive. One therapist wrote

> She begins to squash and press the plasticine, molding it in her hands, squelching, rolling and pulling it into shape. As she continues to do this, I begin increasingly to feel voyeuristic, as if I am watching my patient involved in a distasteful and sexual activity. I wanted to look away. As my patient continues to handle the plasticine in this way I feel increasingly sleepy and cannot think. It becomes a real struggle to stay in the room with her. I just wanted to leave.

This session, as with many reported by therapists, conveys powerfully the projective processes brought into play between the child and therapist, resulting in the therapist's identification both with an onlooker of abuse but also with an adult whose wish is to turn away from what is being done. The therapist's experience watching the child's play changes from that of a benign observer to feeling like a voyeur.

The heightened pre-occupation with precocious and perverse sexuality was evident around sessions leading to therapeutic breaks. In particular, the flirtatious and seductive overtones, the antagonistic and dangerous behaviours during these sessions, seemed to be of an increased oedipal and rivalrous nature. Particular themes which denigrated the mother–daughter relationship, including rivalry and contempt for the mother and the breaking up of the parental couple, occurred at this time. The difficulties in the relationships between mothers and daughters tended to be enacted in the therapeutic relationship around themes of 'being stolen and stealing from' and 'being hated by, and feeling hateful towards' their mothers. A twelve-year-old girl returns from the Easter break and the therapist writes:

> After a while she talks about a boy she likes. However, as soon as she begins to talk about him her mind becomes full of retaliatory figures. She feels her mother will punish her; other girls will want to beat her up. She then tells me she is different from other girls. She tells me this whilst sitting opposite me with her legs wide open, so I could see up her skirt. Furthermore, I found myself in a role of a

judgemental, dowdy, sexless mother, in the face of this sexually competitive daughter figure.

It was during the pre- and post-break sessions that therapists recorded that their own capacity to think and reflect upon the material became increasingly difficult, and tended to be superseded by management of the girls' behaviour and concerns about their external welfare, suicidal impulses, or risk of further abuse. The work became less symbolic and more concrete. The therapists recorded that at these times the work lacked symbolism and creativity, and seemed stifled by denigration and destruction. In many of the girls' minds, the therapy breaks were experienced as a confirmation that the mother/therapist's interest was elsewhere, leaving the patient abandoned. In many of the girls' sessions, it was clear how difficult it was to face the pain of the loss at times of breaks, and how they repeatedly resorted to a preoccupation with sexual and rivalrous thoughts and activities, as a means of filling an impending emptiness and in order to avoid facing the emotional pain.

An impaired capacity for symbolic representation, and hence limitations in thinking, learning and remembering

In the therapy it was often the therapists who were to experience and be aware of the emotional impact of the trauma the girls had experienced such as being left shocked, left in confusion, feeling lonely, frustrated and abandoned. It was not uncommon for a child to create either a whirlwind of activity and excitement or a feeling of being in a morgue; but it was for a long time the therapist, not the child, who was to feel the different states of mind. Emotional pain was communicated to the therapist by the child inflicting real physical pain on herself or the therapist. Internal chaos and confusion was enacted concretely by creating chaos and confusion in the room, and feelings of loss and abandonment were conveyed by missed sessions, or by a child suddenly leaving the room, and in the worst case, by extreme withdrawal into a dissociated state.

This could be understood as acting-out that replaced thinking. The psychological impact of trauma, though pushed out of the child's awareness, remained as unprocessed material, which emerged, or was 'acted-out' in behaviour and psychological symptoms. The psychological mechanisms used by these girls, as indicated earlier, included unconscious defensive processes such as splitting, denial and projective identification, alongside the more conscious symptoms of post-traumatic stress disorder. Words and activity could easily lose their symbolic meaning, and become concretely experienced as penetrating or abusive objects, as illustrated in this excerpt from a session of an eight-year-old girl:

> She played again with the glue stick, using her fingers to turn the stick, making the end go up and down, up and down, with the white sticky stuff slowly getting on her fingers and everywhere. The girl seemed momentarily 'cut off' from any awareness. To me, at this point, there was no other way to think about her activity than how sexually explicit it was. I found myself not being able to think clearly, or to know what to say to her at that moment.

Here, the symbolic meaning of the glue stick provoked a re-experiencing of the abuse, which had to be split off and denied, but was then experienced by the therapist. Sometimes activities within the room provided a potential forum for symbolic activity, such as playing with the ball. For some girls, the beginning of playing passing the ball between themselves and their therapists came to represent the beginning of an increased belief for the child that the therapist was available to receive, contain and think about her experiences. However, for other girls and at other times, the ball game and other games such as 'noughts and crosses' which require two people to play, though potentially creating a situation for meaningful contact, were actually used to 'deaden' any emotional contact or to 'sexualise' the contact. There were particular girls who used the sessions to repeatedly play and relay stories throughout the whole session as though they were engaged in the therapeutic process, but they were actually avoiding any real emotional link or work. The stories as noted by the therapists, became increasingly meaningless, allowing little creative work, or links to be made between patient and therapist.

One therapist writes of a session with a fourteen-year-old:

> She spoke continuously for the whole session. She repeatedly told me stories about stealing, being blamed for things and blaming others for things that were felt to be unjust. To begin with I was interested and tried to understand what she was telling me, and I attempted to think with her about what she was saying. However, she continued to talk, telling me more and more stories about her activities. I then began to realise she was not really telling me anything meaningful; the stories had little point to them other than, it seemed, to fill the room with her own words, and to leave me with my own thoughts. It looked as though there was something going on between us but there wasn't.

As already mentioned, it was usually the therapists who were left feeling many of the different states of mind which the girls were unable to experience for themselves. In particular, splitting and projective identification were the predominant means the girls used to avoid and deny awareness of their experiences, or to avoid any overwhelming feelings, anxieties and thoughts relating to past traumas which might be re-evoked in moment-to-moment interactions with their therapist and others.

The capacity to take in and retain information, to make links or to remember, was very limited for many of the girls at the beginning of the treatment. It was found that a number of them struggled to remember important information, such as the day they had therapy, or their therapist's name, and whether they had come the previous week or not. Significantly, it was noted that the majority of girls had difficulty in remembering their way from the waiting room to the therapy room. On average it took between three and six months before there was confidence in 'knowing' the way to the room.

Many girls expressed distress at not remembering and often it was related to a feeling of the person who provided the maternal function being forgotten. A very disturbed eight-year-old tried to paint a picture of her father, and the paints were so watery that the features of the face kept running into each other. She became distressed, saying she was worried about forgetting him, as though she could not hold onto the memory of her father, who had provided the emotional warmth in the family, but who was also her abuser. Time sequences could easily become muddles and storylines jumbled with children starting in the middle of a story or even starting in mid-sentence. Especially at the beginning of the therapy the girls frequently showed distortions in thinking and perception as well as memory.

An impaired capacity for reflection

Fonagy and colleagues (1997) have suggested that a prime factor in the development of resilience in children is the acquisition of a reflective function. The reflective function is the capacity to reflect upon one's own emotional experiences and one's experiences in relation to others. Fonagy's research focused on the 'quality of mental representations of the self and others', based on Bowlby's (1988) idea of internal working models; Bowlby suggested that when under stress, the child is left to draw upon his own internal resources to help him make sense of his experience. Fonagy suggested that children who have had an early experience of competent parenting within a good and supportive relationship with a primary caregiver, are more likely to acquire the capacity to reflect on their own experiences, through the reflective capacity of the carer, and are thus more likely to be resilient in the face of stress.

It was noted on the project that, to different degrees, there were girls who were more able to exhibit a reflective capacity than others. Three groups began to emerge: those who had indications of a developing reflective capacity, those who were beginning to be reflective, and those who gave almost no sign of reflection, and continued to function by 'acting out'. From the accounts of early sessions, it was noted that there was a particular group of girls who were able to demonstrate a reflective capacity from the beginning and who elicited hope that the therapy would lead to internal change.

Many of the girls in this group told stories about places 'deep in the wood' or in the past 'long ago' which were good places, full of warmth and treasures, or where there would be 'better times' but presently not easily accessible. The stories elicited hope in both the therapist and child that these places could possibly be reached and explored. These stories also indicated that it was likely that these girls had had experiences in the past of being cared for and protected – that is, of experiencing emotional containment.

> One nine-year-old in her second session with her therapist talked about the therapy room as ' . . . being dull, as it didn't have much inside, and that it needed redecoration', leaving the therapist with the idea that she was conveying a hope of an internal redecoration and internal improvement through the therapy.

It seemed that these girls came to the therapy sessions with some sense that experiences, both past and present, could be thought about and reflected upon.

The second group of girls gave evidence that the experience of the 'containing function' of the therapist elicited fragments of their own early experience with a receptive and attentive figure. Hints of such an experience being retrieved are illustrated in a session with this fourteen year old patient, who had hardly uttered a word to her therapist for the first two months of her therapy. She came to her eighth session and

> . . . talked thoughtfully about her pet animals the family used to have at home. But then she said she had been too young to really remember them. Then, after a long silence, she said she thought that there had been a gradual extinction of

their family pets. She said it was her father who had fed, cared for and protected them. Slowly she began to remember that it had been when her father was sent to prison (due to the abuse) that the animals had gradually died. She reflected that it would not be worth getting any more pets as it would not make up for what was lost.

The therapist attempted to link the patient's feelings of loss of the pets to the loss of her father who she felt had taken care of things. However, the patient had not been able to bear this interpretation about her own loss, and rendered herself mentally blank, remaining silent and inaccessible for the rest of the session. It was interesting to note that after this session, the patient was able to find her way from the waiting room to the therapy room for the first time. It is possible to think that in this session the patient might have had an experience of psychically finding her way to a receptive space in her therapist's mind, feeling that her therapist had understood something of her pain and hopelessness.

There were a small number of girls who were unable to use the therapy to begin to reflect upon, or retrieve, any real experiences of a containing and reflective object. These girls indicated that their very early experiences had most likely been without adequate nurturing and protective care. They had immense difficulties relating to their therapists, as they continued to use psychological mechanisms excessively to prevent any emotional contact being made. This particular group tended to be the ones who remained withdrawn, dissociated, or ones in whom concrete and bizarre thinking predominated.

Discussion of the work with the girls

It was evident that many of the girls, before being offered individual psychotherapy, had had little opportunity of working through their experiences both of the early maternal loss they had experienced and the subsequent trauma of sexual abuse. The therapist's function of being available and receptive to the child's internal responses to their traumatic experiences, to think about and reflect upon the child's communications, provided a means for many of the girls to begin to make sense of their past and present experiences.

For unconscious experiences to be understood the child needs a containing figure who can contain and process their feelings, thoughts and experiences (Bion 1962). Fonagy and colleagues (1991) suggested that the child needs an experience of a maternal figure who is receptive and has the capacity to reflect upon their own and the child's experiences. The therapists' function on the project was not only to be available and receptive to the child's internal communications and responses relating to the trauma, but also to give meaning to the unprocessed anxieties, thoughts and fragments of experience which they unconsciously enacted within the transference relationship. The therapists' capacity to receive, think about and reflect upon the girls' experiences with them provided a means for many of these girls to begin to make sense of their past and present emotional experience. Some could then recover, or begin to develop the capacity to reflect.

The majority of the therapists were female, and this may have accounted for the nature of the sexualised material in which the focus, consciously or unconsciously, was on rivalry with the mother/therapist and the fear of envious attacks in retaliation

(Trowell 1997). There may also have been issues for the therapists themselves. Certainly, reports from the supervisors (Emanuel et al 2002) suggest that a pervasive, perverse and premature sexual knowledge and experience made it difficult at times to focus on the therapeutic task. The need for regular supervision is made very forcefully. The four male therapists were apprehensive in anticipation, but during the therapy they were used as benign figures that were frequently maternal, so that they needed to work to hold onto the possibility of being benign and male. However, the numbers were too small to generalise.

The use of interpretations which predominantly focused upon issues of loss and separation as they arose in the transference relationship, led to an increased belief in a relationship that was felt to be open to the child's distress. However, interpretations which predominantly focused upon the external trauma of sexual abuse (and not the enactment of abuse within the transference relationship) did not tend to create internal change. Many of the girls whose therapy tended to focus upon the sexual abuse as an external trauma continued to externalise feelings of both abandonment and abuse in a concrete way. It appeared that in this small group of girls there was little psychological 'working through' of the trauma they had experienced.

It was also interesting to note that where the negative transference was contained, but not necessarily interpreted, this led to an increased belief in a relationship with the therapist that could contain and sustain unwanted aspects of the girls. In particular, it was the therapist's containment of primitive rage and hatred, firstly against the abandoning and unavailable maternal figure and then against the parental couple, which had led to an increased belief in their resilience by the end of the therapy. Overall, by the end of the thirty sessions, all the girls on the project had had an experience of a regular space in which their experiences could be thought about. There were signs by the end of the therapy that all the girls had been able to introject a relationship which was felt to be benign, containing and more resilient. This relationship could receive unbearable and overwhelming emotional experiences and attempt to transform them into meaningful thoughts – even if for some of the girls this was only in an extremely rudimentary form. 'Acting out' behaviour in the therapy room, at home and at school had diminished, and for most of the girls there was an increase in their capacity for symbolic activity and cognitive abilities, particularly in their capacity to remember.

A therapist writes in the notes of the twentieth session with a nine year old:

> Now when she goes to her box and cannot find the pencil, rubber or things that are felt to be 'gone', 'missing' or 'stolen', instead of the heightened panic and distress she used to experience which led her to rip things up, she says 'I think it is here, but I just can't find it at the moment'.

For most girls, there was a marked change in the quality of their relationships, both within the therapeutic relationship but also at home and at school, particularly in more appropriate and realistic boundaries between adults and the child.

> One eleven-year-old girl whose mother had died when she was three, had an extremely antagonistic relationship with her stepmother. The therapy provided an opportunity for her painful feelings of loss and anger about her mother's illness to be re-enacted in the transference relationship. For this girl the therapist's

comings and goings meant that she could begin to mourn the loss of her mother, and also retrieve the good experiences of being cared for by her. For the first time, two thirds of the way through the therapy, this girl was able to turn to her step-mother for support. Furthermore, she was also able to turn to both parents and talk to them for the first time about the abuse she had experienced. It did seem that she had been able to relinquish her hold over her mother which enabled her father and stepmother to be more alive and available to her in her present life.

Overall, these evident changes were often regarded by the therapists as only hints of change, and only 'beginnings' in their capacity to make real and sustained changes, both in their behaviour and their perceptions about themselves and others. At the end of therapy, a number of the girls still struggled to manage themselves and their rela-tionships, and still struggled to believe that they could feel valued and cared for in an appropriate way. However, there was a strong belief that the shifts in the girls' inter-nal worlds were positive but that for some a longer period of psychotherapy might be needed to work through such deep seated issues relating to loss, the breakdown of containment and the further impact of abuse.

The qualitative analysis has been able to indicate that the girls who tended to have made more use of the individual psychotherapy were those who had been able to con-vey, early in the therapeutic process, that they had had an experience in infancy of an attentive and containing figure, even though these experiences had been disturbed and/or fragmented. For these girls the loss of an emotional link with a containing maternal figure had led to disturbances in the child's ego development, particularly introjective and projective processes. For this group of girls, the experience of ther-apy had been an opportunity, through the transference relationship, to retrieve aspects of this earlier good relationship.

The work on the project does suggest that working with issues of sexual abuse can only begin once an internal supportive and resilient maternal figure has been estab-lished. The work with the girls has conveyed powerfully that without the establish-ment of such an internal containing figure, who is felt to be receptive, protective and working on the creative side of the girl, enquiries about and interest in the sexual abuse can continue to feel concretely invasive and abusive.

Work with the carers

Alongside the work with the girls it was very important to consider the stress on the parents and carers. Clinical experience has shown that it was vital to offer a space for parents and carers to think about the implications of their child's referral, the mean-ing of the concerns, and the issues these concerns raised for them and their families, besides offering them support in their difficult task of parenting these very troubled girls. It was therefore a core component of the work of the project to include parents and carers alongside the individual and group therapy for the girls.

Parallel work with carers, both birth parents and foster carers, was built into the design of the study, and a full account of this part of the project is described elsewhere (Miles 2000, Rushton and Miles 2000). The project had limited resources for this work, so that in each case a decision was taken at the assessment stage about the fre-quency of sessions for carers. Whilst birth and adoptive parents were usually seen weekly, and foster parents on a fortnightly basis, overall the level of support, both individual and group, was decided according to need. Parents were seen less frequently if they had less problems of their own and were strongly in support of the girl's treatment. More troubled or demanding carers were offered a substantial amount of help through the project, but with the same time limit as for the girl's treatment, thirty weekly sessions. Where parents were together, both parents were invited to attend, but in the majority of cases the birth mother or foster mother was seen alone.

The aims of the support work

The aims of the work were threefold. Firstly, to support the girls' therapy, and to encourage a positive attitude towards the treatment, so that the girls would attend regularly. Secondly, to address issues of parenting, where mother–daughter relationships had been disrupted, or there were problems with difficult or sexualised behaviour. Thirdly, where it seemed appropriate, to address the parent's own issues. Thus the work with the carers was centred on their parental role, and was not intended to be therapy in its own right, though inevitably their own experiences of abuse in childhood were rightful issues for concern.

The parent workers

Workers in the two main centres, North and South, were recruited across professional boundaries, and all were experienced child care social workers, or specialist workers in adult or child and adolescent mental health teams. In all, twenty-five workers were recruited, each carrying around three cases. Besides the individual or group work with the carers, at times of crisis or renewed risk these workers provided a bridge between the children's therapy, the carers and the outside world. Good communication between workers engaged with the families proved to be of great importance, both in underpinning the girls' continued treatment, in supporting the workers involved with the families in the community, and in an attempt to avoid a mirroring of the often powerful family dynamics in the network. In recognition of the stressful nature of the work, fortnightly supervision was built into the design of the project for the carers' workers.

The parents

Many of the girls were referred by their social workers, whose concern had led them to look for more specialist help that they were not in a position to provide. There was a predominance of very troubled families; only a third of the mothers were living with a partner, a fifth were single parents, and half had been divorced or separated. Often they themselves had had long-term psychological difficulties, anxiety and depression. Nearly half had reported their own childhood experiences of physical or sexual assault, neglect or emotional abuse. They had been struggling over the years with very real difficulties, physical or psychological illness and turbulent relationships. It was against this already troubled background that the sexual abuse of their daughters was often superimposed.

The impact of the abuse

Very many of the parents were themselves in a state of shock when they came to the project, having coped with the trauma of the disclosure of sexual abuse and its aftermath, which had sometimes involved ongoing court procedures. Alongside there had been the impact of the abuse on the family, where sometimes fathers had been imprisoned or had had to leave the home, and the negative effect of the abuse on the wider family support system. Many mothers were feeling isolated and alone, facing practical and emotional problems both for themselves and their children. There were strained relationships between couples, and between parents and their children. Many mothers suffered from an intense and immobilising sense of guilt, superimposed on an already low self-esteem. In addition to the external trauma of the abuse, there was the impact on the internal world of both mother and daughter. Oedipal taboos had been broken, and mothers felt displaced and betrayed. The child, having taken her mother's place, had come between the parental couple, and had been left with sexual knowledge beyond her years.

The work with the carers

The carers' workers needed to be available for the parents, to hear the often sordid details of the abuse, and to acknowledge and contain their rage and their distress. For some, there was anger with the girls and with their partners; for others, intense guilt that they had not known that the abuse was happening. The workers had to bear projections of intense pain and rage, together with distressing accounts of perverse sexuality. The trauma had to be acknowledged and given space before there was any possibility of moving on to think about the issues that the abuse had highlighted for these children and their families.

The importance of family history and attachment issues

There were, sadly, many families where sexual abuse was not a new phenomenon, but where abuse had occurred across the generations. These mothers told their own histories of sexual abuse, unresolved loss, neglect and physical and emotional abuse. Out of this experience they had little sense of their own worth, and they had gone on to repeat past patterns and to marry abusive and sometimes violent men. For these women, their own childhood experiences had been reawakened by the present abuse of their children, often overwhelming their capacity to parent, or to think about the child. Where there was no sense that there had been a reliable attachment figure in a mother's life, it became a far more difficult task for her to provide a secure base for her child. Some parents seemed stuck in their own past traumas and abuse; others seemed able to use the sessions to think about their own distress and move on to become more available for their child's experience and emotional need. For some children, the loss of the abusing father also meant the loss of a central caring adult, with both mother and daughter feeling an acute sense of loss in their different ways.

Parenting issues

Children who have been sexually abused can present severe challenges in their behaviour. This can take the form of inappropriately sexualised behaviour on the one hand, or on the other, intense withdrawal and depression, accompanied by feelings of lack of self-worth. For many of the children on the project, the sexual abuse was but one part of their difficult life experience. At the time of the therapy, some had been removed from their families and were living in foster homes or in residential care. At times in the course of the therapy, the girls themselves could be overwhelmed by pain and despair, becoming suicidally depressed or presenting very difficult behaviour. The work with the parents/carers involved thinking about the child's pain, the possible meaning of behaviour, and trying to rebuild communication between mother and daughter. At times of crisis more active interventions needed to be set in motion. The work could also involve supporting both birth and foster parents in setting clear boundaries for behaviour, particularly where a mother was feeling too guilty to do so.

Parents' own issues

The carers' workers on the project had the difficult task of holding together the many different aspects of the work. They needed to hold in mind the boundaries of their work and the therapeutic work with the child, the continuing safety of the child from further abuse, the parent–child relationship and parenting issues, alongside communication with other workers in the community who carried anxieties about the family. Where appropriate within the framework of short-term work, and where trust had been built, some parents were able to use the therapeutic relationship to think about their own past experience of abuse, their difficult relationships, and their own sexual difficulties.

   Women who have been sexually abused as children have often coped by repressing or dissociating such memories, thus keeping them at bay. If these mothers were to be available to their children in a similar situation, the workers needed to be available to allow them to recover such painful memories, and so to be more able to be in touch with their children's pain. Similarly, where couples did attend together, they were given a space to think about their own relationship under the stress of the abuse, and their difficult parenting role. Following the work on the project, some parents moved on to further therapeutic work.

The impact on the worker

Working with families where there has been sexual abuse evokes powerful feelings in the worker. Whilst it was important to be in touch with the projected pain of the abuse, it was also important to act as a container for such unbearable feelings (Kennedy 1996). The invasiveness of the abuse itself, the profound impact on children's lives, the psychological damage that is done, and the intensity of the feelings involved are often extremely difficult to contain. These feelings can threaten to reverberate both within relationships with colleagues, within the personal experience and day-to-day life of the worker, and in their roles as partner and as parent. Working in abusive situations can also stir memories of abusive incidents in the worker's past, making it difficult to focus on the therapeutic work. We were very aware of the workers' need for support and supervision, both to think about the families but also to keep in mind their own emotional wellbeing.

Postscript

A research questionnaire asked the carers what they had found most helpful for themselves within the project, and for their views about their child's therapy. Their responses showed that what they valued most about their own work was the support offered by the carers' workers. 'It was a life line at a very difficult time'. They were also asked about their views of the girls' therapy: where they were positive in their support of the therapy, this proved to be related to improvements in the girls following treatment. This finding alone underlined the very important part played by the work with carers on the project.

Acknowledgements

We would like to thank the therapists, supervisors, the girls and their families who took part in the project and who made this paper possible, in addition to the research team across all the centres.

References

Beitchman JH, Zucker KJ, Hood JE, DaCosta GA, Akman D (1991) A review of the short-term effects of child sexual abuse. *Child Abuse & Neglect* 15: 537–556.

Beitchman JH, Zucker KJ, Hood JE, DaCosta GA, Akman D, Cassavia E (1992) A review of the long-term effects of child sexual abuse. *Child Abuse & Neglect* 16: 101–118.

Bion WR (1962) A theory of thinking. *International Journal of Psychoanalysis* 43: 306–310.

Bowlby J (1988) *A Secure Base: Clinical Applications of Attachment Theory.* London, Routledge.

Brown GR, Anderson B (1991) Psychiatric morbidity in adult inpatients with childhood histories of sexual and physical abuse. *American Journal of Psychiatry* 148: 55–61.

Cotgrove AJ, Kolvin I (1996) The long-term effects of child sexual abuse. *Hospital Update* September, 401–406.

Emanuel R, Miller L, Rustin M (2002) Supervision of therapy of sexually abused girls. *Journal of Clinical Child Psychology and Psychiatry*. 7: 581–594.

Finklehor D, Hotaling G, Lewis IA, Smith C (1990) Sexual abuse in a national survey of adult men and women: prevalence, characteristics and risk factors. *Child Abuse and Neglect* 14: 19–28.

Fonagy P, Steele M, Steele H, Moran G, Higgen A (1991) The capacity for understanding mental states: the reflective self in parent and child and its significance for security of attachment. *Infant Mental Health Journal* 13: 200–17.

Fonagy P, Steele M, Steele H, Target M (1997) *Reflective Functioning Manual.* London, University College.

Gomes-Swartz B, Horowitz J, Cardarelli A (1990) *Child Sexual Abuse: The Initial Effects.* Newbury Park, CA: Sage.

Kendall-Tackett K, Williams LM, Finkelor D (1993) Impact of sexual abuse on children: a review and synthesis of recent empirical studies. *Psychological Bulletin* 113: 164–68.

Kennedy R (1996) Bearing the unbearable: working with the abused mind. *Psychoanalytic Psychotherapy* 2: 143–154.

Mannarino AP, Cohen JA, Berman SR (1994) The children's attributions and perception scale: a new measure of sexual abuse-related factors. *Journal of Clinical Psychology* 23: 204–211.

Miles G (2000) Working with the parents of sexually abused children. In: Tsiantis J et al (eds) *Work with Parents: Psychoanalytic Psychotherapy with Children and Adolescents*. London, Karnac Books.

Rushton A, Miles G (2000) A study of support services for current carers of sexually abused girls. *Journal of Clinical Child Psychology and Psychiatry*. 5: 411–426.

Russell D (1983) The incidence and prevalence of intra-familial and extra-familial sexual abuse of female children. *Child Abuse and Neglect* 7: 133–149.

Trowell J (1997) Child sexual abuse. In: N Wall (ed.) *Rooted Sorrows*. Bristol: Jordan Publishing (Family Law).

Trowell J, Kolvin I (1999) Lessons from a psychotherapy outcome study with sexually abused girls. *Journal of Clinical Child Psychology and Psychiatry* 4: 79–90.

Wyatt S (1985) The sexual abuse of Afro–American and white women in childhood. *Child Abuse & Neglect* 9: 507–519.

Zanararini M, Gunderson JG, Marino MF (1987) Childhood experiences of borderline patients. *Comprehensive Psychiatry* 30: 18–25.

7 Double deprivation

Gianna Williams

The theme of this chapter will be what I have termed 'double deprivation', and which I will illustrate with material from my work with Martin, a patient whom I saw on a nonintensive basis. There was first a deprivation inflicted upon him by external circumstances over which he had no control whatsoever. Second, there was a deprivation deriving from internal sources: from his crippling defences and from the quality of his internal objects, which provided him with so little support that he was made an orphan inwardly as well as outwardly. Martin was referred at the age of fourteen for aggressive behaviour, stealing and considerable learning difficulties. His reading age was six. He had made a suicide attempt two years prior to referral, when he tried to jump from a second-floor window.

History

Martin was the illegitimate child of African-Caribbean parents, and had been placed in care at the age of two months. His mother died when he was seven years old, but she had had no contact with Martin after he went into care. His father had disappeared at the beginning of the mother's pregnancy. Martin had three placements up to the age of two, when he was fostered by an English couple with a child of their own, a boy four years older than Martin. He was with the foster parents for ten years until fostering broke down at the age of twelve. It seems that the foster parents found Martin increasingly unmanageable because of his stealing and very defiant behaviour, and they had reached the point where they felt 'unable to accept him or have any trust in him'. There is no indication of the impact that the attempted suicide one year before the breakdown of fostering might have had on the foster parents, and how it might possibly have contributed to their feeling at a loss. However, they reported that the difficulties with Martin had considerably increased from the time when he was informed of his birth mother's death.

When Martin left the foster home he returned to a children's home and there were apparently no outward signs of his being distressed about the move. There are, however, many indications in the case history of the foster parents' deep feeling of failure in their relationship with Martin. They saw his coldness and detachment as confirmation that they had never meant a great deal to him. The first contact after the move to the children's home was a phone call which had to be cut short because the foster mother was crying so much that she could not talk. Both foster parents visited Martin at the home but their son refused to join them because 'Martin had hurt his mother too much'. After meeting Martin they left feeling that 'nothing had happened. He appeared to have happily settled himself down'. They said they would prefer to discontinue contact with Martin and have completely lost touch with him since. I have described the breaking down of fostering in some detail, as it is relevant to my main issue of this paper: the 'double deprivation' I mentioned at the beginning of the chapter.

Identification with an idealised internal object

When Martin started treatment he had spent just over a year at the children's home and was attending a large secondary school. The most alarmed and alarming reports came initially from the school, where Martin had become dangerously aggressive to other children. In spite of careful daily inspections, he had developed a talent for smuggling knives into the school and suddenly flicking them open, terrorising other children. On one occasion, which had been followed by suspension, he had pointed a knife at a child's throat and the child had very nearly fainted with fear. Martin did not seem to show any reaction to punishments or reproaches. While provoking violent emotions in others, he himself appeared to be, most of the time, devoid of feelings. As he was to tell me some months later, 'a teacher at my school said that I am the only person he has come across who has *no* feelings'.

When I first met Martin, I also perceived an alarming quality of numbness about him. It was as if, although the suicide attempt he made two years earlier had not succeeded, he was really only going through the motions of being alive, the motions of coming for treatment, very regularly and punctually (in fact he was invariably early), without being in the least in touch with his motivations for coming. His environment was indeed highly motivated on his behalf and, at that time, carrying the weight of all the feelings Martin was not perceiving himself. In fact his numbness, at least in part, was a consequence of his enormous skill in splitting off and disposing of feelings or parts of himself into other people, unfortunately in a very scattered way, as in the terrorising of children at school.

There was only one thing in life which Martin seemed to invest with enormous importance and this was his appearance. I had heard before he started treatment that he often took more than one hour getting ready before going out, and the care he put into the most minute details showed at first sight, even when he was in school uniform. When I saw him during a school holiday, I had a better opportunity to catch glimpses of his personal taste. He paid an enormous amount of attention to the choice of colours; the matching or contrasting of pink and pale green, of various shades of red and orange; he often wore bracelets; chains with a pendant; for a brief period he started wearing one ear-ring. He had many rings on each hand, some of them looked fairly harmless, but at times he arrived at his session with a full set of knuckle rings. It made a particularly striking contrast when he was wearing pale and rather feminine colours. Martin had a very handsome face, but at first it was very mask-like and showed little change of expression. His hair was short, carefully divided in the middle with a straight parting, and slightly puffed on the sides. As I have often seen him use a comb during sessions, I know that this puffing involved an elaborate procedure; a sort of back-combing made very difficult by his frizzy hair.

I mentioned earlier the disconcerting, unreachable quality I perceived in Martin at the beginning of treatment. There was *always* a feeling of his not being all there, which made it very difficult to establish contact with him. But I gradually came to realise that there was often a specific mood attached to the lack of contact. While not listening, or treating whatever I said as if he perceived only a remote sound, he appeared to be totally absorbed in a detail of his appearance; at times it might be something very minor, like removing tiny specks of dust or fluff from his jacket; at times his movements became feminine, almost in a caricatured way. For instance, using his sunglasses as a mirror, he could spend lengthy periods smoothing his eyebrows with his fingertips; or he could become totally absorbed in the care of his nails. Once he came to his session with nail varnish on the nails of both hands. On those occasions he treated my attempt to reach him with an interpretation as if I were a sort of annoying child, or a noise in the background: I should not disturb him while he was busy with something, which was so much more important than anything I could possibly say. Indeed the identification with an idealised internal object was, at this time, very important to him, being, precarious as it was, the only thing which held him together.

One particular session provides a vivid example of the type of projective identification I was confronted with, a form of entering inside an object like a hand into a glove puppet similar to the examples given by Melanie Klein in 'On Identification' (Klein 1955).

Martin was wearing an anorak with a fur-trimmed hood; I was to learn later that its name (it could not be more appropriate in the context) is a 'parka'. He pulled the hood right over his head, then took a comb out of his pocket and started combing the long-haired fur around his hood as if he were curling it with long, sensuous, feminine strokes. He really behaved as if he perceived himself 'parked' inside someone else's skin. The impact of his behaviour was heightened by the fact that on this occasion, as on many others, he was wearing menacing rings on his right hand fingers, but seemed completely oblivious of them.

In this session, and in the ones I have previously described, his verbal responses to my attempts to reach him were in the nature of 'Yes, what is it you wanted to say?', 'I have got no time for your rubbish', 'Tough, you have got to suffer', 'You are talking to a brick wall'. His tone of voice was cold, contemptuous and very hard. Indeed it was like talking to a brick wall, and after some trials and errors, I realised that this was the most important quality of Martin's communication: that he had to put me in the position of the child who tries to make contact with somebody who has no time to listen, a hard and vain mother who says, 'Tough, you have got to suffer', while she is curling her hair and treating with scorn and contempt the weakling who is trying to get some of her attention. I am referring to Martin's internal object, but it also appeared, from subsequent material, to be the phantasy that he had formed about the reason why his mother had left him just after his birth; that she was too vain, hard and self-centred to care for a small baby.

The purpose of Martin's unreachable attitude was now, as it had probably been many times in the past, the one splitting and projecting into somebody else both the feelings that he could not tolerate and a part of himself, the need child he had to disown; at the same time he identified himself with the unavailable object which at time he idealised, felt completely at one with, thus in control of.

When I said to Martin that I thought he behaved with me as if I were a nuisance child, trying to talk to a mother who is only interested in the reflection of her face in the mirror and can't be bothered to listen, a very hard mother, like a brick wall, he answered: 'There is only one way to find out whether you are a brick wall or not. You hit your head against a brick wall; if it hurts, you are not'. The implication of this statement is very enlightening in terms of the development of Martin's defences. He appeared to be saying that the only way *not* to get hurt, if you have got this type of object, is to identify with it, become the brick wall yourself and leave the hurt to someone else. The use of this type of defence brought about the numbness I referred to above, both through identification with an insensitive internal object, and through a depletion due to the splitting of feelings and parts of himself into other people. After all, the foster mother, *not* Martin, was crying on the phone, while he behaved 'as if nothing had happened', and it was the foster parents who subsequently made themselves unavailable for further contact. This chain reaction of rejection had probably occurred many times in Martin's life.

The pressure Martin could put on an external object to give up trying, to give up any hope that he could be reached, was very strong. I think that the forceful impact he had on people in this respect must have deprived him, many times, of positive experiences. He had developed a talent not only for hardening himself, but also for hardening people around him and making them deaf to the real nature of his need. Any further deprivation and experience of an external hard object was reintrojected and cemented the hardness of his internal object.

The Pakistani

Is it understandable that Martin should have such dread of getting in touch with feelings of dependency, when he had inside himself a very insensitive object and he had so often contributed to hardening his external objects? He was not as yet sure that this would not also happen with me, although the sentence I quoted earlier on implied at least a hope that I might bear the impact of his behaviour, and *not* become a brick wall.

Martin's profound contempt and hatred for a split-off, needy part of himself has been a recurrent theme in treatment; it was initially to be known to us as 'the Pakistani'. Martin's prejudice against Pakistanis was fierce and sanctimonious and he had often chosen Pakistani children as the target of his attacks in school. He used to say about them: 'The can't fend for themselves, or they wouldn't have come over here for help, would they?' 'They are inferior, they are savages, not like us British'. This inferior and needy savage had not only to be despised, but crushed and obliterated: 'Oh, I love Pakistanis', Martin said once, 'you hit them and they come for more and more and more until you kill them', and he menacingly caressed the knuckle rings which covered all the fingers on his right hand. It was probably very similar to what he felt would happen to the weakling, the fool who kept hitting his head against an insensitive hard mother; he would not survive it for long. Subsequent material brought much more into the open Martin's anxieties about death, but he was using as 'receptacles' the children he terrorised in school with knives. This type of acting out fluctuated, but it ceased completely at the beginning of the second year of treatment, when signs of integration of this split-off part began to emerge. Martin told me one day: 'I'm not after all the Pakistanis in the world, I'm not man-hunting, I am just after one bloke'. Then he started scribbling. On the side of his box he wrote *his* name, *his* address, and *his* telephone number.

Grievances

As, gradually and very tentatively, Martin began to realise that the Pakistani, he had been bashing, despising and depriving of the help he needed was within himself and he caught the first glimpses of insight into this area of need, of wanting help, and wishing me to retrieve him when he lost touch (the address and the telephone number), so he began to reproach me increasingly for hardness, coldness and negligence, in failing to provide what he needed. He could idealise the aloof, detached, narcissistic quality of his object, only as long as he kept the needy child completely split off. While he used this defence, he was the insensitive mother, he completely identified with her. The feelings that she evoked had to be felt by the despised, trampled Pakistanis, not by him.

As he began to perceive *his* feelings of need, he also got in touch with *his* grievances. His appearance mirrored very strikingly his changed state of mind and the shift of his identifications. He would at times come to the clinic wearing trousers too short for him, a torn jumper, holes in his socks. In the session previous to a holiday break, he was wearing a very thick 'second skin' (Bick 1968): a shirt, two jumpers, a cardigan and his anorak although it was not a very cold day. As soon as he sat down, he touched the radiator as if shivering and said: 'Call this central heating? Cold water running through a mass of metal'. When I linked this reproach for coldness, and his holding himself together with many protective layers, to the forthcoming holiday break, Martin moved to an eroticised and much safer area of grievance: he said I was such a cold person, because I came from a cold country (he was convinced I was Polish) and all we have in Poland is snow and ice, while he comes from Africa where they have beautiful tropical fishes and sunshine. While saying that, his attitude became very seductive, as if he wished to imply that he had all the warmth, the passion, the glamour of Africa, as opposed to me – a metallic object with cold water in my veins (the mass of metal with cold water running through it).

On occasion the grievance had a marked defensive quality to it, and Martin appeared to go to great lengths to put himself in a position where he could reproach me for neglect. From the very first days of treatment, he had come very early to the clinic, at least half an hour, often an hour earlier than his 10 o'clock appointment. We knew from the houseparents that he always left home after breakfast at eight o'clock and that he often walked all the way to the clinic (about four miles) in order to save his fare money. The reasons for coming early were different at different times in treatment; the behaviour remained the same, but its meaning changed many times over the first two years. At the time when grievance began to emerge, coming early appeared to serve a specific purpose. No matter how punctual I was, from Martin's point of view, I had kept him waiting a long time; I was not available when he arrived. It is true that I *had* kept him waiting since the previous session and the sessions were weekly, and thus very far apart. Martin would look very sullen as he left the waiting room. He often brought a comic along and would look through it for the first two or three minutes or look outside the window, very much out of touch with me, then suddenly turn towards the clock, which had obviously moved from ten o'clock and remark for instance: 'Late again', or shrug his shoulders as if to say: 'You are hopeless'. On one occasion he said, referring to the previous session, 'You were half a minute late last time'.

I think that the main defensive purpose served by the grievance was that Martin felt much more comfortable in a known situation, confronted with somebody whom he did not value, someone who could be no good and no use to him, somebody not to be trusted. This was a dimension in which he moved with great ease, a very familiar one. He had not really trusted anybody in his life, and was not prepared to take changes. For instance, his defensive projective identification with the internal insensitive mother had an enormous advantage over a relationship with any live object. It could be conjured up at any moment; it was always available and Martin felt in full control, while he could not fall back on my help all the time. At first, in fact, he could only do that for fifty minutes out of all the hours in a week, and I wondered about a reference to the seven days of the week when he told me once that he had 'seven layers of skin that covered the soft spot': not just a 'crust of the weekend' but a crust of the week. I decided that, as soon as I had a vacancy, I would offer him a second session. Martin reacted to the offer by saying that he would only come if he could choose the day and time. Why couldn't I see him on Saturday mornings? Why couldn't the clinic stay open at weekends. Anyhow he did not need to come twice a week, in fact he did not even need to come once. His spasmodic need to be in control was very clearly spelled out: 'If I were not in control I would not be here', 'If I am not in control, all you have got is the choice of death: hanging, electric chair, drowning, decapitation'.

I thought at first that it would be better to allow him to work through his anxieties and wait for the time when he would be able to say that he wished to accept the second session, but I came to realise that, were he able to say so openly that he needed more help, he would not be so ill and in need of it. In fact, to my surprise, he seemed very relieved when eventually I arranged for him to have a second session without waiting for his blessing. Indeed, he always appeared to experience relief when there was an acknowledgement, in the outside world, of how little he could as yet look after himself and his needs.

Although I felt that it was worthwhile to disrupt the rhythm of treatment in order to increase the sessions, I realised that this change in the known pattern had temporarily shaken Martin's feeling of safety in the therapeutic 'setting' (Meltzer 1967). I also think that the increased number of sessions was at first experienced as a rather cruel tantalising game. If I could give him a little more, then why so little? For instance, Martin brought to one of his sessions the advertisement for a restaurant 'open most hours of the day and night', providing me with a model of how thing should be. One day, looking at the 'emergency numbers' on the telephone dial and talking about emergencies, he said: 'But I am not an emergency, am I? Or I would come every day'. He referred to the time of the session as 'miserable fifty minutes', and told me, after I had referred to myself as 'mother' in a transference interpretation, that 'there are no mothers in a place like this' – he referred to the clinic and, I expect, just as much to a children's home – 'only people doing their job and getting paid for it. There might be some mothers, but that means they have got children at home'.

This reproach about me being no more than yet another part-time person in his life was a very recurrent one. It always appeared to imply that if I put him in touch with a feeling of need, if I was responsible for his knowing that he had a soft spot *inside* himself and not lodged in any odd Pakistani, I could help him only by offering the actual mothering he had been deprived of, or deprived himself of, and a very idealised, always available mothering at that. I should not expose him to the pain of knowing what he had missed without providing it, in the present, if not in the past.

Whenever I fell short of those expectations, and I was bound to *all the time*, I was felt to be playing a cruel tantalising game. I came to understand only later that Martin's repeated accusations that I wanted to make him cry were, at least partly, serving the purpose of turning me into the executioner and himself into the victim who was only fighting in self-defence and was, thus, immune to guilt.

Physical and mental violence

Towards the end of the first year of treatment, while reproaching me for cruelty, Martin threatened me on a number of occasions with physical violence. A key session in this respect was one very close to our first Christmas break. He had spoken and complained about the rain on his way to the clinic, and he had referred to the doll's house (an open plan one in the corner), saying: 'That house is no good: it would let the rain in'. He had put his face out of the window (it was still raining) and wiped his face afterwards. I said that he seemed to be talking about getting his face wet with tears, that he felt that, like the doll's house, I did not provide enough protection against the 'rain-tears'. Martin caressed his knuckle rings with a smile as if getting ready to punch me and said: 'You can get your face wet with rain, with tears, with blood, and yours is going to be wet with blood before mine is wet with tears'. It might be relevant that the risk of physical violence being acted out or, better, 'acted in' treatment (Meltzer 1967) coincided with the end of aggressive behaviour elsewhere. The problem came to be gathered more in the transference. Although physical violence did not ever actually occur, I think that Martin needed to bring about a situation where I would take very seriously the possibility that it could occur and bear the feelings that this aroused.

I found both of Mary Boston's papers (1967, 1972) on her work with a patient from a children's home most helpful in highlighting problems which may be recurrent in the treatment of institutionalised children. Mary Boston (1972, p. 6) refers to the patient's phantasy, greatly reinforced by reality, that his hostile impulses might be responsible for the parents' disappearance and points out: 'Understanding the hostility and phantasies may not be sufficient. The new object, the therapist, has to prove that he can contain the violence and reduce its omnipotence by withstanding it and surviving as the original object in the patient's phantasy did not'. This issue is very relevant in Martin's case. I came to know that his anxieties about the extent of his omnipotence were very strong and that it is certainly possible that his disturbance became exacerbated when he heard of his mother's death because it was experienced by him as a further confirmation, in reality, of the power of his murderous phantasies. He had told me that I would only have the choice of death if I escaped his control. His mother did and she died. Other very overwhelming feelings had also been aroused by her death, as it shattered all hopes that she would ever come back and it was experienced by Martin as the ultimate proof of her narcissistic, selfish withdrawal. Very close to one of my holiday breaks, he said bitterly, 'She is having a lovely holiday, pushing up the daisies' (on her grave).

At the time when Martin was threatening me with his knuckle rings or, suddenly, when he flicked a knife open and stabbed his box[1] ('We'll have to get a new box',

---

1   At the beginning of treatment he was provided with a cardboard box which he seldom opened. It contained drawing material, a ball of string, etc.

'We'll have to get a new Mrs Williams'), he spoke about his mother having died of 'foot and mouth disease' and produced many other gruesome sadistic phantasies. Very divorced from his feelings, they had a ruminatory quality to them and I often felt it appropriate to interrupt the ruminations. He called them his 'walks in the graveyard' and they provided an image of the large portion of his internal world which resembled a graveyard. In those instances there was not a glimpse of guilt feelings as *I* was supposed to feel all the guilt for wanting to make him cry, as his mother had wanted to make him cry. I was confronted with the grievances of a lifetime; he behaved as if he were either phantasising attacks or threatening physical violence in self-defence.

Once the threat of physical violence receded, the impact of the violence did not diminish. It remained as mental violence, but to a certain extent it became easier to work. It is very difficult indeed to gather one's thoughts and interpret when a knife can suddenly appear out of nowhere. (The strength of his projections was enhanced by the surprise element.) Martin let me know that this type of danger was over in a way which was typical of how he showed me he had gained a piece of insight: he gave it back to me in a patronizing sort of way. While talking I was quite unaware of moving my hands. Martin touched one of my hands with a finger, gently pressing it towards the table and said: 'We can just talk, you don't need to use your hands'. By projection *I* had become the acting out patient.

On this occasion I also think that eroticisation of the relationship (touching my hand, the seductive behaviour, the quality of innuendo in Martin's words) has been used as a defence; in this case against tender feelings. Indeed, Martin found any feelings of warmth, closeness, tenderness so painful that he had to dispose of them very quickly. Either he eroticised them and turned them into excitement or he had to 'execute' them. 'My hurt is not my business. I execute it', he once said while fiercely cutting a piece of string that he was holding in his hands in two halves with his own penknife. I think that this sign language provided a very good example of the 'attacks on linking' described by Bion (1959) which were a core of the mental violence in Martin and, possibly, one of the greatest sources of his deprivation.

In 'Attacks on Linking', Bion (1959, p. 20) says: 'I employ the term link because I wish to discuss the patient's relationship with a function, rather than with the object that subserves a function; my concern is not only with the breast or penis or verbal thought, but with their function of providing a link between two objects'. Elsewhere, in the same paper, Bion compares this shift of focus as paying attention to physiology as different from anatomy.

If, using the model proposed by Bion, I attempt to summarise the three most frequent 'attacks on linking' that occurred in Martin's treatment, I shall refer firstly to his emptying of meaning, and thus of feeling, a piece of insight he had just acquired: *attacks on links within his mind.*

He used this method as the quickest remedy against any painful feelings as he much preferred to be in a muddle than to be in pain. He could achieve this purpose by taking a word out of context and 'executing it'. To quote an example: after he had emerged from one of his delusional identifications with the 'vain mother' and, for a moment, seemed really to feel and to understand how little sustenance this narcissistic object could provide for him, there was an abrupt change of mood. He took out of context the word 'character' that I had just used in connection with the vain mother and said, 'Character, character? Oh yes, I like carrots'. It was as quick and sudden as the flicking open of knives. In no time the meaning and the feeling were executed; the part of Martin that knew where it hurts and why it hurts was executed; and the consequence was *a loss of contact between his mind and my mind.*

This loss of contact is the second type of attack on linking to which I wish to refer. Martin was very much in need of a container (Bion 1962), for the feeling he could not bear himself and of the experience that they could be survived, understood and processed for him by an external object. Bion suggests that a very extensive use in treatment of this type of projective identification, 'a stepping stone in development', probably implies that patients have been cheated of the use of this mechanism in infancy. In my view it is very likely that this might frequently apply to children cared for in institutions. But being given what has been needed for so long is often accompanied by very painful feelings. As Bion points out: 'The patient feels he is being allowed an opportunity of which he had hitherto been cheated: the poignancy of the deprivation is thereby rendered the more acute and so are the feelings of resentment at the deprivation' (1959, pp. 104–5). I think that the rapid 'execution' of feelings of being understood, of being in touch, and the consequent loss of contact with me were defences against this type of painful experience.

A third type of attack, intimately connected with the first two, was aimed at *disrupting links within my mind*. Martin very openly expressed his intolerance of my being anything more than a passive container for his projections. 'You are just a great big dustbin stuffed with rubbish: dustbins don't talk'. 'If you find out something about me, just keep it to yourself, will you?', he would say, or 'You are a brain-box'. He did not, as yet, know the content of my sentence; he was fighting the thinking, not the thoughts. If I stopped talking, as a silence was undoubtedly preferable to a battle of wits, he would say, 'Come on – proceed – what is it you were trying to say? Can't you remember?' Indeed this behaviour was not only an attack but a meaningful communication. Martin was once more telling me about a very destructive part of himself, another version of the 'Paki-basher' that was paralysing *his* capacity to think and showing me how it happened. The whole painful issue of the impaired use of his mind, of his incapacity to retain knowledge ('Can't you remember'), to link and to learn was being put across.

I often interpreted this behaviour as a communication, but there was in fact something very crucial in those disruptions which was intended as an attack. Its nature appeared to me very similar to the quality of attacks described by Bion (1962) as follows:

> The couple engaged in a creative act are felt to have an enviable emotional experience. He (the patient) being identified with the excluded party, has a painful emotional experience. On many occasions the patient . . . had a hatred of emotions and therefore, by a short extension of life itself. This hatred contributed to the murderous attacks on that which links the pair, on the pair itself and on the object generated by the pair.
>
> (Bion 1962, p. 100)

And elsewhere:

> . . . envy and hatred of a capacity for understanding, was leading him to take in a good understanding object, in order to destroy and eject it, a procedure which had often led to persecution by the destroyed and ejected object.
>
> (Bion 1962, p. 97)

In my opinion, Martin expressed something which can be understood along those lines when he said, 'I want to overwork that little man that runs around your head, putting together all the data. Why don't you give him a holiday?' 'Why didn't I throw him out of the window and let him have a bit of fresh air?' The attack on linking is here spelled out as a wish to get rid of my 'little man', to disrupt the combined object, to break the link (which in this case appears to be represented by the paternal presence inside the mother) and thus make a creative process impossible. A very primitive type of jealousy and envy, as well as intolerance of psychic pain, were bringing about Martin's repeated attempts at deadening the life of his object and he was left with a very lifeless, cold and frightening object inside. The work of resuscitation took a long time.

It was important for Martin to reach some understanding of the connections between his attacks in the transference and the deadly nature of his internal object. His impairment in learning, in spite of the evidence he gave in his destructiveness of having a good mind, was certainly connected with fragmentation of his internal world. He had been confronted daily, throughout his life, with this deprivation; in this case, fortunately, a reversible one. It is, however, certainly relevant that Martin had himself experienced so many broken links during the first two years of his life. In the turnover of staff within the same institution, and in the three changes of placements, he must so often have lost people he had made some contact with.

First glimpses of the wish to be retrieved

During this second year of treatment, especially in the second half, there were many indications that Martin was relying on my work to re-establish links when they were broken, so that he would not be allowed to get lost in his muddle or otherwise drift away. Although he let me know that he had gained some insight in this area in his manic, patronising way, he had still caught a glimpse of it. 'I have read the Bible', he told me, 'and it says there: 'He who muddles shall perish in the eternal flames and he who speaks the truth shall live forever'.' He also told me that 'you can put a piece of rope to all sorts of good uses, for instance you need it to tie a boat to the shore, so that it doesn't drift away, or you can tie the rope to a buoy'. As soon as he became aware of the double meaning of the word he laughed and said, 'I know what you are going to say'. In the same session, using the string for pulling the curtains, he showed me a very safe knot used by mountain climbers which he tied round both his legs; he said it was safe because it had a double loop. (Some acknowledgement, perhaps, that it is safer to be held by both parents?)

He said that even if he threw himself out of the window he would not fall, he would just hang by his legs. The reference to his attempted suicide was striking, but, as Martin never mentioned it directly, I did not refer to it in my interpretations. There was plenty of material in the sessions that put us in touch with his suicidal impulses and, at this stage, with his fear of them. Martin often asked me why did I not just 'let him rot in peace'; he said: 'Six feet underground is a peaceful place', 'The brain only stops working when you are dead'. 'Dead people lose life, but they gain death'. He also said; 'If I were to kill myself I know the quickest way of doing it. You jump out of a window, head first'. Very often these 'attacks on linking' during a session, his throwing his mind and feelings out of the window and the deadening of his object had a suicidal quality of brutal anaesthesia. I could talk about his suicidal impulses during the session.

However, I do not think that Martin would have dared me to let him drift away into madness or actual death without having developed some trust in an object that would not let it happen. During the second year of treatment, there were indications that he could at times experience a greater feeling of trust towards me and that he was capable, although in a rather intermittent way, of a more dependent relationship. It is possible that this development might have been accelerated by events external to treatment which made him feel at risk.

Martin was supposed to leave the children's home when he was sixteen and over the years he had often said that he wished to join the Army. A great deal of material about the meaning the Army had for him had been brought to his sessions; it stood at first for a 'licence to kill', then more clearly for a 'licence to get killed' – 'a passport to death', as he called it. Although he himself felt much less motivated to join the Army, which would obviously have meant the end of treatment, initially nobody in his environment questioned his 'vocation'. Martin no longer gave cause for concern either at school or at the home, and from the external point of view he had made good progress; if he could pass the exams and join the Regulars, all were in agreement that he should. Martin brought the problem quite openly to sessions when he asked me, 'So what's going to happen when I am sixteen?', and also by bringing to the clinic a picture of one of the homes where he had stayed as a small child. On another occasion he brought a leaflet on 'Local Authority Council and Related Services' and browsed through it, pointing at the 'Territorial and Army Volunteer Reserve' and saying, 'We don't want that, do we?' Then he looked at length at the page listing Child Care and Child Guidance.

I knew that Martin would not have been able to say openly, to anybody as yet, that he still needed a great deal of 'child care and child guidance'. In fact I was surprised that he had gone as far as implying it. I felt a strong pressure towards taking direct steps to relieve his worry about the future, but it seemed more useful for me to deal in treatment with the strong anxieties this situation aroused in him. It was very fortunate that I could rely on a great deal of support from colleagues at the clinic in putting across to the houseparent, the school and representative of social services, how undesirable it would be for Martin to stop treatment at this stage and join the Army. However, one of the problems was where should he go instead; luckily a suitable post or placement could be found. It was also suggested by the school that he could stay on for six months after school-leaving age because he had developed a great interest in photography and he would be able to have some professional training in it.

It was important, in my view, for Martin to know that other people at the clinic were concerned with the practical arrangements in his life. If he had felt that I was organising his future, I think he might have experienced this change in the known pattern as very confusing and tantalising. His reaction to the offer of the second session had given me food for thought in this respect. The crucial problem, if a change of technique is introduced at a given stage during treatment, is the need to set the limit again at some point, and to choose at which point to do so. It would have been very difficult to set a limit which made sense to Martin as to how far I could go and what I could actually do for him, if I had overstepped my role to the least degree. If I was taking care of his future placements, he might well have wondered why I did not offer him a home myself. Because of the extent of his deprivation and his craving for the 'full-time mother' that he could never have in external reality, I believed I could better help him by setting clear limits on what he could expect. If any change were possible, he could start again hoping that I might, at some stage, make up for *all* he had missed; in fact I could only help him lessen the extent of the deprivation which derived from internal sources.

There is an indication that Martin must have had some positive experiences in his early days because otherwise he would have been more impervious to treatment. When he first came it was difficult to get in touch with his wish to stay alive, but it *is* significant that he had not become psychotic (although he used a profusion of psychotic defences), that he *had* stayed alive. Spitz's (1945) work tells us about babies in similar circumstances who did not; Martin had cried for help by producing alarming symptoms, while other institutionalised children go through life dead or hollow inside, without anybody noticing it. At the point when Martin, having gathered his disturbance into treatment, offered a well-adjusted image to the environment and was considered to be fit for the Army, I realised what risks institutionalised children run when they offer the appearance of being intact.

It was a hopeful sign that in the instance I have just mentioned, Martin appeared to be able to stand on the side of his real need to ask for more 'child care and child guidance'. It seemed to me an indication that he was by now in touch with an object within himself who could treat his needs with respect, and ask for them to be taken seriously; a role which he had completely left to me in the past. In fact Martin impoverished, depleted and deprived himself; through the use of splitting and projection, both of the good and bad parts of his self and object. The progressive reintegration which took place afforded hope that Martin's deprivation could gradually be lessened.

It cannot be denied, though, that Martin had also been *deprived* of something by our work. The previous changes of placement had probably been relatively painless. He let himself be moved like a suitcase, a fairly empty one, and left the tears to someone else (remember the foster mother?). But the move from the children's home was hard. When the prospective foster parents came to take him to their house for a weekend, they found him very cosily tucked up in bed with the blanket up to his nose, engrossed in reading a book. He said that he would prefer for the break to be definite, he wanted to go to their house and stay there, not come and go. He was then asked whether he would agree to go to them if he could bring something that mattered with him; as he was so engrossed in reading, would he like to bring that book? Martin answered that he would go only if he could take all his 'family' (house parents) with him. Fortunately it was possible to arrange for him to have regular contact with his house parents (he said he wished to see them once a week), but it is undeniable that the move was yet another loss in his life, and by now he had shed some of the protective layer that made him quite immune to any feelings of loss.

Early in treatment he had told me very proudly: 'I never miss anybody – people miss me'. So I could understand Martin's puzzlement and reservations when he seemed to be asking me in so many ways: 'If it hurts, how can you call it getting better?'

References

Bick E (1968) The experience of the skin in early object relations. *International Journal of Psychoanalysis* **49**: 484–486.

Bion WR (1959) Attacks on linking. *International Journal of Psycho-Analysis* **40**: 308–315, and also in *Second Thoughts*, London, Heinemann.

Bion WR (1962) *Learning from Experience*. London, Heinemann.

Boston M (1967) Some effects of external circumstances on the inner experience of two child patients. *Journal of Child Psychotherapy* **2**(1): 20–32.

Boston M (1972) 'Psychotherapy with a boy from a children's home', *Journal of Child Psychotherapy*, vol.3, no.2: 53–67.

Klein M (1955) 'On Identification', in *The Writings of Melanie Klein*, vol.3. London: Hogarth Press.

Meltzer D (1967) *The Psychoanalytic Process*. London: Heinemann.

Spitz RA (1945) 'Hospitalism: An inquiry into the Genesis of Psychiatric Conditions in Early Childhood.' in The Psychoanalytic study of the child, Volume 1, New York: International Universities Press.

8 Psychoanalytic perspectives on emotional problems facing parents of children with learning disabilities

David Simpson

The parents of children who are handicapped with learning disabilities face a number of very difficult emotional problems which have important implications for their own and their children's development. To have a child who is born or who develops a disability, and particularly a learning disability of whatever cause, is extremely painful, very difficult for parents to bear and mobilises powerful psychological defences with important consequences.

Sources of parents' pain

The sources of the parents' pain are multiple.

Of particular importance is the grief and disappointment which results from losing the child they had originally hoped for. In normal development, prior to a child's birth, during its pregnancy and even before conception, parents usually have either, consciously or unconsciously, a picture in their minds of the child that they would like to have. Sometimes this extends to a picture of the adult person that they would like the child to become. The extent to which this imagined picture of a child is developed in the parents' minds, including how conscious it becomes, is very variable and depends upon the parents' own characters and history. It can however exert very powerful effects.

This imaginary child is an ideal, which often represents, to a varying degree, the parents' own aspirations, realised or unrealised. As it is an ideal, it is essentially unrealisable and in normal development, following the birth of a real child, this ideal is relinquished by the parents through a process of mourning, which is recurrent throughout the child's life. I believe that if the real child is disabled then the increased disparity between it and this ideal imagined child makes this process of mourning much more difficult. In my experience, for parents to have a learning disabled child means to face a painful loss, not dissimilar to losing a child through death, and the grief engendered by them is very difficult to bear. They usually feel intense sorrow as well as anger, which may be directed at the child, although more often at themselves or their spouses. For the parents of learning disabled children the process of mourning their ideal child is rarely worked through and often arrested with important consequences. The capacity of parents to mourn in these circumstances depends upon their existing strengths; which includes their personal strengths, their capacity for mutual support from each other, if there are two parents, and their resources of support from their wider family and social network.

Another very important source of pain for parents with learning disabled children, which clearly adds to the difficulty in mourning the imagined ideal child, is the pain which results from the presence of the child's disability. By this, I am referring to the tangible and perceivable facts of the child's disabilities, which may include an abnormal physical appearance and/or impairments in their capacity for movement or perception (e.g. blindness, deafness) in addition to the child's observable deficits in mental capacity. It is these facts which confront the parent and others with the child's imperfections and difference from others. I believe that it is these facts, about the child, that are the most difficult to stomach. These are not purely a consequence of what the child is not, but also what it is. Difference and imperfection against biological norms is experienced as essentially 'ugly' by human beings. However I think the problem with disability goes much further than simply being a cause of aesthetic displeasure to the perceiver as a result of the discordant nature of the perception. Human disability can cause 'horror' and 'terror'; which are not uncommon reactions in parents to their disabled children. The perception of human disability and its imperfection touches our deep unconscious and raises the spectra of monstrous figures, which are present in all of us. When we see a disabled person we may, like it or not, see a monster and in that case our reaction may be one of repulsion and hatred.

The origin of these monstrous figures and the way they operate in our minds is complex and obscure. Some have become institutionalised in myths and established religions. I think of particular relevance in the area of handicap is the 'Chaos monster', which features in the ancient religions such as that of the Babylonians, Egyptians, Vedic Indians, and threatens to return the world to a precreation chaos. From a psychoanalytic perspective, Britton (1998, p. 54–55) when discussing fears in patients with borderline disorders, suggested that this 'Chaos monster' is the personification of Bion's concept of 'nameless dread' (Bion 1962; p. 117). Nameless dread, which is present to some degree in all human minds, is ultimately derived, in Bion's view, from a failure in a mother's capacity to contain her infant's destructive drive and the anxiety this generates. This results in the development of terrifying monsters in the unconscious mind.

I think these unconscious monstrous figures personify the destructive drive which is present in all of us and which Freud (1920) called the death instinct. This has a biological base; is directed at that which is not us or not like us, and further more is triggered by differences and abnormalities. The learning disabled are particularly at risk and this explains the feelings of repulsion and even murder they sometimes evoke in others. Historically the extermination of the handicapped has been common practice in many societies. Even normal babies are not free from being at risk from these impulses in their parents. I think there is in fact a delicate balance in nature between the survival of the new generations and the needs of the old, which are threatened by them. From a biological perspective the foetus has essentially a parasitic relationship with the mother and infanticide is not an uncommon occurrence amongst animals, nor are such thoughts, and indeed actions, unknown amongst humans. The counter balance to these potential destructive impulses of parents towards their children is the love that parents have for their children and their identification with them. For parents, whose children are learning disabled, this identification is very difficult because they have to struggle against a powerful internal resistance of repulsion and even hatred towards their children. Being aware of these reactions in themselves will be very shocking for these parents, resulting in extremes of feeling, including initial outrage, guilt and shame.

Outrage and associated narcissistic injury, guilt and shame are further very important sources of pain for parents which follow having a learning disabled child and which result from the loss of their ideal child and the presence of its disability. For parents to learn that their child is learning disabled, whenever this occurs, is emotionally traumatic and a sense of outrage and some degree of narcissistic injury is usual. Parents often wonder why this has occurred to them. They usually feel an intense sense of failure; failure that they haven't provided an ideal child and as a result of the reactions that they have to their child, which does not fit with their view of themselves. For some parents, where there is a high degree of narcissistic investment in their imagined wished-for child, having a disabled child can result in extreme feelings of narcissistic injury with attendant outrage and loss of self-esteem. In these parents I believe the imagined ideal child corresponds closely with these parents ideal self or ego ideal. To have a disabled child can leave these parents feeling that their sense of self is damaged and this can evoke powerful defence manoeuvres to which I will return.

Guilt is a very important source of pain for the parents of children with learning disabilities. In my experience, at a fundamental level, a great many parents of children with learning disabilities hold the belief that they are in some way responsible for their child's handicap and as a result of this they are haunted by a painful sense of guilt, which is added to by the guilt they feel as a result of their reactions to their child and the effects of having the child on other people including family members. Clearly if the parents have feelings of hatred and repulsion or experience any damaging impulses towards their child, then these will be important facts contributing to the sense of guilt. This guilt is usually experienced as a persecutory sense of blame; self blame, which in psychoanalytic terms, is understood in terms of blame of the self by the superego. These parents may not only feel they have 'done wrong' but they are 'morally wrong'. They may believe that their disabled child is a punishment from God.

Sometimes parents may expect to be blamed by other people or they might blame others. I think these later reactions are a defence against the more fundamental and irrational feeling that they have caused the disorder. What can be known about the causes of their child's disability and more generally about the causes of children's learning disabilities, can be helpful but unfortunately in my experience is often a hindrance in the situation where parents feel to blame. On a rational level, one would expect that for parents to have a clearly identified cause for their child's condition would help to relieve the parent's feelings of responsibility for this condition. In these situations however, the parents' beliefs that they have caused their children's disabilities are not rational and usually very strongly held. A hereditary genetic cause can add to the difficulties by implying a causal route from the parent's genes and might be confused with blame. Clear causes for learning disabilities particularly for those with mild and moderate degrees of disability, which are the majority, are in fact rare. It is not infrequent to see parents chasing multiple medical assessments in order to find causes for disabilities which I believe has the aim of trying to relieve these parents' underlying burden of guilt. What is unfortunately very rare in these situations, is for these parents' drive for multiple assessments, which rarely satisfy and sometimes results in recrimination towards doctors and agencies, to be understood in terms of the parents' belief that they are to blame and their defences against this. It is my experience that if this sense of guilt can be addressed for parents like this, and this is by no means an easy task, then sometimes these parents can obtain considerable relief, with benefit to themselves and to their children, halting the need for repeated investigation.

I think these parents' belief, in their being responsible for their child's disability and their persecutory sense of guilt, is itself defensive and is rooted in a deeper anxiety. This is what Klein (1935) refers to as depressive anxiety, which is present in all of us, about the state of our internal objects. These include the internal representations, of parental and family figures, including the children, ourselves and our siblings. They exist in our minds in unconscious phantasy and are altered by this. These objects are essential for mental functioning and development and are in fact the building blocks of the human minds. For parents to have real children, who are damaged and disabled, raises the spectra for these parents that their internal objects may be damaged, and that they are responsible. I think this gives rise to depressive guilt in these parents which has a different quality from blame or persecutory guilt in that there is concern for the objects they fear they have damaged. This is like the concern a child might feel for its parent if it felt that it had hurt its parent or caused it injury. This is also much more difficult to bear than simply feeling blamed. I think that our beliefs about our capacities to have children, and their health directly, correspond with our beliefs about the health of our internal objects. For the parents of learning disabled children, where these children are clearly damaged, the potential for depressive pain about the state of their internal objects is much greater and this is reflected in the strength of their defences against this.

Shame is another very important source of pain. Shame is commonly associated with learning disabilities and mental handicap. It can be a very intense, and at times unbearable, painful experience for the parents who have a child with this. Shame is an emotion that depends upon the experience, either in reality or in imagination, of being looked upon by an observer who recognises deficits and impairments, by some standards. Although there may be a benign form of shame, implied for example in the common expression 'what a shame', it is my belief that shame is essentially an emotion that exerts powerful inhibitory, and often destructive effects, on human beings and their development. It has a social dimension and in many cultures it is a major factor determining behaviour in adherence to social rules. I suspect that the origin of shame lies in our childhood relationship with our faeces, which become considered as despicable, and it implies being looked down on and humiliated by a figure that takes a superior position. Shame is also frequently experienced in the oedipal situation by the young child who can feel small and inadequate in relation to its parents and their capacities including their sexual capacities. Children themselves are a symbolic expression of their parents' sexual capacities and for parents to have a child that is learning disabled touches this sense of sexual inadequacy, derived from the oedipal situation which leads to shame. Like children with learning disabilities, the parents of children who are learning disabled often feel looked down on, despised and shamed. This can result in a wish to hide themselves and their disabled children and I believe this has been an important factor historically underpinning the separation of the learning disabled from the mainstream of society in institutional care.

A further very important sort of pain for the parents of children with learning disabilities results from the circumstances of the child's birth and neonatal care.

Learning disabilities are strongly associated with prematurity, low birth weight and neonatal medical problems. These children may require paediatric intervention and are often admitted to special, and sometimes, intensive baby care units. Concern about a diagnosis and the search for a recognised cause of mental retardation, can sometimes lead to the need to carry out investigations that require admission to hospital. Although paediatric services are now more alert to the emotional difficulties, which such admissions can cause, and separations from parents are usually minimised, some degree of separation is inevitable and such admissions are emotionally traumatic, compounding the trauma for parents of realising that their child is disabled or may become so. In these situations uncertainty for parents is the norm and this may include uncertainty about whether their child will survive at all. There is also, often, continued uncertainty for many years as to the child's developmental potential. This emotionally traumatic situation can clearly compromise the early attachment between the parents and their infant which can adversely affect the developing relationship between them through childhood and later life. It is well recognised that mothers whose babies are admitted to special care baby units are at an increased risk of postnatal depression and that the children who have spent time in these units, even without gross disabilities, are at increased risk of later emotional and behavioural problems. To have a child who is learning disabled adds to and compounds these problems, considerably magnifying the parents' pain and the adverse consequences for the child.

The consequences of parents' pain and their defences against it

What are the consequences of these multiple, complex, powerful and clearly interacting sources of pain for the parents of children with learning disabilities. The magnitude of the problem is large and, although there is considerable variation, a number of themes can be discerned.

Despair and depression are unfortunately very common. The shock and emotional trauma of the diagnosis; their insurmountable grief, narcissistic injury, loss of self-esteem, guilt and shame all contribute to either an overt degree of depression in the parents or, in my experience more commonly, a chronic melancholic state which lies below the surface or hangs like a black cloud over the parents individually and over their relationship together. I strongly suspect that the most important factor in this depression is the way that having a learning disabled child touches the parents' deep anxieties about the state of their internal objects, including their sense of self; the depressive anxiety that I have discussed earlier. In the parents' minds, this can often become represented by their very sexual acts, which they can hold responsible for their child's handicap and their family's problems. This despair and depression can be experienced individually and is frequently expressed as a couple. Hostility and discord between the parents of mentally handicapped children is very common and it is well recognised that marital deterioration and break up is a common outcome. This has important consequences for the development of the disabled child and its siblings.

Parental discord can seriously impair a mother's capacity to contain her child's anxiety for reasons that reach beyond the immediate disruptive consequences to the child, of open hostility or separation between the parents. In fact, a mother's capacity to adequately contain and modify her child's anxieties is very much dependent upon the presence, in her mind, of a 'satisfactory' relationship with the child's father.

By the term 'satisfactory' I do not mean a perfect relationship but one which includes mutual respect and love, alongside frustration and other negative feelings, which are an inevitable component of real relationships.

Britton (1989) in considering the development of psychotic disturbances in adults, described how the development of a mind that can bear anxiety, and think, is dependent upon the capacity of a child to tolerate an internal relationship with its parents which involves both love and hate. In this way a child develops a 'third position', in his/her mind, in which he/she is a witness and not a participant. This position is the basis for curiosity and mental development. This is a position where one can mentally 'stand back' and think about oneself or an interaction with someone else. The development of the 'third position' starts in infancy through the baby's contact with its mother. It is the mother's (or primary care giver's) state of mind that is particularly important at this stage although the effects of the actual presence, or absence, and actions of the father and other significant figures should not be underestimated. Of particular importance is the mother's internal relationship with her parents, both her mother and her father. This depends upon her history of development, including her capacity to work through her oedipal conflict, the depressive and persecutory anxiety associated with this and particularly her capacity to develop a 'third position' in her mind in relation to these parents. There is a crucial relationship of mutual influence between the mother's relationship with her internal parents, particularly her own father, and her internal relationship with the father of her child. Both contribute to determining the position and strength of the father or paternal function in the mother's mind which is fundamental in enabling the mother to hold onto her own third position in the face of the pressures emanating from the mother\infant couple which threatens to overwhelm the mother in early child care. The internal paternal function enables the mother to look at her self, to think and deal with the anxiety emanating from her infant and to facilitate the development of a 'third position' for the infant through the child's identification with it.

When a mother has a child who is disabled, her capacity to achieve the 'third position' is seriously compromised, her increased depressive and persecutory anxieties about the internal parents and the deterioration in relationship with the child's father both contribute to this. This will result in a serious further impairment in the child's emotional and cognitive development, over and above that due to constitutional factors. I will return, later in this chapter, to consider further ways in which the psychological consequences of a child's handicap can exasperate the impairment of its intellectual development.

In view of the emotional difficulties faced, it is surprising that so many parents of disabled children do love their children and care for them so well. The defences against sources of pain are extremely important in this. These defences can however become further sources of problems.

In my view three types of defensive mechanism are particularly important; projection, denial and idealisation. I will consider each of them on their own and then consider their combination in a particular form of defensive constellation, which I think, is of fundamental importance in many of the parents and carers of those with learning disabilities.

Projection, used defensively is particular important. Projection involves one person evoking in another their feelings or reactions. Projection is the basis of human communication and has it origins in the way an infant communicates with its mother. It can also be a way of ridding the mind of feelings and thoughts and if excessive it can be detrimental to development. For example, in extreme cases, associated with pathological states of mind in some severe forms of mental illness, the very capacity to think can be projected. Projection between the parents of learning disabled children, of their feelings of blame, despair and depression is a common feature when their relationships become discordant and characterised by mutual recrimination. These parents can also project into their children both their disabled child and any siblings. I will return to this later.

One of the most important defences seen in the parents with children with learning disabilities is denial. This may be gross and near delusional where, for example, the parents, either do not recognise the evidence of anything handicapped about their child or they might recognise the handicap but, through idealisation, believe that it confers special status or ability. It is not infrequent for the parents to speak of the child's special ability in music or art, or even of having advanced intellectual capacities despite evidence that this is not present. Some parents recognise the difficulty in the child but believe their child's disability was a 'gift from God'; something which they must suffer for greater rewards in the eyes of God in the afterlife. This might clearly be the result of an underlying belief, either conscious or unconscious, that the child's disability was a punishment for a sin. Sometimes the parent recognises their child's functional impairments but believes that their child does have hidden abilities that have not been released, even that the child might be holding back their abilities to frustrate them. This situation is clearly complicated by the fact that the child may have more potential than it shows, although not at the level that the parent believes.

A more subtle form of denial, or disavowal of the nature and extent of the problem, is much more common with parents of children with learning disabilities. In this situation a disability is clearly recognised for what it is, on one level, but on another emotional level it is not recognised. Subtle denial and disavowal of the pain of disability may be betrayed in expressions commonly used by the parents of the learning disabled in talking of their offspring, such as, 'she is a rewarding challenge', 'he's always with me' and 'he is such a loving child'.

Although the development of special interests and pressure groups for those with learning disabilities, in general or for specific disorders, is important in providing support and in countering the stigma and shame associated with learning disabilities, they can unfortunately become vehicles for the denial of the reality; emotional or otherwise, of handicap and its defensive idealisation. Sometimes it might even appear that having a disability is superior to not having one; both that it is morally superior, and associated with virtue, and that it is practically better in the way that having a wheelchair for somebody who is physically disabled may be considered an advantage over walking.

Idealisation is particularly important in the parent's defences against the reality of learning disabilities and it goes hand in hand with denial, projection and splitting. I believe that its origin lies in the imagined ideal child, the loss of which is so difficult to bear. For some parents, when faced with a disabled child, that may even feel monstrous to them, this idealised perfect image of a child is emotionally split off from their experience of their child's reality. In these situations, infancy, childhood, and the dependency, associated with them, become idealised. The fact that the child's development is retarded can feed into this. These parents may feel they have a child as an infant for life. Their child's handicap may then be reversed, turning this in phantasy into a gift of immortality for their child and for themselves as parents, for which the child's handicap is the price. Disability is then magically converted to perfection. The cost in this situation of illusion, is that development cannot occur; the parents' disappointment and grief and other emotions are avoided and the working through of these emotions, which is essential for emotional growth, does not occur.

It is my experience, that these defensive identifications are very common in the parents of children with learning disabilities and that their disabled children are often subject to projection into them, from their parents, of both parent's imagined 'ideal child' and its opposite; the 'wrong or sometimes even monstrous child'. In extreme cases this can result in a situation of split perceptions. The child might be seen simultaneously as an ideal, dependent infant, all 'good', and at the same time, or in rapid alternation, as a monstrous wrong child, all 'bad'. One result of this is that the parents can rid themselves of their own feelings of inadequacies. These projections can exert a powerful inhibitory effect on their child's development. The pressure to comply with this idealised image of their children's dependency and disability can prevent the development of the child's capacity to express itself and show what potential it has, for fear that it would be viewed as 'wrong'. In this situation it is very difficult for the child to express its normal aggression and curiosity and to show passion in this. Adolescence, with the associated development of sexuality, is a particular problem. A child's curiosity can be particularly threatening to the parents, in these situations, because it threatens the very basis of their defensive system of idealisation and denial, touching the underpinnings of the painful feelings that the parents are unable to bear. Curiosity is actually the basis of intellectual development during childhood and thrives on the parent's positive responsiveness to this. Aggression and passion are also requirements for intellectual development. If the child's passionate curiosity and aggression are inhibited it will suffer further intellectual stunting, over and above its inherent problem. Unfortunately, many learning disabled children, in these situations, feel compelled to comply with their parents' defensive structures, to protect their parents from the reality of their disability, which they fear will lead to their parents' psychic collapse. In doing so they further limit their capacities leading to what is sometimes called 'secondary handicap' (Sinason 1992). I believe that this is a fundamental problem that affects all those concerned with learning disabilities, including parents and professionals, and emanates from peoples' difficulties of giving up their illusions, to face the painful realities of disability. In another paper (Simpson 2004) I have called this the way in which learning disability can become a 'refuge from knowledge'.

The siblings of children with learning disabilities are also subject to these projections and to the effects of these defensive constellations. It is not infrequent for them to feel they have to replace their handicap sibling and become the ideal imagined child of their parents. These children can feel under inordinate pressure to be well behaved and to succeed academically; for example, where one child in a family is learning disabled while its sibling has an exemplary academic record through school and university. Unfortunately siblings, in these situations comply with these projections at personal cost, and they may be unable to fulfil themselves and to express their aggressive and sexual nature, for fear that it does not fit with their parents' ideals.

Conclusion

I believe that a psychoanalytic understanding of the sources of pain faced by the parents of learning disabled children and the types of defences used by them is of particular value in informing those who seek to help these parents. This includes those who wish to help practically; through medical, social work and psychological interventions and particularly those who wish to engage in helping them with the emotional consequences of their child's disability through counselling or psychotherapy.

In view of the reality of learning disability, these parents have very powerful defences and they clearly need them. These defences must be respected, which is a requirement of any therapeutic work, which must be sensitive and compassionate. However a balance is needed between the need to maintain defences to prevent pain and the danger of collusion with these defences as a result of the powerful psychological pressure on professionals to fall in with the parents' tendencies to denial and idealisation. When faced with the common defensive constellation of learning disability acting as a refuge from knowledge; then professionals working with learning disabled patients, like the learning disabled patients themselves are in danger of an unconscious compliance tending to avoid the psychological reality of disability and staying well away from sources of disappointment, loss, guilt, shame and other difficulties. In my experience, if these subjects can be sensitively broached and particularly if the fundamental sense of blame that so many parents feel can be addressed, then progress is possible. Mourning can then proceed for these parents and with it emotional growth can occur for them and their offspring.

References

Bion WR (1962) *A Theory of Thinking. Second Thoughts*. New York, Jason Arronson.

Britton R (1989) The missing link: parental sexuality in the Oedipus complex. In J Steiner (ed.) *The Oedipal Complex Today*, pp. 83–101. London, Karnac.

Britton R (1998) *Belief and Imagination*. London and New York, Routlege.

Freud S (1920) *Beyond the Pleasure Principle*. Standard Edition VIII.

Klein M (1935) A contribution to the psychogenesis of manic-depressive states. In *The Writings of Melanie Klein*. Vol. 1, 344–369.

Simpson D (2004) Learning disability as a refuge from knowledge. In D Simpson, L Miller (eds) *Unexpected Gains: Psychotherapy with People with Learning Disabilities*, pp. 69–82. London, Karnac.

Sinason V (1992) *Mental Handicap and the Human Condition: New Approaches from the Tavistock*. London, Free Association Books.

Part 3

Parents, families and professional networks

9   The court, the couple and the consultant: Is there room for a third position?

Judith Freedman[1]

I want to consider a new area of work with parents, which results from legislative attempts to protect children within families. I am specifically concerned with proceedings related to allegations of child abuse, whether sexual, physical or emotional. Parents involved in these proceedings may feel that the professionals only focus on the children, and no one is interested in understanding their needs.

It may seem obvious to mental health professionals that in order to improve the situation for children, it is important to understand and address the needs of parents. The Children Act (1989) attempts to translate this understanding into legal imperative. The Act departs from previous family law by emphasising the need to work in partnership with parents in families where child abuse has occurred or is suspected. The Act encourages local authority social workers to assist parents and to give them every opportunity possible to demonstrate adequate parenting capabilities. In practice, this means that parents receive support first by work with their local authority social worker. If these early interventions fail to achieve a safe environment for the child, then the statutory agency must turn to the courts to determine how best to ensure the child's welfare.

The Children Act provides that the parties in these proceedings should make available to the court expert evidence on the psychological make-up of the family. As Lady Justice Butler-Sloss said in a recent case, 'when dealing with children, the court needs all the help it can get.' (Wall 1997, p. 485). At the Portman Clinic, we have long worked with couples who present with sexual perversions and violence. The advent of the Children Act has led to our becoming involved with the family law system as expert witnesses: legal representatives for local authorities, for guardians-ad-litem, and even parents themselves turn to us for assessment of parenting abilities when child abuse is a concern.

An important feature of these proceedings is that they are nonadversarial. Justice Nicholas Wall explained this in a recent paper (1997):

> It does not mean that difficult issues of fact which have to be resolved by rigorous investigation and detailed cross examination do not arise in proceedings relating to children. What it means is that the welfare of the child is the court's paramount consideration and that the duty of the court is to reach a decision

---

1 The author wishes to thank Mrs Dorothy Lloyd-Owen for her collaboration with the clinical work presented in this paper.

which is in the best interests of the child concerned, as opposed to a result which favours a particular party to the proceedings.

(p. 485)

This means that there is a double focus in the aim of our work. We take as our task the provision of a parent-based assessment, but in so doing we must keep paramount in our minds the welfare of the child. Thus, the aim of our assessment is to examine the *result* of the parenting that the couple can provide, particularly their ability to keep the children safe from abuse.

In the course of the assessment, we seek to understand who the parents are as individuals and as a couple and how their psychological make-up affects their ability to parent. We do not undertake to determine whether child abuse has occurred. This we leave to colleagues in social work, paediatrics and child psychiatry, who have access to forensic evidence to determine if the children were abused. Rather, we see as our brief two other areas: first, we communicate to the court a psychodynamic understanding of the couple as parents; second, having outlined any areas of difficulty for the couple, we assess their ability to engage in therapeutic work that might address their problems. The court explicitly asks us to provide a view of the parents independent of the conflict that already exists between the local authority and the parents.

A complication is inherent in this arrangement. This is the question, who is this assessment for? In our usual practice as couple therapists, we are accustomed to seeing people who ask for an assessment. We consider their request for help to be an essential indicator of the couple's motivation to undertake an assessment. The implicit contract in therapeutic work is that we agree to relay back to the couple the results of our assessment.

By contrast, we undertake these assessments explicitly for the court. Indeed, we begin our interviews by explaining that we cannot keep confidential what happens in the assessment and that we must report everything of importance to the court. As Lady Justice Butler-Sloss said, '*the court* [my italics] needs all the help it can get.' Not the couple needs all the help it can get – although frequently this is the case – but the court on behalf of the children. Whether we are engaged by a local authority that seeks to take children into care, by parents who want to keep their children or by the guardian-ad-litem, all parties jointly agree to the assessment with the understanding that the results will be considered by the court.

This understanding significantly influences the behaviours of those involved in the assessment. In particular, it is likely that the parents will seek, both consciously and unconsciously, to align us with one side or the other of the conflict. Hence, my question in the title of this paper – in work for the court, is there room for a third position that is independent of the contesting parties?

I want to suggest that in these conflicts between couples and the courts, the possibility of a consultant providing a third position is determined by the couple's joint ability to face reality. Most often, we are approached for an assessment when the authorities say that the parents have abused the children and the parents deny or minimise the abuse. So long as this remains the case, only two positions seem available; that is, they did it or they did not do it. This is a critical impasse, since the possibilities for rehabilitation are minimal for parents who cannot accept their destructive thoughts and deeds (Kennedy 1997). Our task is to see if it is possible to provide a third position. An example of a third position could be a report that suggests that the parents probably abused the child, but that we can understand something about their behaviour and that we can propose ways forward through treatment.

The avoidance of reality in couples

Difficulty in facing up to painful realities – such as the existence in oneself of destructive thoughts and deeds – we believe causes problems for parents in caring for children and limits their ability to engage in treatment. Although we are interested in what happens to the perception of reality between a couple, we must first consider the ability of both partners as individuals to face reality. Klein suggested that this capacity is an oedipal development. She thought that the crucial factor is how the child deals with the deprivations he experiences as a result of the oedipal situation, particularly in having to give up the close bond to a nurturing mother. She wrote:

> At a very early age children become acquainted with reality through the deprivations which it imposes on them. They defend themselves against reality by repudiating it. The fundamental thing, however, and the criterion of all later capacity for adaptation to reality, is the degree in which they are able to tolerate the deprivations. . . .
>
> (Klein 1926, pp. 128–129)

Freud and Klein both saw the acceptance of reality as a mental state that is constantly vulnerable to anxiety. If anxiety overwhelms an individual's sense of reality in an enduring way, then a psychological disturbance may result. Freud (1924) described how in neurosis as well as in psychosis there are:

> attempts to replace a disagreeable reality by one which is more in keeping with the subject's wishes. This is made possible by the existence of a *world of phantasy*, of a domain which became separated from the real external world at the time of the introduction of the reality principle. This domain has since been kept free from the demands of the exigencies of life, like a kind of 'reservation'.
>
> (p. 187)

I think that Freud suggested here a way in which some experience is segregated but not totally split off from the internal world. This is quite different from complete denial. Rather, experience held within the domain is available to the person, but it is not subjected to the requirements of reality. Freud's notion of a domain can account for a range of mental disturbance, depending on what proportion of the real external world is contained within the domain.

Britton (1989) expanded Klein's concept about the experience of deprivation during the oedipal situation to suggest that the child has to contend with his new awareness of the reality of the parental sexual relationship. He wrote:

> The initial recognition of the parental sexual relationship involves relinquishing the idea of sole and permanent possession of mother and leads to a profound sense of loss. . . . Later, the oedipal encounter also involves recognition of the difference between the relationship between parents as different from the

relationship between parent and child: the parents' relationship is genital and procreative; the parent–child relationship is not.

(pp. 84–85)

Britton suggested that Freud's domains are a kind of 'oedipal illusion', an area of experience in which the child or later the disturbed adult continues to deny the 'law of the oedipus complex – the law that distinguishes the sexes and the generations, provoking not only jealousy but also envy of the parental couple for their sexual and procreative capacities' (p. 99).

The denial of this fundamental law is critical, because the blurring of distinctions between the generations is a central aspect of child abuse (Chasseguet-Smirgel 1985). I think that what Britton has proposed here can become an important precursor to child abuse. A child may, for whatever reason, turn away from the reality of the parental sexual relationship and segregate this experience in an area that is never consciously acknowledged. If this child reaches adulthood without confronting the reality of parental sexuality, then he or she may not be able to respect the distinction between the generations. In this mental state, it may become easy for him to evade the psychological law that prohibits sexual or even violent contact between the generations. There is then a risk that he may enact this confusion by abusing children.

Britton suggested that the child's acceptance of the existence of a relationship between the parents adds the missing link to the already existing relationships that the child has with both parents. He proposed that this allows for a boundaried triangular space with 'the possibility of being a participant in a relationship and observed by a third person as well as being an observer of a relationship between two people' (p. 86). In other words, there is a triangular relationship bounded on three sides by dyadic relationships – child with mother, child with father, and mother with father.

This introduces a complexity of relatedness far greater than exists in dyadic relationships alone. Another way to conceptualise this difference is to consider that the child's first relationships with mother and father are the prototype for his division of relations into good and bad. Bringing mother and father together requires the child to integrate his notions of good and bad into a more complicated picture (Trowell 1986).

When the child allows the parents to come together in his mind, it becomes possible for him or her to take up new positions as either observer (of the parental couple) or observed (by his parents). Britton wrote:

> If the link between the parents perceived in love and hate can be tolerated in the child's mind, it provides him with a prototype for an object relationship of a third kind in which he is a witness and not a participant. A third position then comes into existence from which object relationships can be observed. Given this, we can also envisage *being* observed. . . . Anyone . . . who has treated a psychotic patient or been involved in a psychotic transference will know what I mean when I refer to times when this seems impossible, and it is at those times that one realises what it means to lack that third position.

(p. 87)

I think that we are concerned with three different triangles in family court work. First, there is the relationship of the parents with their child in the family. This is the relationship with which the court is concerned. Second, there is the relationship of the parents to the social worker. In both triangles, but particularly the second one, parents may experience themselves, unconsciously and alternately, as the child and as the adult. The relationship with the social worker, who is perceived as an authority figure, generally reawakens and mimics aspects of the important early relationship between the parents, as children, and their own parents. The third triangle involves the couple, the court, and the consultant and is, perhaps, the most elusive of all.

I want to suggest that when we undertake court assessments of couples where child abuse is suspected, we are entering a space in which there are long-held domains of estrangement from reality. We have to explore the couple's ability to expose themselves to reality, stimulated by the insistence of the court. The questions of whether they can observe and be observed thus become crucial. Indeed, couples often tell us about this when they complain bitterly about social workers monitoring them. The social workers and the consultant, hopefully, bring with them the oedipal capacity for observing and being observed. If they can resist the pressure from the parents to take one or the other side in the dispute, the possibility exists that new insights may emerge from which the parents can learn. There is always the very real risk when this happens that the parents will hate the professional observers for getting them to face realities that they have avoided for a long time.

In moving from talking about the couple as individuals to talking about them as an interacting pair, we need to consider whether they are able to acknowledge reality as it exists between themselves. The evasion of reality within couples is mediated through the mechanism of projective identification.

Projective identification and the evasion of reality

Klein (1946) originally described projective identification as a mental mechanism used by individuals to project unwanted aspects of the self into an object. Couple therapists have expanded this concept of a defence mechanism from the intrapsychic to the interpersonal realm. Central to the expansion of this idea is the notion of the complementary effects of mutual projective processes. Thus, one partner in a couple projects unwanted psychological aspects into the other partner, who he or she perceives as willing to accept that particular projection and integrate it into his or her personal identity. In return, the other partner projects a complementary aspect of him or herself into the first partner. Zinner (1976) listed some of the resulting polarities that are commonly found in couples: emotionally labile/cold and logical; strong/weak; frigid/lusty; helpless/effective; rageful/even-tempered; depressed/cheerful.

Despite the usefulness of projective identification in shedding light on interpersonal relations, it is an intrapsychic mechanism. This means that individuals use projective identification to avoid internal or intrapsychic conflict. The result, however, impacts profoundly on the couple's relationship. Zinner (1976) wrote:

> [projective identification] wreaks havoc on the marriage because it requires, to be effective, a continuing state of conflict within the dyad. This conflict need not be overt but may be implicit in the form of polarised perceptions that marital partners have of each other. These polarizations preempt the possibility of sharing feelings and of collaborative behavior.
>
> (p. 157)

This account of the fate of projective mechanisms within a couple makes it clear that what begins as the defensive manoeuvres of one partner, designed to lessen personal anxiety, also has a profound effect on the couple as a whole. Zinner specifically mentioned the waylaying of shared feelings and collaborative behaviour. I suggest that the avoidance of these collaborative activities both results from and leads to interferences in the couple's ability to perceive reality. For example, parents who cannot empathise and cannot work together are at risk of failing to protect their children. As individuals, the parents may care for the children adequately. However, in the distrustful environment that they create as a couple, children may no longer be safe and secure, because the parents cannot question concerns with each other.

Dicks (1967) took up a related aspect of the polarities described by Zinner. He described idealisation as the 'main defence mechanism in marital relations'. Dicks proposed that idealisation allows a turning away from the reality of uncomfortable mental states:

> By denying the reality of ambivalent hate or anger, and by the variants of projective identification, one or both spouses attribute to the partner those bad feelings they must now own themselves, or else make the partner all good and exalted while themselves taking on the guilt and the badness.
>
> (p. 43)

An example of this scenario presents frequently in family court work. A referrer asks us to see a father who, allegedly, has sexually abused the children. The referrer tells us that the mother was unaware of what was happening. We then must consider the possibility that whilst consciously the mother kept herself unaware of the abuse, unconsciously she may have encouraged her partner to perpetrate it. Thus, the partner may have expressed for her a destructive part of her own internal world that she cannot bear to face.

A segment from a treatment of a couple, who I will call the Smiths, will illustrate how it emerged that a wife subtly encouraged her husband to act in an abusive way that she ostensibly disliked. Some years earlier, Mr Smith sexually abused his young stepdaughter, a child from his wife's first marriage. Mrs Smith claimed that she knew nothing about what was happening and chose to stay with Mr Smith. In so doing, she lost her daughter and the subsequent babies born in the Smith marriage, who were removed in court proceedings.

A couple therapy session began with Mrs Smith complaining that Mr Smith never does any of the housework. Mr Smith protests that he does some, but Mrs Smith does not acknowledge this. He then likens it to her suggesting to him recently that he could have an affair. Both these things, he maintains, push him toward abusing a child. At first, none of us can understand how both things could incite him to child abuse. A connection occurs to me, and I suggest that he is talking about how Mrs Smith makes him feel useless. 'Yes, that's it', he smiles. Mrs Smith looks puzzled. I explain that Mr Smith feels useless when Mrs Smith says, 'you never do anything', or 'I don't feel sexually attracted to you so why don't you have an affair'. He then has the impulse to turn to a child with whom he could feel more important.

This material began to shed light on Mrs Smith's quite active but unconscious complicity with her husband's child abuse. In the course of the therapy it gradually became apparent that Mrs Smith might have encouraged Mr Smith to sexually abuse, in part because of her own unacknowledged hatred of her children.

This vignette explains the rationale for our insistence on seeing both parents together when we are asked to assess the potential risk they present to children. In our view, assessment of only one parent does not allow the full picture to emerge. We seek to assess the quality of parenting that a couple provides. Within the couple context, the individuals may find themselves more or less constrained in their efforts to face reality, observe themselves and be observed, and protect their children. This is the focus for our work.

A clinical illustration

I will turn now to a description of a case that illustrates these points. (I should like to emphasise that I have thoroughly disguised the clinical material I have used in this chapter.) The referral began with the local authority social worker phoning to ask me to prepare a report for the court on Mr and Mrs Jones. She explained that the couple had a newborn baby, their first child together, and the local authority was concerned about her welfare. The local authority was worried because Mr Jones already had three convictions for child physical abuse, one of them on Mrs Jones's son. Earlier interventions from social services had resulted in Mrs Jones's four older children from a previous marriage leaving one by one to live with their father. These children now were alleging that Mr Jones had abused them sexually as well as physically. The local authority had intervened already to place Mrs Jones and the new baby girl separately from Mr Jones. The parents opposed this and wanted Mrs Jones and baby Mary to come home.

This case is somewhat unusual, as it involved allegations of both sexual and physical abuse of the children. We realised at the initial meeting of the professionals that the local authority was primarily concerned about the unproved allegations of sexual abuse and saw this as the greatest area of potential risk. They identified Mr Jones as the main source of concern. A 'risk assessment' was requested on Mr Jones, taking account of his convictions for physical abuse and the allegations of sexual abuse.

The questions about Mr Jones were in striking contrast to the questions posed about Mrs Jones. These included assessing her parenting abilities, her ability to protect Mary and the possibility of Mrs Jones caring for Mary on her own. As is usual, there was a question about the nature of the marital relationship, but this did not seem to relate to the overall concerns about risk.

By the end of the professionals' meeting, we were concerned about the sole focus on one parent as a risk. We find that this is a familiar issue in our opening negotiations, one that requires us to work with the referrer about the importance of shared pathology within a couple. With this family, we suspected that the local authority had failed to consider the possibility that Mrs Jones was complicit in the abuse, and we wondered why this might be.

Unusually, and in retrospect symptomatically, the local authority seemed unsure about what previous records were relevant. Staff disclosed papers to us piecemeal over the next few weeks. We were interested to discover what the social workers had left out of the meeting, even though it was available to them in their files. These revealed a long history of incidents involving Mrs Jones and problems in her care for the children of her first marriage, even before Mr Jones came onto the scene. These included Mrs Jones hitting her eldest child in the playground, neighbours saying that the children were not properly fed and reports of the children begging for food. The children suffered various injuries without clear explanation, the most serious of which was a baby fracturing her skull when she fell out of her highchair.

It also emerged that Mrs Jones had a previous partner who had a conviction for child sexual abuse before he met her. Mrs Jones had stood by this partner, just as she later stayed with Mr Jones after he was convicted for slapping, punching and kicking her son during arguments. When Mrs Jones's daughters disclosed sexual abuse by Mr Jones, Mr and Mrs Jones both said that they were lying. There were no legal proceedings regarding the sexual abuse. Mrs Jones promised on various occasions to keep Mr Jones out of the home, but she consistently failed to do this.

By now, we suspected that there was something about this couple that prevented others from taking seriously the problems in the mother's care of the children. We began the assessment interviews holding that issue in mind.

We offered a series of appointments: first, a joint meeting with Mr and Mrs Jones and both assessors; next, separate interviews for each parent with one of the assessors; then, a session with Mr and Mrs Jones together with baby Mary; and finally, a concluding session with Mr and Mrs Jones.

The couple arrived halfway through the time for the first interview. They told us that they were devastated by the actions of the local authority to protect Mary. They saw these as unexpected and unwarranted. They did understand that the intervention followed from Mr Jones's previous convictions for assault on children. However, as they described these incidents to us, they minimised and denied what happened. Had we not read documents pertaining to these events, we would have had difficulty believing that courts of law could have made convictions. Both Mr and Mrs Jones lacked affect when they told us about the incidents. They described the injuries as tiny red spots and emphasised that they did not view them as serious. Mrs Jones told us that if she had thought that Mr Jones had seriously injured her son, she would have kept him home from school, as other parents would do. She seemed to imply that parents normally keep children at home to hide injuries they have inflicted on them.

Already in the first interview, we could begin to see how this couple kept their experience of the physical abuse of children divorced from reality. It seemed that their main aim in the interview was to convince us of their innocence. We can recognise this as the polarisation of views described earlier. Thus, Mr and Mrs Jones seemed to imply that they could conceive of only two positions for us: either we accepted that they were innocent or we joined social services in deeming them guilty. They seemed disinterested when we wondered about interesting details that emerged in the interview. For example, we learned that all three episodes of physical abuse involved issues around food and that Mr Jones gave as excuses the fact that he was sleep deprived each time.

In the individual interviews, Mr Jones related a traumatic childhood. As a young child, he lost a brother. In the aftermath, his parents divorced and his mother had her first mental breakdown when he was seven. For the next several years, Mr Jones and his surviving siblings moved between relatives and foster placements until their mother could look after them again. When Mr Jones was 14, his mother remarried. Mr Jones and his brothers argued a lot and engaged in physical fights with their new stepfather. Eventually, Mr Jones moved out and began a series of relationships with women, none of them long-lasting until he met Mrs Jones.

The mood of the interview was sad, with Mr Jones frequently dwelling on lost relatives and brushing away tears. It was difficult to remember that this was a man who was accused of physically and sexually abusing children. The abuse seemed out of keeping with the picture he presented of himself.

In the next individual interview, the focus was on the accusations of abuse. Mr Jones denied the sexual abuse. He amended his account of the physical abuse to reflect a somewhat lesser degree of minimisation and said that he knew that what he did was wrong. He emphasised that he would undergo any kind of 'course' required, if it would result in the family staying together. However, he was unable to consider factors that might have precipitated the abuse. When I suggested that he had related incidents in which he might have felt powerless or deprived, he looked blank in response.

Mrs Jones had two interviews with my colleague. On the first occasion, she brought baby Mary, who slept for most of the time. Mrs Jones seemed not to pay attention to Mary or to what she herself was thinking, feeling and saying throughout the interview. She seemed pre-occupied, indeed besotted with Mr Jones. She idealised him as 'good and safe with children', despite the allegations. She said that if he had done anything wrong, she would have sent him away. However, she insisted that he had done nothing wrong.

Her past history offered some clues to her difficulty making links between her internal and external experiences. She revealed that her father sexually abused her sister, starting when Mrs Jones was about nine. Mrs Jones shared a bedroom with her sister, but she professed not to know about the sexual abuse until her sister disclosed it as an adult. It seemed that Mrs Jones's need not to know has persisted from childhood through to adulthood. This was evident when she went on to report that she allowed her father free access to her own daughters. She also continued to dismiss the girls' allegations that Mr Jones sexually abused them.

In the second interview, Mrs Jones's neediness and vulnerability were more apparent and expressed through somatic concerns. She idealised Mr Jones as someone who could care for her.

By the end of the individual interviews, a picture was emerging of Mr Jones as sad and masochistic, unable to express anger openly, and of Mrs Jones as cut-off from her feelings and idealising of her husband. They both felt that it was Mr Jones who should be punished and undertake personal change. This was the state of affairs when we met with the parents together with baby Mary.

Mr Jones held Mary for most of the interview. It seemed to us that whichever parent held her, it looked rather uncomfortable for Mary. Despite this, she protested with only an occasional whimper and most of the time tried to get to sleep. Usually in an interview with a baby present, we want to focus on the interactions between parents and child. On this occasion, it seemed difficult to remember that Mary was present. Instead, the interview proceeded almost as another couple session.

Mrs Jones began on the offensive. First, she complained that the family centre staff did not seem very concerned about the safety of children, whereas she presented herself as an expert on these safety issues. Then she complained about the insensitive manner in which the social workers dealt with them.

Eventually, we asked about their thoughts regarding what they might need to work on for themselves. Mrs Jones immediately said that the problem was Mr Jones's temper. She attributed this to his extremely high caffeine intake and his insomnia. He had not realised until recently that these two things could be related.

We then asked Mr Jones what problems he thought that his wife might need to address. He had great difficulty in answering this question and quickly began to talk instead about how he needed to control his temper. It soon became evident that in this couple all the problems about management of anger and anxiety were projected into Mr Jones. They both talked about him as an obsessive worrier who lies awake at night thinking about the bills that arrived that day. He thought that he should pay them immediately. These worries were quite real for this couple, who had considerable financial difficulties. Yet, Mrs Jones said that in the face of these bills, she did not worry. Instead, she busied herself with cooking or crafts. In other words, her approach was one of avoidance. We pressed Mrs Jones about what she does with her anger. This seemed to be a perplexing question for her. However, when we referred to her various somatic complaints and suggested that perhaps her anger goes into her body, she seemed to understand.

Mary entered the discussion again only when the parents mentioned that she was undergoing screening tests for possible serious medical problems. We noted that Mrs Jones described the medical details as if she was very knowledgeable, but she seemed unable to experience what she was saying emotionally, so that she did not sound worried at all.

We found ourselves in this interview in a complex situation. Mrs Jones's tendencies to project her concerns and to express herself somatically were very present. Mr Jones seemed willing to take on for himself all the burdens of worrying and of anger, but we still could not reach Mrs Jones about these issues. Most worrying of all, baby Mary seemed to drop out of awareness during the session.

A week later we met with Mr and Mrs Jones for the last session. We introduced it by saying that we were interested to hear about what they had learned thus far. They were puzzled. It soon became clear that Mrs Jones in particular had viewed the entire assessment process as an opportunity for the couple to prove what good parents they are. She felt confident that they had done this. The couple then took up their customary positions, with Mr Jones saying that he knew he did wrong and that he would go on whatever anger management course we wanted.

Mrs Jones's view of the assessment already demonstrated how the couple had avoided the experience of observation by turning it into a performance of good behaviour. If they had engaged in the experiences of observing and being observed, then the possibility of meaningful exchange could have resulted in new insights. Instead, Mr and Mrs Jones quickly re-established their familiar marital projection, in which he had all the problems with the management of anger.

We were now ready to address this projection. We said that in our opinion, they together created a dangerous situation for a young child. We explained that we had observed Mrs Jones keeping herself worry-free by getting Mr Jones to do all the worrying for her. She then appeared as someone who did not know what was going on while he became more and more agitated and eventually could hurt a child. This picture was very difficult to represent to the couple. They talked over it, disagreed with it, and finally said that they did not understand it. We gave evidence from the past, but Mrs Jones refuted it and continued to talk over us, while Mr Jones rushed in to take the blame. We suggested that a similar process was emerging in the room, only this time, the couple were leaving us with the worries about the child.

After we had spelled out our views for the fourth time, we clarified that we were not attempting to blame Mr Jones, but rather we were saying that we thought both of them represented a risk. We explained that we did not feel that Mr Jones going on an anger management course alone would help much, as it was the interaction between the parents that was dangerous.

We invited the couple to think with us about this problem, but they could not. It was clear that they were panicked. They realised that we did not accept their solution of fixing something in Mr Jones, but instead we were asking them to consider the contributions both of them made to the difficulties. Faced with this request, Mrs Jones concluded that they would not be allowed to keep Mary. She cried bitterly and apologised to her husband.

In this context, a striking reversal of positions suddenly occurred. Mr Jones took up the quiet or, as he called it, the placid role whilst Mrs Jones showed us her murderousness. She said that if she needed to protect Mary, she would knife anyone who might harm her. She also complained about her eldest child, saying that the girl had to leave because either she or her daughter would have murdered each other.

This shift lasted only momentarily. We went on to speak to Mrs Jones about how she was brought up not to know about the incest that was occurring between her father and her sister. We said that she was repeating the role of her mother, who did not know and therefore allowed this to continue. Mrs Jones's view was that she had not known, so how could anyone hold her responsible?

Mr and Mrs Jones left us in a rather distressed state. We felt that we had not managed to get them to share our concerns.

Unbeknownst to us at the time, the family centre staff was reaching similar concerns about the parenting this couple provided for Mary. Just days before, Mrs Jones had left Mary in her highchair, allegedly strapped in, but Mary had fallen out and hit her head. Mr Jones shouted abuse at his wife. It was eerie that this same accident was recorded with one of Mrs Jones's older children.

Sadly, Mr and Mrs Jones were not able to use our interpretations to examine how as a couple they failed to provide safety and security for Mary. They battled on, holding onto the idea that Mr Jones would attend an anger management course.

In the months that followed, I filed a written report for the court and also attended to give evidence. I will summarise what I said to convey the psychodynamic understanding we give the court. I reported our findings about the difficulties for both parents alone, as well as together as a couple. I described Mrs Jones's inability to face the painful realities of needs and vulnerability. I spoke about the aggression that is required for a parent to address these issues, both for herself and her children. I speculated that Mrs Jones had an underlying fear of having to face something unbearable and that this fear dated back to her childhood experience of having not to notice that her father was abusing her sister.

I said that Mr Jones seemed quite depressed and masochistic. It appeared that this mental state began with his deprived childhood experience, particularly his belief that he needed to rescue his depressed mother. He replicated this pattern in his adult relationships with women, with whom he became masochistic.

As a couple, Mrs Jones's avoidance of painful realities and Mr Jones's willingness to take on the worrying for both of them, resulted in occasions when anxiety mounted and a child was harmed. I noted that Mr and Mrs Jones had allowed us to observe a very important reversal in their positions but that it was only sustained momentarily. Indeed, it required the threat of losing their baby for Mrs Jones to allow a brief emergence of her own murderous feelings.

The judge concluded that Mary was at risk with her parents and ordered her removal from their care. He further made a finding of fact that, based on the evidence available, it was likely that Mr Jones had sexually abused Mrs Jones's older daughters. The significance of this is that it will be extremely difficult for Mr Jones to gain custody of a future child without showing evidence of real personal change.

With Mr and Mrs Jones, our observations led to a more complicated picture of the difficulties in their interaction than was available before. I suspect that during the court proceedings, they experienced me as allied with the authorities against them. Certainly, their dark looks conveyed that feeling. I hope that over time they may come to realise that we did not present a picture of a bad mother or a bad father but rather of two parents struggling with the results of their own childhood deprivations.

Unlike the other work presented in this book, the aim of these court assessments is not therapeutic. Parents may find the contact helpful, but this is not the primary aim. One extremely damaged mother in a highly abusive family managed for the first time, after the assessment, to sit through lengthy court proceedings that resulted in the loss of all her children. This suggests that parents may find some degree of containment in these assessments. I think that this results from our listening to who they are as people, even as we keep the wellbeing of the child, their child, in mind. This is something that these parents have not managed to do, and I think that this is the third position we offer to them.

References

Britton R (1989) The missing link: parental sexuality in the Oedipus complex. In: J Steiner (ed.) *The Oedipus Complex Today: Clinical Implications*, pp. 83–101. London, Karnac.

Chasseguet-Smirgel J (1985) *Creativity and Perversion*. London, Free Association Books.

Dicks H (1967) *Marital Tensions: Clinical Studies towards a Psychoanalytic Theory of Interaction*. London, Routledge & Kegan Paul.

Freud S (1920) Beyond the Pleasure Principle. In Standard Edition of the Complete Psychological Works of Sigmund Freud, London, Hogarth Press.

Freud S (1924) The loss of reality in neurosis and psychosis. In Standard Edition of the Complete Psychological Works of Sigmund Freud, London, Hogarth Press.

Kennedy R (1997) *Child Abuse, Psychotherapy and the Law*. London, Free Association Books.

Klein M (1946) The psychological principles of early analysis. *International Journal of Psycho-Analysis* 7. [Reprinted in: *Love, Guilt and Reparation*. London: Hogarth Press, 1975.]

Trowell J (1986) Physical abuse of children: some considerations when seen from the dynamic perspective. *Psychoanalytic Psychotherapy* 2: 63–73.

Wall N (1997) Judicial attitudes to expert evidence in children's cases. *Archives of Disease in Childhood* 76: 485–489.

Zinner J (1976). The implications of projective identification for marital interaction. In: H Grunebaum, J Christ (eds) *Contemporary Marriage: Structure, Dynamics and Therapy*. Boston, MA, Little Brown. [Reprinted in: JS Scharff (ed.) *Foundations of Object Relations Family Therapy*. Northvale, NJ, Jason Aronson, 1991.]

10 Dangerous cocktails: drugs and alcohol within the family

Martin Weegmann

'In the long run my dad gave me a gift. It took me years to realise it, but I came to see that I did not have to drink like him or to be like him'

(Barbara, adult child of an alcoholic parent)

'we shall finish with a plea . . . that a child and family perspective be taken with respect to alcohol problems, and that, likewise, the importance of alcohol problems with respect to child and family problems be appreciated'

(Velleman and Orford 1999, p. 266)

Introduction

The misuse of substances represents one of the most pressing psychosocial and physical problem areas in Western societies. The risk radiates to others, since for every one person misusing drugs and alcohol, several others may be affected, with those closest at hand suffering most. The numbers of people with substance use problems who are also parents must, it is estimated, run into many hundreds of thousands. An early report on children growing up with alcoholism spoke about the 'forgotten children' (Cork 1969). Since this time, however, considerable research has accrued regarding the kinds of experiences that children might have in growing up with alcoholism in the family. Similarly, research is steadily growing on the experiences of children growing up with drug-addicted parents (see Rivinius 1997, for example). Research, however, does not always translate into social awareness, so the recent Home Office commissioned report, *Hidden Harm* (2003), is a welcome attempt to publicise the difficulties of children of drug users in the UK.

In my understanding of much of this extensive research on the effects of addiction in the family, it would seem important not to generalise about the situation of children exposed to such difficulties. Equally, it is important not to extrapolate any simple conclusions from what children might have experienced to later, adult adjustment. By definition, clinicians or therapists see 'casualties' and might fail to take into account those individuals who are less (globally) affected and/or who appear to make relatively normal transitions through adolescence into adulthood. Fonagy (1998, p. 88) quotes a quip to which psychoanalytically oriented therapists might be prone, the failure to realise 'that *data* is not the plural of *anecdote*'! Velleman and Orford's (1999) extensive research on adults who were the children of problem drinkers clarify some of these issues and distinctions, suggesting that many children are resilient and that children *are* likely to be more disadvantaged by exposure to, for example, parental violence and family disharmony, than due to the presence of drink problems per se. The overall *quality* of home life and presence of protective and mitigating factors needs to be assessed, at different stages in the development of the family; as with other areas of developmental psychopathology, it makes sense to conceptualise the problem as involving one of vulnerability/risk. Consequently, the stereotypical picture of the substance-misusing household as one of complete chaos is clearly a misleading generalisation. Although, I have indeed seen family situations where there was a breakdown of all normal boundaries, with children being exposed to the worst kinds of excess, abuse and neglect, I have seen others in which the substance misuse by a parent was relatively contained, kept out of sight or ignored and the children well cared for. Of course, there are many families which exist somewhere in the middle of this continuum, perhaps distorted in some areas by substance misuse, whilst relatively well-functioning in other areas. Taking a systems view of the family, there is a wide range of possible accommodations and adaptations to the fact of substance misuse, from family systems almost entirely dominated and structured by chemicals to those which manage to 'by pass' the user and maintain normal, or near-normal functioning and boundaries. Families also change over time, so that substance misuse might affect family members quite variously depending on age or phase of the family life-cycle (see Steinglass et al 1987).

With this problem-range and complexity in mind, this chapter offers a psychodynamic perspective on substance misuse, based around two clinical examples. In both cases I have highlighted some of the implications there had been for the wider family system, stressing the importance, as Velleman and Orford state, of keeping the 'family perspective' in mind.

'Out of it': psychodynamics of addiction

One of the most tragic aspects of addiction is that it is establishes closed circuits of behaviour and thinking. A person's repertoire of responses to situations becomes stereotyped and their interests can narrow down to the point that only the next bottle or fix becomes important. Substance misuse thus becomes antidevelopmental, suspending the individual in time and space, stopping growth in its path. Being 'out of it', dislodges the user from normal temporality and awareness of self and the environment. Freud (1930) captured some of these aspects of intoxicants in a characteristically eloquent manner, 'one knows that, with the help of this "drowner of cares", one can at any time withdraw from the pressures of reality and find refuge in a world of one's own'.

Vignette one: Helen

Helen used cocaine. I will concentrate on what the drugs did to her mind, so to speak.

> 'I first used drugs when my partner had been violent towards me. Before that he had always been verbally critical. An old friend said that I always looked miserable and offered me something to "put the smile back on my face". And that's what they did, at least in the early days and I found myself able to cope again, or at least get by. They (the drugs) were like a barrier in the snow. Somehow I felt at that stage in my life that this was my lot and that it was better to be high some

of the time whilst being punched, than being abused *and* miserable. After he left I got help but did not tell the counsellor about the drugs, 'cause I figured it was not important to tell her. The drugs continued because this time they helped me to forget what he had done to me. It was quite some time later, after I got scared about what they were doing to me, that I managed to stop. I knew all along that my children were not getting the best deal and that not seeing violence and arguments was *not* all they were entitled to'.

Helen spoke with clarity about her use of drugs and the function that they had played in her mental and relationship life. She was able to make connections between the drugs as a way of coping with severe relationship trauma and states of despair, so that her friend's suggestion for her to use something to 'put the smile back' had an immediate appeal. The idea of a 'barrier in the snow' was a graphic description of the role of drugs in her psychic life, creating some form of protective shield, but at the cost of increased dissociation (by the way, 'snow' is sometimes a word for cocaine). Thereafter, even when the violence had stopped, the substance misuse spread and was increasingly co-opted into her everyday functioning. One might say, using Steiner's (1993) idea, that the use of drugs increasingly constituted a 'psychic retreat', a place to which she could withdraw, thus providing a measure of safety. As drug use had by this time become normative, she saw no discrepancy in not talking to her counsellor about them; they were *hers* and so Helen felt no need to worry or talk about them. They were a best-kept secret.

Helen also made links between her turn to drugs and earlier difficulties in growing up in a household dominated by verbal brutality and sporadic violence between her parents, although not addiction. She commented, 'I was already an addict waiting to happen'. I was not convinced of this, or at least that her statement was to be taken literally, since it is impossible to predict who will and who will not turn to drugs compulsively in later life. However, in using this self-description, I think that Helen was expressing an important idea, fitting into what could be called a story or narrative of her problems and recovery. If she saw herself as 'addict waiting to use', she could place her substance misuse in the context to childhood adversity. It was a way of making sense of her past and a helpful warning of her *continuing* vulnerability to returning to drugs. Thus, Helen used a version of the formula, 'in recovery, never recovered'.

Helen's recovery proved solid and she did not relapse (based on information obtained at long-term follow up, post-treatment). Forming a positive relationship with a second therapist, years later than the counsellor, she was able to rebuild her life and sense of self. Fortunately she had been able to heed the message when she had started to become scared by the consequences of the drugs. Whilst they had initially 'drowned cares' and promoted a degree of independence from her circumstances, they were at risk of becoming out of control; Helen knew that somehow they had opened up a dangerous gap inside and she was less in touch with herself as a result. Likewise, she knew they had introduced an invisible barrier between herself and her children.

Krystal (1977, p. 91) talks about one of the dilemmas of the addict as consisting in being 'unable to claim, own up and exercise various parts of himself' and perhaps with Helen this centred around the ability to exercise maternal functions, for herself and her children. Helen was able to acknowledge and to rectify the fact that her children needed more than the obligatory care that she had hitherto been able to provide. She started to see herself in a new light and to value her many qualities. The snow had melted.

In many ways, Helen was a classic example of an individual who, as a result of childhood adversity, had 'more to overcome' than many and had consequently a greater likelihood of forming problematic relationships and/or developing psychopathology. Psychodynamic observers have rightfully emphasised this wider vulnerability to later difficulties and negative pathways into adulthood, including substance misuse.

Childhood abuse and neglect can form the backdrop against which inability to modulate emotions and poor self-regulation arise (see van der Kolk and Fisler 1994). This is a familiar psychodynamic theme of difficulties around self-containment and knowing the self or mind. Taylor et al (1997) details how inadequate emotional containment during childhood can leave individuals without the means to process and mediate feelings so that, in growing up, such individuals lack 'emotional literacy' and can resort to primitive, sensori-motor efforts to discharge or to produce affect experiences. The compulsive use of substances can thus be seen as a 'disorder of self-regulation'. The term 'mentalisation' has been increasingly used to describe an important aspect of how individuals manage themselves, how they 'build up a mind' and, related to this, how they interpret the minds and intentions of others. Fonagy and Target (1998, p. 93) argue that children with limited or disrupted 'mentalisation' are unable to respond flexibly to situations and to the 'symbolic, meaningful qualities of other people's behaviour'. Thus, in Helen's case, cocaine use seemed to have been a way of retreating from the difficulties that surrounded her, with simulated 'highs' replacing the need to think about and appraise her situation. Early exposure to violence had no doubt contributed to a lack, at the time, of an ability to negotiate or establish crucial boundaries.

In a series of publications, American psychiatrist and psychoanalyst Edward Khantzian has vividly described the powerful self-medicating role that substances can play. Drugs can create feelings or dampen them, can stimulate or reduce feeling-intensity, can tone up or tone down the experience of mental life. Of course, drugs create damage and yet their use can offset the difficulties posed by an individual's problematic environment and past. Capturing this paradox, Khantizian (1993, p. 269) suggests that drugs 'substitute dysphoria and a relationship with suffering they do not understand or control for one they do understand and control'. The acquired control is illusory, with the addict chasing his/her tail. The search to 'feel better' is a seductive one.

It is important to state that difficulties around trauma, affect-regulation, poor mentalisation and so on, which increase vulnerability to later substance misuse are also likely to *result* from chronic substance misuse. Substances *also* undermine normal emotional feedback mechanisms, create *new* experiences of trauma or loss and diminish the ability to care for the self. In the words of a proverb, 'A person takes a drink and then the drink takes the person'. People can, after all, experience a difficult adolescence or adulthood even when they did not experience a difficult childhood. With the progressive use of substances, we witness a kind of de-mentalisation of experiences, together with other reversals of development that can happen in response to later challenges in life.

In my view, one of the strengths of a psychodynamic view of addiction is less than any supposed, general view of the nature of the 'addict', but more so its unremitting emphasis on the sources *and* consequences of addictive vulnerability (see Weegmann 2002). Good psychotherapy with addicted individuals needs to be graded, based upon a continual assessment of the person's motivation, their view of their situation, strengths and limitations and the creation of a reliable therapeutic space, within which unfolding problems can be considered. Once a person has relinquished the substance, supportive and exploratory approaches in therapy can be carefully balanced. One of the aims is to increase an individual's psychological resources and capacity for mentalisation, counteracting the temptation to get 'out of it', or, in the language of Alcoholics (and Narcotics) Anonymous, 'to change the way we feel'.

Now let us consider the possible experience of a child who grows up in a family dominated by substance misuse. The document *Hidden Harm* refers to a feeling which children of drug-misusing parents often report, that their parents were 'not there' for them. 'Not being there' is the counterpart to the parent's being 'out of it'.

'Liquid containers'?: growing up with addicted parents

Vignette two: Barbara

Barbara (quoted at the start) had grown up with alcoholism in the family, had acquired serious drink problems and subsequently became abstinent with the support of Alcoholics Anonymous and group psychotherapy. The material comes during year two of group therapy:

> 'These last few weeks, I've had so many feelings from when I was small, so many small things which make me angry to think about. It's like with everything they always put drink first – like if we were on holiday, it would be the pub all day and if I was ill that was a problem because they might be too hungover to look after me. So I had to look after me. They were always in some kind of mood – with themselves, loud when they were drunk, feeling sorry for themselves the day after, or guilty when they were off it for a few weeks – then I was given a lot of freedom, but punished when they were back on it again. I did not know whether I was coming or going.'

As Barbara spoke she was shaking and would periodically glance at me (the therapist).

Because drinking was normalised, Barbara had had no evident means of 'seeing' the alcoholism at home. Where both parents drink, the problems are compounded since the child cannot rely on a sober parent. She did, however, recall a gradual sense that her family was not 'like others' and awkwardness when the topic of family life was discussed at school. It was only when she managed to stop drinking and face reality that she was able to re-evaluate her parents and see the problems, which, to outsiders, might have been all-too apparent. One might say, using a metaphor from Heidegger (see Inwood 1997), that the parental drinking could only be 'unconcealed' once Barbara had created a 'clearing' in her own mind and once she had emerged from the fog of her own drinking. From this vantage-point, she was more able to construct a new and clearer description of family life, re-evaluating 'lost time' as well as future possibilities. Recovery and therapy had given her the means to and permission to have a story to tell.

During this phase of therapy, I noticed how Barbara was engaged in mourning aspects of her childhood situation, revisiting small details and patterns of family life. Barbara now noticed sequences of behaviour in family life, such as: drinking parent – intoxicated parent – withdrawing/sick parent – dry parent. There were related affective patterns, such as: tension – disinhibition – moodiness – guilt. Barbara felt anger and sadness, focused around the thought that 'alcohol came first'. With the help of group discussion, we helped Barbara to consider how her own affective responses had become tied in to the reaction and behaviour of her parents, as she learned the art of maintaining vigilance, scanning her parents for signs of the state they were in and, above all, maintaining safety. Her vigilance of me in the group, the nervous glance, was, I surmised, an expression of her need to maintain safety in the therapy and to take account of my possible responses. Amongst the kind of things which I said to her during this period were, 'I think you feel the need to be careful in what you say and to check, because I might feel like a parent in this particular family/group', and, 'In your glancing at me every so often, I think you looking at my reactions; I think it's vital for you to feel that I am really taking in what you say and can be a witness to some of what you have been through'. Of course, the rest of the group helped in all kinds of ways in the clarification of these micro-responses. Barbara had initially experienced analytic group therapy as 'too spontaneous' and worryingly free of 'rules'; anxieties, such as these, were consistent with her experiences of a family life dominated by confusing priorities and inconsistent (liquid) rules. Her containers had not been reliable and much of the time, realities were simply drunken away. Of course, she repeated this with her own drinking.

I have found the Lichtenberg et al (1992) concept of 'model scenes' a particularly helpful one in assisting traumatised individuals, like Barbara, to conceptualise broken and truncated childhood experiences. Careful descriptions of affective and interactional patterns, known as 'model scenes', represent an acquired understanding of what an individual had to contend with, based on clarification of the *actual experiences* involved and how the person made sense of them; in other words, how such experiences formed the materials around which the internal world was built up. Such model scenes are constructions, rather than the only or definitive way of seeing what happened and are thus open to revision as therapy unfolds. It was, clearly, an important therapeutic achievement that Barbara was able to recapture and ultimately to mourn the consequences of these complex sequences and nuances of behaviour and family interaction. By giving conceptual representation to salient developmental experiences, Barbara's model scenes helped her to extend mentalisation and allow revisions of psychic life.

The co-presence of safety and danger

A new member joined the group who, struggling with drug problems, dropped out after some weeks. Barbara was furious with me for having 'spoilt a good group' and believed that I had brought in the other patient to test her (i.e.. Barbara). She began to doubt my judgement, since this other patient had 'not been suitable', in her view. Six months later, I announced a plan to introduce two other new members, which led to mounting panic and hostility on her part. She was deeply worried about my decision, the fact that I had the power to decide and feared I was endangering the group's existence.

My impression of group life prior to the arrival of the new person was similar to that of Barbara's, in that a good degree of cohesion had been established with increasing feelings of closeness and loyalty between members. It was as if my decision to alter the composition and, moreover, to 'bring in a junkie' as Barbara said, had shattered this cohesion and relative safety. There were a number of dimensions contained in Barbara's reactions to this and the later prospect of new members.

To start with, this whole episode seemed to demonstrate the fragile nature of Barbara's progress in certain domains. The idea of 'bringing someone else in' disturbed the status quo and I sought her detailed associations to the idea, as I did for others in the group. She made a link to her father coming home ('coming in') and to the sense of needing to be watchful as a youngster, also to having to 'read' her mother's mood when on and off the bottle. Clearly, a 'junkie' had a specific significance for Barbara and I wondered whether it represented both an intoxicated parent and an intoxicated Barbara – a reminder of herself at an earlier stage. Either way, it threatened chaos. In the light of this, I explored Barbara's profound fears of being re-traumatised and re-exposed to the situations of childhood/adolescence.

People with restricted mentalisation can and do experience changes as concrete threats. In this example, Barbara was thrown into panic, unable to reflect upon her feelings in response to me, my decision and the presence of the other person (the 'junkie'). She could not envisage my actions as having been well-intentioned, even if fallible, nor discern my interest in assisting the new person, but saw it as a cruel test. One of the problems arising for abused and neglected people is that they do not have a consistent experience of their caretakers as being able to hold them in mind and anticipate their needs; consider how, for example, Barbara felt that being ill was resented by her parents as this meant that they might have to expend energy in looking after her. Patients like these can, in a very real sense, grow up, 'to fear minds' (Fonagy and Target 2000, p. 858).

Rey (1988, p. 457) wrote a valuable paper posing the question of *who* the patient brings with them into therapy. He speculates that patients bring with them a number of 'people' and dilemmas, including an unconscious request to 'bring about the reparation of important damaged internal objects without which the reparation of the subject's self cannot happen normally and happily'. I agree with this, but would add that the patients also bring in transpersonal patterns and the damaged values they have lived with. For example, not only were Barbara's parents damaged in various ways, but as a result she had no stable concept of a 'sober household', even though she was managing to provide this for her own children. In my understanding there was a thin line in her mind between me as a figure different to her parents – leading to a real appreciation that I had helped to build up a cohesive and supportive (family) group – alongside a fear that I might ruin the group's collective efforts and lose sight of her. This was crystallised in her feeling that I had spoilt a previously harmonious group and introduced danger. I had to bear her experience of me, at this point, as unwise and uncaring and believe that her hostility towards me was a reaction to the fear that I was endangering her to once more. I said something like, 'I think it is crucial for you to expect that I can provide you with a sober group and keep your needs carefully in my mind and when you think I might not be doing this, or lose sight of you, you are terrified that the whole thing will fall apart'. There was a reparative theme and a destructive aspect, struggling with each other. I added that I thought it was encouraging that she could let me know how she was feeling because this meant she had not given up hope of getting through to someone.

The reference to sobriety, like the term 'junkie', had a specific meaning for Barbara and it was important to her that I understood the role that Alcoholics Anonymous played. It was essential that I did not see it as a rival group and appreciated that through the fellowship Barbara had found a 'sober family', providing structure and clarity. I wondered at times whether Alcoholics Anonymous provided something like the 'secure base', from which she was able to used the therapy group for exploration (see Weegmann 2004).

Thinking under fire?

Bion used the term 'thinking under fire' to characterise some of the situations and pressures under which the therapist operates. It is an apt metaphor for threat. On one occasion, for example, Barbara said she wanted to 'wipe me off the face of the earth'; all I could do was to sit still, even though I was shaken, shocked and momentarily frightened. It was only later, that I could formulate the notion that someone's *existence* was at stake (including the group's existence). There are, however, other descriptors which come to mind with this group of patients, who have experienced the extremes of addiction in their parent(s). One of these could be, 'thinking under stupor', whereby the therapist has to tolerate the patient's experience of confusion and the patient's *uncertainty* in being able to reach a consistently *clear-minded* part of the therapist. This may be the product of repeated experiences of parental intoxication, inconsistent messages and failed or inadequate acts of reparation, mixed in with all the anger and grievances built up by the patient.

Another possible expression, closely related, could be that of 'thinking under dissociation', in which the patient cannot be sure that the therapist will be able to bring significant psychic *clarity*, together with the fear that what has been kept apart might now be brought together into a dangerous collision. Fonagy (2000b) talks about traumatised patients who 'defensively inhibit their capacity to mentalise', partly in order not to have to think about the parents' state of mind or what was done to them by others. A nonconscious collusion or pattern can form in which the child's dissociation reproduces the dissociations of the parent(s) and in this climate all kinds of 'madness' can occur and pass unnoticed. We have noted how Barbara became a drinker, even a 'worse drinker', than her parents. However, Barbara's later reflection to the effect that her father's alcoholism was ultimately a 'gift' (see the quotation at the beginning of the chapter) was a testimony to her ability to move beyond confusion and to forgive.

I will add that Barbara continued to make progress and adapted well to the later newcomers. I saw an increasing ability to trust in the group and her therapist as well as an emergent playfulness. She began to look more relaxed with the to-and-fro of the group situation, to tolerate spontaneity. Winnicott (1964) reminds us that worry-free play is an important developmental attainment. If we link this up to other psychodynamic ideas, then play also represents a loosening of the concrete and an expansion of mentalisation, so that the individual can indeed 'play' with their mind and entertain alternative possibilities (see Lichtenberg and Meares 1996 and Fonagy and Target 2000a).

Keeping the family in mind

Family interventions can take many forms, from seeing the whole family, the parents or other family subsystems, but also, by keeping the family in mind even whilst seeing the individual patient. The psychotherapist has a valuable contribution to offer in this regard to conceptualising the family, in their understanding of a notion of the 'internal family', which the patient brings with them at a symbolic level. Barbara was not alone in the therapy group in re-creating some of the experiences and dilemmas of early family life and in re-creating with me the problematic relationship to her parents. I was aware that in treating Barbara, that not only did she bring internal parents with her, but, also, that she was a parent herself, trying to provide a good foundation in life for her own children. Supporting her children differently was, indeed, one of her original motivations in seeking help. Thus, from my point of view, I was aware of both trying to help the *patient* in her and also the *parent* in her. I knew, as she did, that her children would not have completely forgotten, even if they might have forgiven, her own alcoholic behaviour and that the future was happening *now*.

Conclusion: some considerations in working with children and family members

A number of considerations can be borne in mind in working with those affected by addiction. I begin with some general points, followed by more specific observations.

- Specialist addiction services usually concentrate on the needs of the (individual) substance misuser and can therefore overlook the needs of those in the wider relationship or family context. They may feel ill-equipped or ill-trained to deal with the family member as well as the user. It is important, therefore, to try to move such services out of a narrow conception of practice and to incorporate more systemic thinking, which has implications for training and resources.
- Child and family services may traditionally have underestimated the effects of addiction within family systems, especially when addiction is not openly presented as the problem. Denial and secrecy add to the complications of assessment. There needs to be, I suggest, an increased awareness of the prevalence and operation of addiction in family systems (see Rydelius 1997).
- Hodgins and Shimp (1995) has devised a careful approach to identifying children of alcoholics. Amongst the questions we might ask a child at risk would be: Have you ever thought that one of your parents had a drink problem? Did you ever argue or fight with a parent when he/she was drinking? Have you ever heard your parents fight when one of them was drunk? Did you ever feel like hiding or emptying a parent's bottle of alcohol? Did you ever wish that a parent would stop drinking?
- A psychotherapeutic perspective can assist enormously in the conceptualisation of damage and resilience. This is best combined with a systemic perspective, so that the clinician can appreciate how minds and family systems become distorted and aligned to the needs of the substance-misusing parent(s). Individual defences against anxiety thus come into being. Some of the pressures which can be brought to bear on youngsters is described well by Beletis and Brown (1981): 'what is most visible and problematic – the alcoholism – is most vehemently denied,

children are early caught up in the difficult task of joining the denial process, or facing continuous threats to their own perception of reality' (p. 189).

• With respect to individual and group psychotherapy, it is likely that key dimensions and family life will be re-enacted in some form during the course of the treatment, as we saw in the case of Barbara, dimensions which might include, for example: the meeting and non-meeting of needs, issues of control, trust, judgement and perception of reality, dealing with truncated and/or hyper-attuned affective life. Group therapy in particular provides important opportunities for mirroring, identification, support and reality-testing, a sober resource that can eventually be internalised if all goes well.

Acknowledgement

I would like to thank Ewa Piwowoz-Hjort for her help.

References

Beletis S, Brown S (1981) A developmental framework for understanding the adult children of alcoholics. *Journal of Addictions and Health* 2: 187–203.

Cork M (1969) The Forgotten Children. Toronto: Addiction Research Foundation.

Fonagy P, Target M (1998) Mentalisation and the changing aims of child psychoanalysis. *Psychoanalytic Dialogues* 8(1): 87–114.

Fonagy P, Target M (2000) Playing with reality III – the persistence of dual psychic reality in borderline patients. *International Journal of Psychoanalysis* 81: 853–873.

Fonagy P (2000) Attachment and borderline personality disorder. *Journal of the American Psychoanalytic Association* 48/4: 1129–1146.

Freud S (1930) *Civilisation and Its Discontents*. Standard Edition. New York: WW Norton.

Hodkins D, Shimp L (1995) Identifying adult children of alcoholics; methodological review and a comparison of the Cast 6 with other methods. *Addiction* 90: 255–267.

Inwood M (1997) *A very Short Introduction to Heidegger*. Oxford, Basil Blackwell Publishers.

Khantzian E (1999) *Addiction as a Human Process*. New York: Jason Aronson.

Khantzian E, Wilson A (1993) *Substance abuse, repetition and the nature of addictive suffering*. In: Wilson A and Gedo J (eds.) Hierarchical Concepts in Psychoanalysis. New York: Guildford Press. p. 263–283.

Krystal H (1977) Self- and object-representation in alcoholism and other drug dependence: implications for therapy. In Blaine H, Julius (eds) The Psychodynamics of Drug Dependence. NIDA monograph, Washington DC: Government Printing Office.

Hidden Harm (2003) Home Office: Advisory Council on the Misuse of Drugs.

Lichtenberg J, Meares R (1996) The role of play in things human. *Psychoanalysis and Psychotherapy*, 13/1. p. 7.

Lichtenberg J, Lachmann F, Fossage J (1992) *Self and Motivational Systems*. Hillsdale, NJ, The Analytic Press.

Rey H (1988) That which patients bring to analysis. *International Journal of Psychoanalysis* 69: 457–470.

Rivinius T (1997) *Children of Chemically Dependent Parents*. New York, Brunner/Mazel.

Rydelius P (1997) Annotation: are the children of alcoholics a clinical concern for the child and adolescent psychiatrist today? *Journal of Child Psychiatry and Psychology* 38: 615–624.

Steiner J (1993) *Psychic Retreats: Pathological Organisations in Neurotic, Psychotic and Borderline Patients*. London, Routledge.

Steinglass P, Nennett L, Wolin S, Reiss D (1987) *The Alcoholic Family*. London, Hutchinson.

Taylor G, Bagby R, Parker J (1997) *Disorders of Affect Regulation*. Cambridge, Cambridge University Press.

van der Kolk B, Fisler R (1994) Childhood abuse and neglect and loss of self-regulation. *Bulletin of the Menninger Clinic* 58(2): 145–169.

Velleman R, Orford J (1999) *Risk or Resilience: Adults who were the Children of Problem Drinkers*. The Netherlands, Harwood Academic Press.

Weegmann M (2002) Growing up with addiction. In: Weegmann M, Cohen R (eds) *Psychodynamics of Addiction*. London: Whurr.

Weegmann M (2004) Alcoholics Anonymous and fellowship groups: a group analytic view. *Group Analysis*, **37**/2, p. 243–258.

Winnicott D (1964) *The Child and Family and the Outside World*. London, Penguin Books.

11 Working with borderline personality disorder

Joseph Mishan

Andrew sat back in his chair, eyed me and smiled. 'Hello' he said, 'I hope you had a nice holiday.' I nodded. He continued: 'I hope you won't take this personally or anything, but well, it's like I've seen Dr Sanders for a couple of hours while you've been away, and I have to say, I got more from him in those two hours than I got from you in the last year'. Instantly needled, I tried to keep the tension out of my voice. 'Uh uh. I wonder why that might be?' 'Well', he replied, a slight glint in his eye, 'I thought you might be able to tell me that.' Rage swelled in me, my stomach tightened. Andrew looked cool, surveying me. I thought, God after all I've done for you in the last year! I'd like to wipe that smile off your face. And Dr Sanders of all people: he was so medical model! But then maybe Andrew had a point: I had forgotten to send that form off about the housing before I went. And Dr Sanders was a qualified professional psychiatrist. He had probably given Andrew the anti-depressants he was always on about. At least that was something tangible. Suddenly I felt dreadful. My self-confidence sagged. Rage turned to hopelessness. I didn't know what to say in my defence. An awkward silence descended as I struggled with a welter of emotions.

This account of a meeting[1] with a patient diagnosed with borderline personality disorder illustrates the extremes of emotional temperature these individuals can evoke in their carers. This can give rise to serious problems in treatment and management and to schisms between professionals. While it cannot grant immunity from being affected, analytic understanding can help sustain the capacity to think while in the swell of emotional assault.

The category of personality disorder is often used casually by professionals to refer to individuals who are particularly difficult. They are sometimes felt not to have a diagnosable mental illness by the psychiatrist and are therefore uncomfortable enigmas. They can be continually demanding but respond to professional help with neither improvement nor gratitude. They generate desperation, resentment and frustration, and accusations of malingering. This category of patient often poses a serious challenge in the health care system. 'Personality disorder' can sometimes be used as little more than a term of abuse, or a signal of despair.

---

1 All persons described in the vignettes are fictional but based on real clinical experience.

The psychiatric perspective

Speaking from a diagnostic (descriptive) perspective, ten personality disorder types have been described by the Diagnostic and Statistical Manual of Mental Disorders (DSM-IV). In practice, patients rarely belong to only one type and the DSM manual usefully proposes a 'clustering' system, which proposes three subcategories. These are cluster 'A', 'B' and 'C'. Cluster 'A' are 'odd or eccentric' types and include paranoid, schizoid and schizotypal personality disorders. Cluster 'B' are the 'dramatic' personality disorders: histrionic, narcissistic and antisocial and borderline. Cluster C patients are 'anxious and fearful', i.e. obsessive compulsive, avoidant and dependent types. In this chapter we will focus on the borderline personality disorder within cluster B.

The psychiatric perspective defines this disorder in terms of typical overt behaviour, whilst an analytic standpoint describes the internal dynamics involved. On a psychiatric or descriptive level, borderline personality disorders (BPD) are characterised by lability of mood and impulsivity. Moods may switch from powerful highs to empty depression with little middle ground often in response to the mildest criticism or to perceived abandonment or rejection. Moods may precipitate the threat of, or actual non-lethal cutting, overdosing, alcohol or drug taking. Self-image, including sexual orientation, is unstable. Brief psychotic episodes may occur. Although they may come across as completely at ease within average social exchanges, borderline patients feel threatened by intimacy; relationships are marked by betrayal, violence and disruption. There is a very high co-morbidity with other diagnoses so that most borderline patients are also diagnosed with other problems such as depression, eating disorder, substance abuse or anxiety states. Perhaps not surprisingly, the history of such individuals is marked by broken relationships, abuse, substance abuse and a poor work record. Their childhoods are likewise chaotic, with strife, violence and marital breakdown between parents; alcohol and drug abuse often plays a part in this. Sexual and physical abuse is common, perpetrated by the parents or by friends or relations. Obviously, there is little consistent affection and concern within such a family; instead competition, humiliation and threat may be normal currency.

An analytic perspective: splitting, projection and projective identification

The analytic perspective offers an explanation of this picture in terms of internal dynamics and early relationships. It suggests that the internal psychological world of the borderline is dominated by un-integrated and extreme attitudes. Emotions and internal representations (such as the parents), which in the normal/neurotic individual would be more connected nuanced and ambivalent, are rigidly defined and separated. For example, the borderline patient might view their mother as wonderful and completely without blemish, and their father as utterly despicable. Hate is dissociated from love as black from white. One borderline patient even refused to utter the word 'father', because he was in her view so utterly contemptible; the possibility of loving and hating the same person could not be borne. This internal disconnectness is described in analytic language as 'splitting' and refers to a tendency to divide that which truly belongs together. Thus the other may be felt to be totally bad at one moment and virtually perfect the next, whereas a more realistic appraisal would be neither entirely one nor the other. Splitting creates harshness and polarity. It also makes the formation of a stable identity problematic. One young man was noted to dress in a variety of clothing during an extended assessment. His outfits suggested businessman, drop-out and 'gothic' by turns. He claimed to be 'experimenting' with different identities, but his presentation conveyed to the therapist extreme uncertainty about who he was, his values and his future. This unformed quality is often reflected in sexual orientation; the patient might claim adamantly to be homosexual, but may change orientation during treatment as if on a whim.

Characteristically, such patients gather numerous carers around them who are all responding to different needs and requests such as housing, financial and counselling needs. Often, one or more professionals may be held by the patient to possess a special understanding while others are viewed with disdain and can do nothing right. The hapless professionals may be caught up in the patient's view of them, generating a special pride in the one case or anger and hatred in the other. The frequent result is that the two sides, reflecting the internal world of the patient split into good and bad, end up warring over who the patient is and what they need. Main (1957) gives a very pertinent account of the 'special' patient and their projections into the therapeutic team. This putting of feelings, thoughts or attitudes that belong to the self into others is referred to as 'projection'. Hated, painful or unwanted parts of the self may be allocated to another person, who is then identified with as the unwanted part of the self. This is projective identification. The target person may also be induced to feel and enact the projected attribute, in this case not only is something projected, but the object of the projection 'identifies' with the projection. In the above vignette, Andrew projected a feeling of anger and then inadequacy and depression into his carer in response to the holiday break. This protected him from these feelings and allowed him to remain calm and aloof. Paradoxically although these psychological manoeuvres are an attempt to protect the self and hold it together, splitting and projection further weaken the self. In this example, Andrew is weakened in the sense that he no longer has access to feelings of loss. He is also persecuted by the potential return of these feared and hated feelings, which are now felt to reside in the carer. In consequence, the carer may then be perceived as a threat because he contains the unwanted feelings. Projection of parts of the self may be so extreme that very little of the internal world remains and the patient may not be able to think or have emotions and may then feel empty.

Self-harm

Projection and splitting are radical psychological attempts to protect a fragile self from disintegration. When this fails, physical methods are resorted to. Self harm such as cutting or substance abuse can have a variety of functions and meanings. It may be:

- Communicative. Fonagy and Higgit (1992) described a female patient who, when she felt unable to describe her state of emptiness to the psychiatrist in a casualty department inscribed the phrase 'I am lost' into her leg with a razor. This act, as might be imagined, would have had a powerful communicative effect on the psychiatrist who could hardly have avoided the horror, pain and helplessness felt by the patient.

- Distance-maintaining. Abandonment and rejection is one of the most central pre-occupations of the borderline patient. Self-harm evokes a response in those around the patient, and may re-assure them that others are still engaged and mindful of them.
- Attacking. The wish to retaliate for some hurt, by inflicting pain or torture may be achieved symbolically through an attack on the person's own body, which at that moment is imagined (consciously or unconsciously) to be the target person.
- Soothing. Mental states of unbearable pain may be soothed by cutting which is felt to be a relief as the poisonous 'bad' blood is released. Physical pain may also distract from a mental agony. Drugs may be soothing, and alcohol may 'drown' mental distress.

In practice, soothing punitive and communicative functions may all be combined at differing levels in the one act.

A 35-year-old man recalled that at the age of 14 his anger and despair about his father's drunken stupors reached such a pitch that he burned himself with a cigarette in view of his father. His father responded by telling him to stop it because he was dropping cigarette ash on the floor.

The self-harm in this case might be seen to be communicative in terms of the pain and alarm he wanted the father to experience on his behalf, punitive in that it was meant to be an aversive experience for him, and (perhaps less prominently) a way of distracting from the intensity of his own emotional state.

Caring for the borderline patient: the countertransference

Caring for such patients often engenders powerful disturbance. The carer feels con-taminated, intruded upon and oppressed, or alternatively immensely potent and omniscient. In either case the sense of reality and ordinary proportion is lost, and feel-ings take on a 'larger than life' quality. This response to the patient's conscious and unconscious communications is referred to as the 'countertransference'. Its quality is a mirror to the patient's world which is harsh, conflictual and intense.

One experienced junior doctor felt so provoked by a patient's continual suicide threats that he finally exploded with 'at least it would give him something to do that week'. In this way the doctor was driven to enact a punitive and abandoning part of the patient. Equally, this intense countertransference may lead to fantastic rescue attempts.

A 28-year-old woman was attending out-patient psychotherapy for depression on a regular basis for three months when unusually, she did not appear for two sessions and left no message. The therapist, aware of her history of suicide attempts and that they had been discussing disturbing themes, phoned the GP who agreed to do a home visit. With some difficulty, the GP managed to get the patient to agree to see her therapist the same day to discuss possible admission to hospital. In the event the therapist spent over two hours with his patient, during which more disturbing material about sexual abuse emerged. Convinced that his patient had reached a critical point in therapy and that he had a special understanding of the dynamics, the therapist arranged another two-hour session for the following day. These intensive sessions continued for the rest of the week. Finally, the consultant on the unit noticed the frequent appearance of the patient and questioned the therapist about it. Much to the fury of the patient and the chagrin of the therapist he separated the two. He arranged an inpatient admission for the patient, and weekly supervision sessions with the therapist.

In this case the therapist was drawn into enacting the patient's fantasy of exclusive one-ness with an other; something which was later confirmed when the patient asserted that the therapist would surely know what she thought without her even having to say it.

To summarise, the borderline patient's internal world is harsh, fragmented and extreme. The patient is subject to oscillation between feelings of tremendous potency, and of terrifying non-being. The smallest comment from another can produce a tidal wave of emotion. This internal maelstrom is moderated only by recourse to actions and psychological manoeuvres, which in the long-term perpetuate fragility. Proximity to such emotional intensity inevitably invades and distorts the carer's own feeling states and normal objectivity.

Clinical work: the mafia and the pathological organisation

One explanatory model is of particular use in organising and understanding the borderline patient. This model sees the borderline patient's problem as being the result of internal conflict. Rosenfeld's paper on 'destructive narcissism' (1971), refers to the way in which ordinary positive self-esteem or narcissism becomes fused with a powerful aggressive instinct. This fusion creates a grandiose and envious force that dominates the rest of the personality. In a well-known passage Rosenfeld writes:

> 'The destructive narcissism of these patients often appears highly organised, as if one were dealing with a powerful gang dominated by a leader, who controls all the members of the gang. . . . The main aim (of the organisation) seems to be to . . . control the members of the gang so that they will not desert the destructive organisation and join the positive parts of the self or betray the secrets of the gang to the analyst. To change and receive help implies weakness and is experienced as wrong or as a failure. . . . In cases of this kind there is the most chronic resistance to . . . progress.'
>
> (p. 249)

Rosenfeld is describing not just a defence such as projection or splitting (although these defences are involved), but a defensive organisation or system around which the whole of the personality becomes configured. Such an organisation is stable and hard to shift. Similar 'organisations' have been described by other psychoanalysts such as Sohn (1985), O'Shaughnessy (1981) and Steiner (1987). One of the main functions of the organisation is the setting up inside the person of a part of the self (the destructive narcissistic 'gang' in Rosenfeld's account) which purports to provide all needs and offer simple solutions to the suffering and needy part of the self. Any need for anything from outside the self is seen as a weakness, and a threat to the fantasy of complete self-sufficiency, and therefore subject to rigorous suppression or attack. For example, the person may be persuaded that if only they relied entirely on the organisation or gang they would never have to suffer loneliness or abandonment again. The needy and suffering part is kept in thrall by this apparently all-providing and superior, caring part. The 'solutions' offered are destructive to the self (such as overdose) or to relationships with other people (such as cutting links with others). If this promise fails to keep the needy part in its grasp, and the person does turn outside for help, then they are threatened or punished, perhaps by having to commit an act of self harm, or by internal confusion. It should be remembered that the pathological organisation, like any other defence does offer at least immediate relief to painful states of mind. Steiner (1987) points out that personality-disordered patients often suffer from an 'agro-claustrophobic' dilemma. In this the person is caught between a fear of an over-close relationship with others which threatens to engulf and stifle them (the claustrophobic pole), and the fear of total isolation by abandonment (the agoraphobic pole). The individual oscillates between one fear and the other, unable to find a comfortable distance from other people. The pathological organisation offers a haven from this conflict whilst apparently providing all the individual's needs. Steiner adds that:

> 'At times the anxieties of relinquishing the protection of the pathological organ-isation seem very real and the patient will vividly convey the horrors he would have to face if it were to be abandoned. At other times however, the need for it is less convincing and the impression develops that the organisation is turned to not so much out of necessity but because dependence on it has become a kind of addiction.'
>
> (p.337)

In the latter case the patient will have some insight into the true nature of the organisation but will in any case adhere to it. This suggests collusion between the organisation and the patient. Steiner also points out that the pathological organisation may take other forms, such as a desert island or a room.

Engagement with such patients is extremely trying. The professional is in competi-tion with the pathological organisation which offers the dependent needy part of the patient simple and immediate solutions, which enviously attack and devalue any help offered. In these cases it is important to keep in mind that although one might be speaking to one part of the patient, the other is also present and aware.

Kirri was a 32-year-old single Greek man who was referred to a day unit by one of a multitude of professionals who were all involved in his care. He was considered to be resistant to treatment and highly manipulative. He frequently made suicidal threats and had a history of overdoses and cutting. These threats and acts produced in his carers first extreme anxiety and then barely disguised exasperation and rage. At first difficult to engage he soon made equal demands upon the day unit. He left messages on the answerphone which hinted darkly of suicide. Attempts to talk to him about these messages and his actual self-harm were met with bland reassurance that they were of no real consequence, and anyway if he killed himself no one would care.

It was conjectured within the team that the needy, frightened part of the patient was being split off and projected into the staff by a ruthless part of the self which was determined to rise above pain and fear. This produced in the staff the pain, anxiety and rage that belonged to this part, and left the rest of the patient able to indulge in destructive acts with impunity.

Alistair, a 26-year-old married man, was referred to the psychotherapy unit with possible psychotic symptoms. After many weeks of poor attendance he was eventu-ally engaged in the day hospital, and it emerged that although not psychotic, he had a fragmented inner world. He described being dominated in his head by a persistent voice which continually told him that he was no good and not wanted; that any kindness was just façade and would be followed by betrayal. The voice's solution to Alistair's fears of abandonment was that he should kill himself, so that they would be at peace in a painless eternity. At first, all attempts to bring to his attention the harm he was doing to himself, his marriage and to his few relationships through his continual threats of self-harm were greeted with indifference or scorn. He said if people really cared about him they would let him finish the job once and for all instead of keeping him in his hellish limbo. Instead of improvement, sympathy with his plight seemed to increase the fury of his attacks on himself and his threats. After some months and with considerable hesitation, he revealed that he had made a promise to the voice that he would hurt himself in return for his attendance at the unit. This seemed to be a compromise between the voice and the day unit; it demonstrated his loyalty to the pathological organisation whilst allowing him some access to help.

Alistair seemed to be acting under the influence of a powerful part of him, which claimed to have the solution to his underlying fear of abandonment. The solution, according to the voice, was his death which would bring everlasting peace.[2] This promise was, of course, tremendously tempting given that it purported to offer an instant and final solution to Alistair's main fear. It avoided the struggle, hope and disappointment of dependency on real external figures. Meanwhile, the sane feeling part of the patient which knew death for what it was and feared the sadistic attacks, was often projected into others. When he did try to make contact with others he was punished by being harangued by the voice until he cut himself.

If possible, the carer needs to understand the patient's attraction to the pathological organisation whilst challenging its distortions and promises. For example, the idea of death as everlasting peace might be questioned. The patient's capacity to resist the organisation may be enhanced by 'talking to' the captured vulnerable part of the patient who may be trying to reach the outside world, or be quietly suffering. Some patients may be consciously caught between allegiance to the organisation and the need for authentic emotional closeness with real people. Again this dilemma should be acknowledged; the patient may not know who to trust or whose version of reality to believe.

A 34-year-old man, Steven, who had recently started at the day unit, phoned after a Bank Holiday break to say that he would not be coming to the unit that day. He said that he had no need for further help since he now knew for sure that he needed to kill himself, since this was the only way to ensure that he was not hurt by staff and by the unit not being there when he needed it. It was evident to the member of staff who took the call that in saying this he had come some way to acknowledging that the unit was important to him. The staff member therefore felt that he might be reachable. He said to Steven that perhaps over the weekend he had felt neglected and needed the day hospital very badly, but that since it was not there his only solution and comfort seemed to be suicide. However, the staff member expressed doubt about death as a blissful union with his dead mother (an opinion he had previously expressed), and further wondered whether Steven hoped that he, the member of staff, might be able to rescue him from a lonely death. Steven acknowledged that he was

2 In this case, and in many others in which destructive forces are idealised, death is fantasised concretely as everlasting peace, or union with mother, not as the cessation of existence.

very scared but he still felt that, regrettably, the best way to reduce his suffering was death. The discussion continued, with the staff member acknowledging that Steven might be caught up with an uncertainty about whether to trust the staff of the unit or the familiar deathly (dead mother) part of him which seemed to be offering such an immediate and tempting solution.

In this engagement it may be seen that the member of staff takes a middle position, not identifying strongly with any part of Steven's internal world; neither the rescuer nor the destroyer. However, he does challenge the 'solution' promulgated by the pathological organisation (but also acknowledges their attraction). This kind of response to a patient in whom self-harm and suicide is a constant possibility takes some nerve on the part of the carer, and requires a relative freedom from the need for immediate action dictated by a real or imaginary policy or a culture of blame. External pressure of this kind will push the carer into precipitant acting out of that part of the patient which has been projected and disowned (e.g. the terror of death and the wish to live), and this will simply perpetuate the split. Judgements about when the patient is truly in danger and when they are not are very difficult, because they are inevitably contaminated by projections from the patient. Inevitably, inviting the patient to think about and to question the pathological organisation will increase the conflict between the patient and the organisation, as it is this which the organisation is there to prevent since thinking always brings perspective and separation. There will be increased acting out as an expression of this conflict. This is a difficult time for staff and patient alike and communication and cohesion amongst the staff team is crucial. Whether to take action or not in any given case will depend on a number of factors and it is usually clearer (although never clear) after thinking through with the team.

The development of borderline pathology

The genesis of borderline pathology is, predictably, linked to upbringing; the development of the internal world of the infant is closely bound up with the way they are cared for and thought about by the parents. Empirical studies of families suggest that physical and sexual abuse is very common (Boyer 1987) and that the parents do not provide adequate involvement, support and protection within the family (Walsh 1977). However, Kernberg (1975), stresses genetic endowment in which the individual has strong aggressive and envious drives.

Wilfred Bion (1962) put forward a theory of emotional and cognitive development which was based on the mother's response to her infant's projective identification. In his view the development of thinking and thus the ability of the infant to process their own thoughts and feelings, and the capacity to learn, depend partly on innate factors such as tolerance of frustration and envy, and partly on the mother's capacity for 'reverie'. The infant normally uses projective identification to communicate his or her state of being to the mother. This means that the infant in a state of pain, fear or frustration will induce in the mother a similar state of discomfort (perhaps by crying in a piercing fashion). A mother, who has a reasonably balanced state of mind, receives this discomfort and makes a thoughtful response. For example, she may change her baby's nappy, offer a feed, etc. She may get it wrong at first, but importantly she can stay with the problem until she meets her baby's need. The transformation of a bad feeling into a tolerable or good one – say hunger into satiation – is seen as a process of mental 'digestion' in which something is taken in by the mother and then re-presented as it were, in a more tolerable form. Thus the infant's experience of some tearing pain in its stomach is transformed into the need for food when the mother offering food deals with the pain. The pain in the stomach begins to take on a more defined and meaningful shape. The mother's capacity for transformation of projective identification is her capacity to 'contain' her infant's state of mind. Bion suggests that over time, the infant takes into itself the mother's capacity to metabolise, to think about, its mental and physical state. This capacity promotes tolerance of frustration, which is necessary for the infant to learn from the real world. The development of an internalised mental processing capacity contrasts starkly with what happens when things go wrong. If the mother's ability to contain her infant is poor, as might be the case with a borderline mother, containment gives way to a counter-projection by the mother of the infant's pain. The mother gives the pain back to the infant, for example by shouting at it to shut up. This gives rise to what Bion evocatively describes as a 'nameless dread' in the infant. The infant is enveloped by the return of its projection made bad, formless and terrifying because it is stripped of meaning. If this is the predominant form of interaction, the infant takes in the mother's propensity for getting rid of feelings and frustration, and therefore cannot contain frustration long enough to learn from its experience of the world. A capacity for metabolising does not develop; rather the individual will come to depend on an arrogant omniscience. The internal stage is then set for the development of psychosis or borderline pathology.

The borderline parent

After years in therapy it began to occur to Roger that he seldom recalled a time when his mother seemed aware of him as a person in his own right. This was an unwelcome development since he had previously felt that he and his mother had a special and close relationship. He began to feel that this very closeness had a particular quality in which his mother's moods and anxieties prevailed over his own. She would confide in him about her feelings about his father, including her sexual revulsion towards him. These confidences made him feel privileged and special and yet, as he now recognised, uncomfortable and even contaminated. In one very emotive session, he burst out: 'I was just a vessel for my mother; she just poured her shit into me. She never cared how *I* felt!' One memory took on new significance. At the age of about six, he went into his mother's bedroom at night because he felt scared of a thunderstorm. She became irritated when he was not reassured by her words, and shouted at him that the problem was in his head and that he should go and deal with it. He vividly remembered crawling back under his covers, the fear of the thunderstorm being displaced by a creeping terror that he was going mad. At the age of 13 he started cutting himself superficially when faced with frightening events in his life, such as bullies at school. This helped to calm him.

In the thunderstorm memory, a thoughtful and comforting response by his mother, would have necessitated taking in her child's fears and tolerating and soothing them, something she may not have had room for given her own anxieties and fears of intimacy. It can be seen how his mother's irritation and her insinuation of his madness, magnified his fear by introducing a more powerful and formless fear. At the same time, Roger's capacity to deal with his own emotional life (particularly the feeling of fear) was impaired because he took into himself his mother's propensity to refuse and expel emotional disturbance. Without the equipment to tolerate and think about his emotions, they continued to be experienced only as unbearable tension from which only cutting provided relief.

A mother was referred to the psychotherapy department with a history of depression that was so severe that she hardly left her small flat where she lived with her 2-year-old daughter. She brought her daughter to the interview strapped into her pram. During the interview she made no reference to the infant nor made any attempt to attend to her in any way. She complained about incessant noise in her flat from neighbours in particular, which she insisted was making her depression worse. She had applied for insulation from the council but to no avail. After about twenty minutes her daughter, a fair-haired shy girl dressed in brown dungarees, began to wriggle and press against her straps. Immediately her mother reached into her bag and produced a bottle which she tried to insert into her daughter's mouth. Her daughter responded by taking it out and throwing it on the floor, and for the first time began to cry. The mother's attempts to return the bottle exacerbated her daughter's distress and her cries grew louder and her struggles more desperate. The interviewer noted his own response, which from the first was to pick the child up out of its restraining straps and cuddle her. The mother became increasingly irate, finally bursting out with; 'You see! She just won't take anything even when she's hungry. She just wants to make more mess and noise which she knows I can't stand!' And turning to her now distraught infant; 'Why don't you take your bottle when you're hungry you little brat! Oh, just shut up!' The interviewer felt that the room was now full of rage, panic and uncontained distress just flying about, and it was all he could do to just sit there and keep sane.

It was obvious to the interviewing therapist that the child was not hungry, but wanted to get free of her pram straps. Her mother had misinterpreted her daughter's behaviour as hunger, possibly because she was in need herself (i.e. it was a projection), or possibly because she wanted to silence her daughter by filling her mouth. Either way, she had not taken in the cause of her daughter's distress. Instead, she had pushed back her own anxiety in the form of the bottle.

Eventually, this child may accede to her mother's insistence on silence and take into herself a fear and intolerance of 'noisy' feelings. Emotions will be experienced as a disruption in the wished-for calm, quiet or no-feeling (which may further represent the union with mother). She may then take steps to rid herself of her affective life, including the capacity to process it. This may be achieved by any of the typical borderline defences described here, such as projection, splitting, cutting or substance abuse. (There is another discussion of these processes in Chapter 12.)

Research and treatment

There are a number of different approaches to the treatment of personality disorder. These range from cognitive-behavioural to psycho-social and pyscho-analytic or some combination of these. Drug treatments may be used for depression, anxiety or psychotic phenomena in combination with the psychological treatment. Short periods of in-patient treatment are often necessary at moments of crisis. Research on effective treatment for borderline patients has shown the vital importance of a cohesive and well-organised team approach. Bateman and Tyrer (2004) suggest that:

'part of the benefit the severely personality disordered patient derives from their treatment comes through their experience of being involved in a well-constructed, well-structured and coherent interpersonal endeavour. It seems that . . . what may be helpful is the internalisation of a thoughtfully constructed structure . . . and above all the experience of being the subject of reliable, coherent and rational thinking. [This group of patients] . . . may . . . have been deprived of exactly such consideration and commitment during their early development.'

This cohesion is, according to Bateman and Tyrer, probably more important than the theoretical model used. However, whatever model is used the relationship between the patient and the worker must be recognised and worked with; a therapeutic alliance between carer and patient cannot be taken for granted. For this reason, the 'divided function' model of care in which different professionals are involved exercising different functions, such as therapist, psychiatrist or social worker, is problematic. The patient's propensity to splitting and to provoking strong emotional reactions means that individuals in such teams may come into conflict with each other, unless there are regular meetings and good collaboration. Where the 'divided function' model of care is used therefore, it is vital for members of the team to be aware of the borderline patient's propensity to sharply divide their carers into good and bad. This awareness will mitigate against acting on impulse in response to these projections, and promote a more thoughtful response. This splitting may also occur between services, for example between social workers (who may be involved in the difficult and painful task of negotiating care of the children), and the Community Health Team who may be in a position to be more simply supportive of the parent.

The Halliwick Day Hospital treatment model exemplifies what Bateman and Tyrer call the 'specialist team model'. In this day hospital, a group of multidisciplinary staff work together using a psychoanalytical framework informed by attachment theory[3]. Group analytic therapy, structured therapy groups and individual therapy are offered within a community setting. The team includes a psychiatrist, nurses and OTs working under a consultant psychotherapist. Each member of the team takes a particular role for each patient, such as individual therapist or dealing with aspects of housing or care of the patient's physical health. These divided functions are tightly held together by the shared theoretical approach, by regular meetings which include supervision in which countertransference feelings are given special attention, case conferences on each patient and feedback after groups, and of course by virtue of the fact that they all work within the same building. This cohesion allows thoughtful and consistent boundaries to be set, for example in the case of time out for serious acting

---

3 The therapists in the Day Hospital use a treatment manual to guide their interventions. The treatment (mentalisation-based treatment, 'MBT'), is based on recent formulations by Bateman, Fonagy and others (Bateman and Fonagy, 2004). In this model the infant fails to fully develop the capacity to 'mentalise'. Mentalisation entails making sense of the actions of oneself and others on the basis of intentional mental state, such as desires, feelings and beliefs. It involves the recognition that what is in the mind is in the mind and reflects knowledge of one's own and others' mental states as mental states. This capacity is enfeebled in borderline patients and so group and individual therapy actively focuses on developing their understanding and recognition of the feelings they evoke in others and the feelings evoked in them by others.

out. Also the team can consciously allow and tolerate a certain amount of splitting by the patient if this is felt to be a necessary defence for the patient at that time. For example, an idealisation of one member of staff and a denigration of another may arise, or denigration of the groups in favour of the individual therapy is not uncommon.

Alison, a 40-year-old woman at the Halliwick felt so threatened by other male patients in her group that she refused to attend. She demanded that an older man, Mark, be removed from her group because she found him intimidating, and that the men should be warned by staff about their aggression. She gave vent to her feelings in her individual session (with a female member of staff) which she greatly valued, but was usually silent and sullen in the group. Her complaint put the staff in a difficult position.

Mark did tend to be intimidating towards other patients, and Alison had been sexually abused in her childhood which had made her mistrusting of men in general. In the next case conference it was conjectured that her individual sessions may be functioning as a protective enclave against her own denied and projected aggression which was attributed to the men in her group. However, her subjective experience of vulnerability was also acknowledged, and it was decided that for the present she would be allowed to continue with her individual sessions until she was ready to rejoin the group. Over time she became increasingly involved with her own issues concerning herself, her children and her husband and her animosity toward Mark and the men in her group faded. She began to recognise her own hatred of herself and, worst of all, her hatred of her own aggression.

The emphasis in the Halliwick Day Hospital is on examination of relationships in the here-and-now, and the testing out of assumptions and fantasies made by the patient about these relationships. This includes the patient's feelings about the Day Hospital and the staff in it. The attention paid to feelings about the day hospital reduces the chance of the patient dropping out of treatment, which is very common with such patients.

Conclusion

Borderline patients frequently test our professional selves to the limit, and sometimes beyond. They penetrate into our more personal feelings about ourselves; our competence, tolerance and even our identity. They resist and derail well-meaning 'delivery of care', and we are forced to attend to the internal world and its manifestations in the relationship. The analytically informed approach described here provides markers in this murky region whilst allowing us to remain human, thinking and in touch. Even so, enactment and error are inevitable and the presence of supportive colleagues is vital. But despite all its challenges, working with borderline personality disorders offers a vivid and immediate experience which brings us up against the best and the worst in ourselves.

References

Bateman A, Fonagy P (2004) *Psychotherapy for Borderline Personality Disorders: Mentalization Based Treatment*. Oxford: Oxford University Press.
Bion W (1962) A theory of thinking. *International Journal of Psycho-Analysis* **43**(4–5).

Boyer L (1987) Regression and countertransference in the treatment on a borderline patient. In Grotestein JS, Solomon MF, Lang JA, (eds) *The Borderline Patient*. Hillside, NJ, The Analytic Press.

Fonagy P (1991) Thinking about thinking: some clinical and theoretical considerations in the treatment of a borderline patient. *International Journal of Psycho-Analysis* 72(4).

Fonagy P and Higgitt A (1992) Psychotherapy in Borderline and Narcissistic Personality Disorder. *British Journal of Psychiatry* 161: 23–43.

Kernberg O (1975) *Borderline Conditions and Pathological Narcissism*. New York, Aranson.

Main T (1957) 'The Ailment.' In: The Ailment and Other Psychoanalytic Essays. Main T, London: Free Association Books.

O'Shaughnessy E (1981) A clinical study of a defensive organisation. *International Journal of Psycho-Analysis* 62: 359–369.

Rosenfeld H (1971) A Clinical Approach to the Psychoanalytic Theory of the Life and Death Instincts: an Investigation into the Aggressive Aspects of Narcissism. *International Journal of Psycho-Analysis*, 52: 169–178.

Sohn L (1985) Narcissistic organisation, projective identification, and the formation of the identificate. *International Journal of Psycho-Analysis* 66: 201–213.

Steiner J (1987) The interplay between pathological organisations and the paranoid-shizoid positions. *International Journal of Psycho-Analysis* 68: 69–80.

Walsh F (1977) The family of the borderline patient. In: Grinker R, Warble B (eds) *The Borderline Patient*. New York, Jason Aranson.

12 Working with families who see help as the problem

Marion Bower

This chapter is about families who abuse their children physically, emotionally or by various types of neglect. The abuse may be subtle or overt, but it is chronic and long-standing, often going back several generations. What they have in common is that they are immensely difficult to help. Great efforts may be expended only to be sabotaged or break down or the family move either geographically or to another agency. Agencies are often divided between those who are very worried and those who are unconcerned. Collaborative work is intensely difficult even between members of the same agency or agencies who normally work well together.

In a classic paper Fraiberg (1975) suggests that families like this are 'haunted' by the ghosts of past abusive figures. She describes two aspects of these families which make the professional task intensely difficult. Firstly, the intensity and compulsiveness with which the parents re-enact their own past experiences with their children. 'The parent it seems is condemned to repeat the tragedy of his own childhood in terrible and exacting detail.' Secondly, families such as this rarely seek help and those who try to offer it will be treated with suspicion or hostility. Fraiberg puts this very clearly 'there may be no readiness on the part of parents to form an alliance with us to protect the baby. More likely it is we and not the ghosts who will appear as the intruders.' Put more simply, as far as the family is concerned the professionals are the abusers.

The experience of being perceived as cruel or abusive is deeply disturbing to those of us in the helping professions. There has therefore been a tendency to rationalise the responses of these families. For example, parents are seen as being afraid that their child will be taken away, or have had bad experiences of helping professionals in the past. More subtly it is acknowledged that parents own past traumatic experiences predispose them to mistrust offers of help. While all these explanations may have some truth in them, I think that for some families they are only partial explanations of why helpful interventions are evaded, attacked or break down.

Using traditional Freudian theory Fraiberg suggest that parents who behave abusively towards their children are not simply lacking adequate models of parental care, but that the abusive behaviour serves a defensive function. Fraiberg points out that not all parents who have been abused go on to abuse their own children. She suggests that what distinguishes those who re-abuse from those who do not, is that the non-abusive parents retain an affective (emotional) memory of their painful or disturbing experiences. (Fraiberg does not discuss what enables some people to process and remember unbearable experiences. This is obviously a very crucial matter which I will discuss later in this chapter.) Parents who subject their children to similar abuse to that which they experienced are examples of what Freud referred to as the repetition compulsion. What cannot be remembered becomes repeated. Intolerable emotional experiences are repressed and discharged through action, which bypasses the feeling element.

Using Anna Freud's concept of 'identification with the aggressor' Fraiberg suggests that abusing parents identify with their abuser and inflict on their children the same emotional or physical pain they experienced themselves. From the parents' point of view this behaviour is used unconsciously as a psychological defence system, the parent evades unbearable emotions which are projected into the children. This makes it clear why parents find it so difficult to change their behaviour. Offers of help and expectations of change threaten their much needed psychological defence systems.

How then are we going to make change in these families. Fraiberg's approach was to offer the parents an opportunity to be cared for and emotionally understood as well as offering help to the children. The idea being that once the parents' distress could be heard they could hear the distress of their children. This approach is similar to the new emphasis on family support as part of the child protection process. While this is clearly a humane and reasonable approach, it is also the case that it does not always lead to the sort of change we would hope for. Fraiberg's own case examples show many breakdowns and reversals in the work, often after long periods of very intensive input. I think most of us can think of similar situations, in fact this phenomenon is so common in social work that it is almost taken for granted. I am not suggesting that no change can take place, but that we need a sophisticated understanding of the type of family defensive organisations we are dealing with in order to plan and intervene realistically.

I think that it is necessary to add to Fraiberg's account ideas from modern Kleinian and post-Kleinian thinking. The concepts of internal object relations and pathological defensive systems allow us to look at the totality of the family's interactions as a defensive system and the way in which workers are drawn in to enacting the defensive system in a way which perpetuates it. I will start off looking at the theory and how it can be applied to family functioning. I will then give case examples of two slightly different types of family defensive systems. Finally, I will consider some of the implications of these ideas for training, practice and institutional functioning.

The development of pathological defensive organisations in individuals and families

Modern Kleinian and post-Kleinian object relations theory provides a helpful framework for understanding how the interactions between a child and its parents and other family members become internalised and subsequently enacted when the child grows up to be a parent. Central to this theory is the concept of an unconscious internal world of object relations. Joan Riviere (1952) defines this very clearly, 'It is a world of figures formed on the patterns of those persons we first loved and hated in life, who also represent aspects of ourselves . . .'.

The internal world is not an exact mirror of the people in the child's external world; it is formed through complex interactions between the child's personality and those of the parents. As I will describe below the child projects their own emotional states onto the parents who are then internalised in the form they are perceived through the lens of the child's love and hate. An example of this is the conscience or super-ego, formed from the internalised parental prohibitions. Freud noted that this is often more harsh than the actual parents, which he attributed to the projection of the child's aggression onto the parents. Figures in the internal world are not static, but exist in relationship to each other and the self. The nature of these figures and the quality of their relationships determine how the child, and later the adult, relates to others in their world.

Klein discovered that even in benign family circumstances from the beginning of life the baby is beset by powerful feelings of love, hatred and aggression, which the early ego cannot yet cope with. Initially the baby deals with this by projecting all the bad feelings outside of itself and tries to internalise good experiences. There is an urgent need for good figures which can be internalised to become a core of strength in the ego. Initially the mother is split into a very good, idealised figure and a very bad figure, aggression and hatred are directed at the 'bad' mother and there is a need to maintain this split to preserve a sense of goodness. Klein calls these early psychological defences the paranoid-schizoid position. If all goes well the more developed ego allows the baby to perceive the mother as a whole person who is both good and bad. The baby becomes aware that the mother who is damaged and attacked in phantasy is also the good and loved mother. Feelings of guilt and acute emotional pain accompany this awareness, and the child wishes to put right the damage and make reparation to the loved mother both in reality and phantasy. This is what Klein refers to as the depressive position, the presence of an actual undamaged mother (or carer) is crucial to help the child negotiate this painful state of mind, which is also linked to its capacity to perceive reality.

Although this theory appears to concentrate on internal states in actuality it lays a new emphasis on the importance of environmental factors. Klein herself puts this very clearly:

> 'Unpleasant experiences and the lack of enjoyable ones, in the young child, especially the lack of happy and close contact with loved people, increase ambivalence, diminish trust and hope and confirm anxieties about inner annihilation and external persecution; moreover they slow down and perhaps permanently check the beneficial process through which in the long run inner security is achieved.'
>
> (Klein 1940)

Building on the work of Klein, Bion identifies an aspect of the mother's care and response to the child which I think is a crucial aspect of emotional resilience. This is the capacity to receive and process the child's projections of unbearable emotional states; he calls this the capacity for containment. This maternal capacity is over time internalised by the child, who becomes able to give name and meaning to states of mind. I think it is the presence of this capacity which distinguishes the parents whom Fraiberg describes as those who have suffered abuse but who do not re-abuse. It suggests the presence in the child's life at some point of a parent or other person who possesses these qualities.

Where a mother is not emotionally available to her child, the child will increase the intensity of projected distress. When this is not responded to there will be an internalisation of an object relationship where distress is met by an impermeable object. It is this type of internal object relationship which is externalised and enacted when one person or agency is very worried and another is oblivious.

In the types of families that we are concerned about as social workers there is not simply an absence of loving and containing figures, although this is very serious in itself, but the presence of actively cruel or violent adults who not only fail to contain or respond to the child's emotions, but may use the child as a receptacle for unbearable states of mind of their own. This is a potentially catastrophic state of affairs for the child, as there are no genuinely good figures to internalise or help the child manage their own aggression or hatred. In this situation an extreme type of splitting and denial of external and internal reality may arise and the child will idealise the bad destructive figures in his or her world. The idealisation of power and cruelty involves a hatred of real dependency or need. The projection of cruelty and aggression onto parents who are like this in reality can lead to the internalisation of figures whose cruelty and violence is amplified. The child's internal world is therefore filled with very cruel figures and very damaged figures. As the phantasies of damage cannot be offset by reality, the child feels potentially threatened by a sense of persecution or annihilation. In this situation powerful psychological defence organisations emerge. Rosenfeld (1971) described a type of defensive organisation he called the mafia. Cruel or aggressive aspects of the self are idealised and offer 'protection' from pain and anxiety to vulnerable aspects of the self. As with the mafia the price of protection is loyalty to the organisation enforced by bullying and intimidation. Attempts to leave may bring on a violent attack. Rosenfeld noted that when individual patients with this type of defensive organisation begin to turn to the analyst for help they often dream of an attack by a delinquent gang.

A young woman with a history of traumatic losses held herself together by deriving excitement from her membership of a group of other young people involved in drinking, drug-taking and various forms of risk-taking and delinquent behaviour. Following the breakdown of her relationship with a violent man, she became severely depressed and was offered psychotherapy as part of her NHS treatment. The patient initially responded very well to this and began to cut down the drink and drugs and apply to college. She asked her therapist to extend her therapy, however immediately after making this request she had the following dream. 'She was followed by a frightening gang of people armed with knives; a man grabs her and cuts her throat'. Following the dream the patient became increasingly contemptuous of her male therapist who she described as a 'sad bastard'. She began to cut down attendance at her sessions and took up with another violent partner. Shortly after this she broke off her therapy.

In this example we can see how a gang in the patient's internal world attack her by cutting her throat when she begins to depend on her therapy. This is reflected in an enactment in the external world where the patient attacks her therapy by 'cutting' it down, and turns to a violent 'protector'. These types of external enactments often occur in individuals and families as a response to social work help. Before going on to give examples of this I would like to briefly discuss how defensive organisations becomes externalised and enacted in families.

As Fraiberg suggests, Freud's concept of the repetition compulsion explains the way in which unbearable emotional experiences are repeated and re-enacted as an alternative to being experienced as mental states. Klein's theory of 'projective identification' allows us to understand how aspects of the self can be projected into others. Family members can be chosen for their 'fit' with projections, however as Bion pointed out, projections can have a real effect on the behaviour of the recipient. A woman may project her own violence into a violent male protector, and a man may choose a woman who represents his own vulnerability. Continuing mutual projection can increase the man's violence and the woman's passivity. The birth of a baby in such a family re-activates parental feelings of vulnerability and primitive anxieties held at bay by the defensive organisation. This fuels further acting out with the baby becoming the receptacle for unbearable emotional states in the way described earlier. As this process develops the family becomes an externalisation of the parents' pathological internal defensive organisation, with tragic consequences for the children.

This type of individual defensive organisation bears considerable resemblances to a type of gang family which is very familiar to social workers. These types of families are superficially stable and coherent and are often known to social workers over several generations. Relationships with social workers can be hostile and suspicious or superficially friendly. In reality there are chronic serious difficulties often including abuse, neglect and involvement with crime and violence. There is intense loyalty to the family, even among children who have been abused. The family see themselves as 'protecting' their children from a hostile outside world and often adopt children from other vulnerable families. Difficulties come into the open when social workers try to challenge the family's view of themselves or their care of their children. When this happens workers will usually be subjected to subtle or overt threats, intimidation or even violence. This process is extremely difficult to withstand, particularly for an individual worker, and is often a reason why quite gross abuse can go unrecognised and unchallenged. Individual members of the family may turn to professionals for help, but this is often difficult to sustain, and there is often a return to the protection of the gang, as in the example described above.

Rosenfeld's concept of a gang-like defensive organisation makes a division between good/dependent aspects of the self and bad/destructive aspects. Social work thinking tends to be underpinned by a similar abused/abuser split. This simplistic view of the position of the victim can lead to the assumption that it is enough to remove the victim from the abusing situation. This ignores the catastrophic effect of abuse on the internal world.

Milton (1994) describes this situation particularly vividly. In discussing work with women who have been victims of sexual abuse she says:

> '. . . It is vital to address what is perhaps the most serious aspects of the victim's plight: her corruption in childhood via excessive stimulation of her own hatred and destructiveness, which becomes erotised and, and her identification with the aggressor, often as a means of psychic survival. . . .'

Steiner (1992) has suggested that in these situations the 'good/dependent' aspects of the self have become corrupted and good and bad aspects of the self inextricably mixed. In this situation the defensive system is held together not only by violence but by perverse bonds, often of a sado-masochistic nature. Steiner suggests that an individual with this type of defensive organisation can be identified with either a victim or an aggressor or at times be a helpless spectator of a sado-masochistic relationship. 'At the same time he cannot free himself because to leave would be to abandon elements of himself which he has projected.' It is common when working with families with this type of defensive organisation for workers to feel themselves as either an abuser or abused. The first case example in the next section illustrates this type of difficulty.

Case examples

In order to preserve confidentiality I have used a mixture of my own case material and case material I have heard about while running case discussion groups for social workers. No individual family is represented by the case material.

Trying to escape the gang

Tracy, aged 18, and her daughter Kelly, aged 2 months, were referred to an area social services team by the social worker in the hospital where Tracy had had her baby. Staff at the hospital were concerned by Tracy's rather rough treatment of the baby, and her boyfriend Dean had been verbally abusive to nurses trying to help Tracy, and they suspected him of stealing some money from the ward.

The social worker, a black woman, went to visit Tracy and Dean who were living with Dean's mother, Mrs W. When the social worker arrived Tracy was trying to bottlefeed Kelly who was crying loudly. The social worker remarked sympathetically that it was hard work with a new baby. Dean's response to this was to stand threateningly over the social worker and tell her that she was an 'interfering black cow, we have ways of dealing with people like you'. The social worker felt frightened and vulnerable, aware she was alone in the flat with the two of them. However she told them firmly that she had a job to do, and was not there to be abused. She suggested that they visit her in her office the next day and made it clear that if not, she would be returning with a colleague.

To the social workers surprise Tracy followed her into the street, still carrying the baby, she promised she would come to the office, adding 'Dean is very possessive and his Mum says that all you want to do is take away the baby.' The following day Tracy turned up with Kelly, accompanied by Mrs W, who waited outside, 'I told Tracy I'd be there if she needed me', implying that she considered Tracy to be at risk with the social worker. While Kelly slept Tracy told her that she could not remember anything before she was 11, but she had been in care since she was 16, following sexual advances made to her by her stepfather while her mother was pregnant with a new baby. Her mother had refused to believe her although her stepfather had a history of sexual offences against young women. The following year Tracy had threatened another girl in the childrens' home with a knife, 'I didn't like the way she looked at me', following this she ran away to London to live with a cousin, and went to live with Dean when she became pregnant. Tracy said that she and Dean and his Mum were having a lot of rows and they would not let her contact her Mum. She showed the social worker a large bruise on her leg where Dean had kicked her as she left the house to visit the social worker, however she emphasised that Dean had not hit the baby.' I keep her quiet.'

By now the social worker was feeling very concerned, and suggested that they could think whether Tracy might be better off in a hostel where she could be supported with her baby and would be allowed to make contact with her mother. Tracy seemed dubious, 'me and Dean are like twins really.' At this point Kelly woke up, and the atmosphere became anxious and tense. As Tracy pushed the bottle into the crying baby's mouth she struggled to drink but gasped and vomited it back up. The social worker found it difficult to watch, but was not sure how to intervene. She asked Tracy if she had tried to breastfeed. Tracy said 'I stopped because I didn't like the way she looked at my breasts.' Eventually Kelly calmed down enough to drink and fell asleep. Tracy wanted to leave, 'I don't want her to wake up again.' The social worker suggested that Tracy should come and see her the next day and in the meantime she would enquire about hostels and they could discuss this. As Tracy went to the door her scarf slipped off. She asked the social worker if she would pick it up and put it on as her hands were full. The social worker was deeply uneasy about this. She felt it would be unkind to refuse, but she wondered how Tracy would experience the physical contact. With considerable misgivings she did what Tracy asked. Tracy did not return to see the social worker. When she visited the W's with a colleague they told her that Tracy had run off back to her mother, they blamed the social worker for 'driving her away'.

Discussion

It seems likely that Tracy had experienced neglect or abuse prior to the incident which brought her into care; she is a vulnerable young woman who has also acted in a violent manner. She takes refuge with violent and possessive 'protectors', Mrs W and Dean, who also seem to represent aspects of herself, for example she sees Dean as her 'twin'. The birth of the baby who has real dependent needs, as well as representing the dependent aspect of herself, threatens this defensive organisation. She wishes to turn to someone genuinely helpful and protective, rather vividly represented by the way she follows the social worker into the street, clutching the baby. However her 'protectors' physically attack her for this disloyalty, Dean kicks her, Mrs W tries to turn her against the social worker, 'she only wants to take your baby'. In the meeting with the social worker we can see that this is not just an external threat to her getting help, but an internal conflict. If the real baby or the dependent aspect of Tracy 'wakes up' it will be under attack. Tracy projects her adult sexuality into Kelly and is unable to breastfeed her. This in effect attacks the feeding relationship. In a similar way Tracy (unconsciously) creates a situation with the social worker where the worker is either experienced as rejecting or seductive, this leads to a breakdown of the feeding/helping relationship. In my experience people who are afraid that social workers are about to steal their baby will rob the worker of the opportunity to look after the dependent aspects of themselves.

I think that it is important in these situations to be aware of the way in which the interactions of family members function as a defensive organisation, and the pressure on the social worker to enact a role which fits in with the organisation, in this case a figure who is abusive or rejecting. We can see how projective identification is used to rid family members of intolerable emotional states. For example the social worker's feelings of being frightened, vulnerable and alone on her home visit, were probably feelings that Tracy and Dean might have felt when left alone with a baby they were ill-equipped to deal with. Dean exploits areas where the social worker may feel vulnerable. Of course it is likely that this defensive organisation is both caused and based on Tracy's early experiences, however it remains alive in the present and is both an obstacle to her receiving help and a real threat to her baby.

The brick wall

This is an example of a family where the defensive organisation is less stable. I call these borderline families. In these families one or both parents are likely to have a borderline personality disorder, however these families will also move closer to the border of concern about their children, although this is experienced as intense persecution. They may turn to professionals for help with a child who is perceived as a dangerous persecutor. 'He's driving me mad/going to be the death of me'. If some progress is made and the parent is slightly more in touch with feelings of guilt and responsibility, or aware of depending on a professional for help, these feelings are experienced as a threat of emotional breakdown. Most often it is not the parent who breaks down but the helping relationship and the workers are left with the feelings of guilt and inadequacy. There is often an intensification by the family of gang defences.

Andrew, aged 13, was referred to a child guidance clinic at the suggestion of his school. He had been excluded following a series of violent attacks on other pupils, which included holding a smaller child under water in a swimming pool, and stabbing a girl in the back with a pair of scissors. School were concerned that he had shown no remorse for either incident. Andrew was brought to the clinic by his mother, Mrs G, and his stepfather, Mr H. The social worker was struck by the physical contrast between Andrew and his mother, both small and angelic looking and the huge and menacing Mr H, who walked with a stick. Mrs G announced that Andrew was 'killing' her and her husband with the pressure of the constant visits to school. However, in a subtle way she seemed rather proud of the incidents. A question about Andrew's father revealed that the relationship with Mrs G had been extremely violent, and Mrs G had suffered several broken arms and two miscarriages following violent blows to her stomach. She had also had two terminations prior to Andrew's birth. As Andrew listened to this narrative tears poured down his cheeks. When the social worker commented on Andrew's sadness Mr H reacted with contempt, 'he's a pathetic wimp'. Mrs G appeared to ignore this interchange and said that Andrew was like his father and she was thinking of ringing his father to ask if he would 'discipline' Andrew if the clinic could not help. Andrew went pale. The social worker felt simultaneously responsible for Andrew's safety and unable to challenge Mrs G's cruel threat.

While the adults were talking Andrew had been drawing a picture of a small shark with two larger sharks. When the social worker asked about the picture he said that it was sharks playing in a tropical lagoon, he drew a series of dots below the small shark's eyes. When the social worker commented that it looked as if the shark was crying, Andrew said, 'no its blood and the big sharks will attack him'. For the second appointment only Mrs G and Andrew turned up, Mrs G said that Mr H did not like all this talk about feelings. She said 'Tell her Andrew'. Andrew said that he did not want to come any more. However Mrs G was willing to discuss the situation in school a bit more and agreed for the social worker to contact the school's psychologist whom she appeared to find practical and unthreatening. Andrew spent the time carefully drawing a brick wall. When the social worker asked about the wall Andrew said 'it's a dead end'. The social worker said it seemed to be the end of coming to the clinic. Andrew said 'I don't want to come because you're trying to make me feel bad about what I've done.'

Although the family did not attend any more a report produced by the clinic and the school psychologist led to Andrew's placement in a small highly structured and supportive school. For a year there were no more violent incidents. Then Andrew defied his mother's request to tidy his room. Mr H refused to discipline him, Mrs G then hit Andrew so violently with a stick that Andrew was placed on the child protection register.

Discussion

Andrew's picture of the sharks in the lagoon represents the shared internal world of his family. Vulnerable feelings like tears are attacked with shark-like cruelty. At another level I think that the 'tropical lagoon' is also a representation of the mother's uterus where the vulnerable babies have been killed. Andrew's attack on the child in the swimming pool may be another enactment of this. This cruel internal world is also projected onto the clinic, so that Andrew is afraid to be alone with the social worker. Andrew also clearly expresses the feeling on behalf of himself and his mother that any sense of guilt for the violent attacks will expose them to a cruel and merciless superego, and a brick wall comes down on attempts to explore this. Feelings of guilt and responsibility were projected into the social worker, who found it impossible to confront Mrs G with her violent threat to Andrew.

Borderline individuals and families need to split professionals to receive help, in this case the 'good' educational psychologist and the 'bad' clinic social worker, however this can be offset if there is good communication between agencies. Weakening of individual or family defensive organisations exposes members to feelings of vulnerability and anxieties about breakdown, so there is a need for strong institutions or professional networks to provide support. It is important to bear in mind the role of all family members in the defensive organisation. In the example above, Mrs G's choice of a less violent partner, and Andrew's lessening aggression meant that Mrs G was less able to project her own aggression, which exploded in the attack on Andrew. The outcome of this was increased support for Mrs G. Children usually play a crucial role in parental defensive organisations, however parents whose children have been removed are rarely offered help. This may leave them at the mercy of breakdown or more often leads to them having or acquiring further children.

Making changes

In this chapter I have tried to show ways in which families use complex, interlocking defensive systems to maintain an equilibrium which is damaging to all its members. To tackle this type of defensive organisation head on is virtually impossible. In Chapter 13 Britton discusses the need for small but necessary steps to be taken with the types of families I have just described. He also adds to that that it is important for workers to be aware of *small but significant changes*. The role of the supervisor in helping workers recognise progress can be a very important one, as despair and inadequacy will be projected into the worker.

It is often easier to achieve change by 'picking off' individual members of the family, although work may need to be done to achieve this. Often this happens by a child coming into care. In Chapter 7 Williams describes work with a boy whose foster placement had broken down and is violent at school. She describes the role of psychotherapy to tackle the internal defensive organisation, but also emphasises the importance of work with the children's home and the school. When work is going on to undo an internal gang there is a need to provide a strong external structure to support this. As professional networks and institutions play a key role in change I will finish by discussing some aspects of this.

The role of institutions and theory

I have tried to emphasise the difficulties faced by workers in dealing with families which function as pathological organisations, this includes the projection of unbearable states of mind and massive pressures to enact aspects of the family dynamics. For the sake of clarity my case examples so far have dealt with individual workers and families. However, just as these families need a strong institution or professional network, so work with these families is very dependent on the nature of the worker's institution and their relationship to it. Complex enactments between families, workers and institutions may take place. These projections and enactments can become incorporated into institutional dynamics and these compromise the capacity of both workers and institutions to recognise risk and act appropriately on behalf of vulnerable children. I will give a couple of examples of this process.

A family with a multigenerational history of sexual abuse was presented at a case discussion on a social work course. As is usually the case the process of the discussion reflected some of the dynamics of the family and the difficulties of working with them. The three children were placed with two different foster parents following physical injuries and sexual abuse by their father. Their mother, Mrs S, had chosen to remain with their father. Mrs S had been sexually abused by her own father who was now dead. The maternal grandmother was offering to foster the children to 'keep the family together', the children were said to be 'strongly attached' to their grandmother. The social worker had to make recommendations to the court about their care. The social worker felt that the existing foster carers were not entirely satisfactory as they had allowed some unsupervised contact with an uncle who also had a history of abuse, she felt under pressure from her manager to go along with a kinship care arrangement.

At the start of the discussion the worker presented a complex genogram and family history which took up over half the time, the seminar members felt lulled and numbed by the detail, each suggestion from the group was met by further accounts of the history of family abuse, eventually one of the seminar members said 'No more of this, I can't stand it'. When the seminar said 'no' to the abusive narrative, this seemed to free the worker who commented that despite the family history of abuse her department did not seem to learn from it, as the grandmother had not been able to protect her own daughter and had expressed no guilt or regret. This seemed to be projected into the social worker who felt guilty about the limitations of the care her own department had provided. In families which function as pathological organisations helpful links and routines become perverse ties and rituals which prevent thinking. In the same way, concern about family history can be used as a refuge from facing the present needs of children. Practice guidelines can become a ritual which cannot be questioned, potentially helpful attachment theory becomes perverted when it does not distinguish between secure attachment and loyalty to a corrupt 'protector'. In these situations careful examination of the facts is essential.

With the support of the seminar the social worker could examine the painful facts of the case. However this capacity to face reality is lost in families functioning as pathological organisations. When the social worker stopped the 7-year-old boy masturbating against his 4-year-old sister and suggested he talk to her, he climbed into a toy box and said 'this is my coffin'. For him this may be an identification with his dead abusive grandfather, for the family the multigenerational abuse functioned as a deadly refuge from unbearable emotional states. When departments or workers are faced with trying to make change in deeply disturbed and damaged families with limited resources, it is hard not to resort to pathological defences.

In this case the family's omnipotence and denial of damage was mirrored by the omnipotent expectation by the court that the worker could come up with a plan which will 'put right' children who have been hugely damaged in ways which might never be entirely reversed. The manager was tempted to adhere to a guideline that would make fewer demands on the budget, but denied the grandmother's history. In these situations there is often a difficult balance to be struck with what is possible both in terms of the budget and the possibilities of change. Workers may evade this pain and uncertainty by masochistically submitting to departmental 'commands' or feel righteously aggrieved on behalf of their clients. Departments may bully workers who make robust and well-thought-out plans to meet the needs of damaged and vulnerable clients. (I would like to emphasise that it is not only social services departments which succumb to pathological defences in my experience, they are just as common in therapeutic institutions.)

I have written elsewhere (Bower 2003) on the importance of psychoanalytic theory as an intellectual container which helps workers process the powerful emotions and disturbing projections which arise in contact with disturbed individuals and families. In this chapter I have tried to illustrate how an understanding of pathological organisations contributes to the assessment of risk and making realistic plans to help families. However, on its own theory is not enough, workers need the support of structures and institutions. Families which are functioning as pathological defence organisations usually need a network of workers and institutions. A shared theoretical model can facilitate these links, although a genuine respect for a different point of view is just as important. Collaborative partnerships between clinics and social services or social services and schools restore the institutional equivalent of a supportive parental couple. However, the nature of these families (perhaps something we are all prone to) means that these links will always be under attack, and constant work and awareness will be needed to maintain them.

References

Bower M (2003) Broken and twisted. *Journal of Social Work Practice* **17**(2).

Fraiberg SH, Adelson E, Shapiro V (1975) Ghosts in the nursery: A psychoanalytic approach to the problem of impaired mother–infant relationships. *Journal of American Academy of Child Psychiatry*, **14**: 387–422.

Klein M (1940) Mourning and its relation to manic depressive states. In *Love Guilt and Reparation, The Writings of Melanie Klein* Vol 1. (1975) The Hogarth Press, London.

Milton J (1994) Abuser and abused: perverse solutions following childhood abuse. *Psychoanalytic Psychotherapy* **8**(3).

Riviere J (1952) The unconscious phantasy of an inner world reflected in examples from literature. In Klein M et al (eds) *New Directions in Psychoanalysis*. Karnac, London.

Rosenfeld H (1971) A clinical approach to the psychoanalytic theory of the life and death instincts. In Spillius E (ed.) *Melanie Klein Today*. Routledge, London.

Steiner J (1992) *Psychic Retreats*. Routledge, London.

13 Re-enactment as an unwitting professional response to family dynamics

Ronald Britton

The notion which is expressed in the title of this chapter is that contact with some families may result in professional workers or their institutions becoming involved unknowingly in a drama which reflects a situation in the relationships of the family or within the minds of some of its individual members; and that this is not recognised but expressed in action. As the action appears to be that of professionals going about their business, i.e. interacting with the family, colleagues or other agencies, the fact that these transactions are shaped by an underlying dynamic is unlikely to be perceived. This may eventually call attention to itself by its repetitive nature or by the impasse which seems to follow a variety of initiatives. Indications of the presence of a prevailing unconscious process influencing professional responses may be the intensity of feeling aroused by a case; the degree of dogmatism evoked; or the pressure to take drastic or urgent measures. In other cases, in contrast to this, the professional 'symptoms' are inappropriate unconcern; surprising ignorance; undue complacency; uncharacteristic insensitivity or professional inertia.

This last characteristic is illustrated in the case of a boy referred to a Child Guidance Clinic by the school he attended, or more precisely rarely attended. A new teacher at the school had reactivated concern about an old situation. In the past the School Welfare Officer had been very troubled about the boy who appeared to be neglected by his mother, with whom he lives alone. The Welfare Worker had involved the Social Services Department in the case, as the boy could not learn at school and seemed undeveloped emotionally and socially. A regular arrangement was made for a woman social worker and the mother to meet to discuss the problems of both child and parent. The outcome was the perpetuation of this arrangement for a long time with its purpose lost and its effect negligible. Frustrated by her own lack of impact on the school attendance, the Welfare Officer had effectively ceased to be involved in the case. Like the boy's father in the early years of his life, she left the scene.

The psychiatrist at the clinic, having gleaned this information, felt his best course of action was to consult with the social worker already involved with the family, a common clinical approach. Thus began a protracted, desultory, 'consultation' with the social worker, in which the 'work with the family' was discussed. For a time the school showed signs of considerable frustration at the lack of new developments but then seemed to lose interest, leaving the two professionals still involved with the case in a relationship very like that of the boy and his mother, or the boy and his school, which was repeated with the mother and the social worker. There seemed to be in all the situations related to the case the emergence of a characteristic pattern of object-relations, i.e. a pair staying together in an unsatisfactory, nonprogressive relationship from which frustration was nevertheless excluded and instead felt by the person whose failure to make an impact eventually led them to withdraw or depart. A configuration like this could be discerned in a number of interpersonal contexts. It could also be a description of an intrapsychic situation in which freedom from frustration and its consequences was achieved by the elimination of any real desire or expectation from the individual who thus became the cause of discouragement of others who were provoked by this inertia into attempting to kindle some desire for change. Here we seem to be dealing with repetitious actions which transfer a pattern of relationships from one situation to another in which new participants become the vehicles for the reiterated expression of the underlying dynamic. The repetition compulsion may be a dynamic in the sense of being a compelling force determining events but in another sense it is essentially static. The basic situation remains unrealised and unchanged whilst new versions of it proliferate. The cast changes but the plot remains the same. This is well described in the psychoanalytic literature as occurring in the lives of individuals; here I am referring to a similar phenomenon in the lives of families and groups.

A number of psychoanalytic concepts are implicit in this account. One is the recurrence of a specific pattern of events and relationships. This phenomenon referred to as the 'repetition compulsion' was first described by Freud in a paper published in 1914 called 'Remembering, Repeating and Working-Through' (Freud 1914). He linked it to the established idea of transference, which he said 'is itself only a piece of repetition . . . of the forgotten past, and not only on to the doctor but also on to all the aspects of the current situation . . . the patient yields to the compulsion to repeat . . . in every other activity and relationship . . . at the time.'[1] In the same paper he described the tendency to replication of unconscious ideas in action rather than thought for which the term 'acting out' was subsequently adopted.

My characterisation of a process in the case described above whereby frustration is denied and extruded from the relationship of the couple and provoked in a third party can be seen as an example of 'projective identification'. Melanie Klein (1946) coined this term to describe a phantasy of the self or more often parts of the self entering into the identity of another person; if this is preceded by denial of those aspects in the subject then they are perceived as attributes of the object of the process. Thus in this case the third party appears to be one who wants change or development and the couple feel no urge to transform or clarify their situation. The situation could be described as an omnipotent unconscious phantasy that those aspects of themselves which would experience such desire, and its associated frustration and helplessness can be split off and located in someone else. However, there is more to it as the behaviour and experience of others is actually influenced by the process. Wilfred Bion (1974) commented on this and together with other analysts who followed Melanie Klein has enlarged the use of the term to include the effect on the recipient of such 'projections'.

> I am not sure [he says] from the practice of analysis that it is only an omnipotent phantasy; that is, something that the patient cannot in fact do . . . I have felt and some of my colleagues likewise that when the patient appear to be engaged on a

---

1 I do not intend in this chapter to explore the fuller meaning given to the concept of Transference in subsequent psychoanalytical work by Melanie Klein and others.

projective identification it can make me feel persecuted, as if the patient can, in fact, split off certain nasty feelings and shove them into me so that I actually have feeling of persecution or anxiety.

(p. 105)

This would then link the notion of projective identification with that of 'countertransference', an older term defined as 'the analyst's unconscious reactions to the individual analysand – especially to the analysand's own transference' (Laplanche and Pontalis 1973). As these two authors point out, some take the countertransference to be that in the analyst's personality which is liable to affect treatment, others to that brought about by the transference of the analysand. Though this is an important distinction (implying as it does that the analyst has a special responsibility for the former) in practice, in the consulting room the two may not be separable since the one plays on the other. As Lagache (1964) points out, the transference and countertransference are reciprocal parts of a whole, involving both of the people present.

One way that the analyst may remain unaware of his countertransference is that he, like the patient, may act it out, instead of experiencing the psychic situation. A good deal has been written about the way an analyst may increase his understanding of his patient by scrutiny of his own irrational feelings and impulses in the analysis. Rosenfeld (1965), like Bion, has emphasised that projective identification may be a form of unconscious communication from the patient. It may be, however, that it is in his behaviour with the patient, including his choice of interpretation, wording, tone, timing, etc., that the evoked 'countertransference' may be evident, as a re-enactment of an unconscious object relationship in the analysis. Betty Joseph has drawn attention to this, emphasising that 'the more the patient is using primarily primitive mechanisms and defences against anxiety, the more the analyst is . . . used by the patient unconsciously and the more analysis is a scene for action rather than understanding' (Joseph 1978).

It is a recurrent discovery that processes described as occurring in the microscopic world of psychoanalysis have relevance outside it. I believe this to be the case with the concepts just described: Freud in first describing 'repetition compulsion' said, 'The patient yields to the compulsion to repeat – in every other activity and relationship . . . at the time' (Freud, op. cit., p. 150).

I would like to paraphrase this in relation to the ideas expressed above and say that the more primitive mechanisms and defences against anxiety are being used, the more is every professional contact likely to become a scene for action and for the professional to yield to the compulsion to repeat or re-enact an unconscious situation. The term countertransference is commonly used to describe the feelings the analyst becomes aware of, or what he sees to be his emotionally determined expectations and apprehensions in contact with his patient. I would like therefore to use the words 'complementary acting out' to denote the counterpart to countertransference in deeds rather than words; that is, the enactment by the analyst of reciprocal object relationship to that acted out by his patient. By extension I propose to use this term to describe unconsciously determined action (or inaction), by professionals when this is evoked by their involvement in certain cases.

I have been impressed by the way this may continue beyond the immediate contact with the family and seem to infect the relationships of colleagues or different agencies. In some cases the pattern of response of education departments, schools, social services or doctors takes on uncannily the shape of the family; quarrels are pursued between workers who seem as incompatible in their views as are the parents; high-handed intervention by senior colleagues echoes the domination of a family by the intrusions of an opinionated grandparent. In another case a succession of professional agencies not only failed to accept responsibility but uncharacteristically failed to communicate with each other or acknowledge other workers; existence, thus echoing the family pattern of a child who had been at different times abandoned by both his parents, long since separated, who related to him independently without acknowledging each other's existence.

Such examples have become familiar in examining the circumstances of situations referred to the Tavistock Clinic for help when there is disagreement, stalemate, or what are felt to be intransigent problems. The sphere of action, however, need not be so obviously related to emotional difficultly or disturbed behaviour. The nature of 'complementary action' may only become evident when a particular configuration is seen to recur in varied forms. The formulation of this may give a meaning which the separate acts, by their apparent diversity, have obscured. Thus, in the example I am about to quote, the way I choose to present the facts already represents my view of the case, i.e. as a coherent attempt to dispose of a psychological difficulty through a particular kind of action. It is clear that the events were perceived at the time as a series of situations unrelated to each other and demanding action in their own right. It is therefore evident that my view may be mistaken and might appear arbitrary or fanciful. As a hypothesis it can only gain strength if it has predictive value.

The case concerned a girl, her family and a hospital. It was characterised by a preoccupation with removing some presence felt to be dangerous to the girl. She was recently sexually mature. One organ under suspicion was removed lest it contain the malignancy which had previously killed her grandmother. A second organ, known to be diseased in her mother, was suspected of causing the girl's symptoms and was excised only to be found to be quite healthy. The girl attempted to remove life itself by suicide. The hypothesis, that an unconscious phantasy was operative, that something malignant and female must be got rid of, seemed plausible. If this hypothesis was correct this imperative, though unconscious, belief influenced the decisions and behaviour of the girl, her parents and a number of professional advisers at different times. One way of expressing this underlying phantasy would be to say that there was a powerful anxiety that something catastrophic would follow from the development of a mature, female, sexual presence (or in the psychoanalytic sense the emergence of a danger, female, 'bad' object). In this family, you might say, there was a shared phantasy that there was something threatening about femininity; that women contained the seeds of destruction or malignancy. A family history of women of two earlier generations spending time in mental hospitals lent credibility to this version when it emerged a little later.

The working hypothesis gained support, however, by subsequent developments. Further mystifying symptoms provoked a superficially different but basically similar response within the hospital staff. The malignancy was now located not in an organ or tissue but in the girl's relationship with her mother; specifically it was thought that the food produced by the mother provoked the disease. The solution was again removal, this time of the girl from the home, into care: I would emphasise here that this apparently new initiative, which in a psychodynamic sense is so repetitious, came from the professional staff as their response to the situation with which they were in contact. If they were steered by unconscious forces, these forces were operating in them, called forth as it were by their experience with this family.

The quality of this story provoked the feeling that these events belong in a dream. In a sense that may be true. To return to Freud's notion of acting out – he says, 'The patient does not remember anything . . . but acts it out. He reproduces it, not as a memory but as an action' (ibid., p. 150). We can substitute for memory in this definition all other forms of mental activity. Hence action seems not simply a substitute for memory but for 'realisation'. If we follow Bion (1970) in seeing the endeavour to contain emergent states within the 'mental sphere' as a constant struggle for individuals and groups, the case can be seen as a failure of 'psychic containment'. First, within the girl whose phantasies were not expressed in thoughts, or dreams, but in the development of hypochondriasis and the location of a feared disorder in the body organ. Second, within the family whose anxieties were not expressed in ideas but enacted in the dramas which spilled over into the hospital. Finally, in the professionals drawn into the case who took atypical drastic steps rapidly more than once and were stirred into repetitive action rather than reflection, even though very concerned about the case.

Bion's view (1967) is that thinking is a development forced on the psyche by the pressure of thoughts and that a breakdown in the apparatus for thinking or dealing with thoughts may lead to a psychopathological development. He suggests 'that what should be a thought becomes a thing in itself, fit only for evacuation'. We might add, 'and dramatisation'. He links this capacity for thinking to the dominance of Freud's 'reality principle' and its failure as a regression to the pleasure principle. This, in turn, hinges on the achievement of what Melanie Klein (1975) called the 'depressive position'. As Hanna Segal suggests (1973, p. 76), 'in the depressive position, the whole climate of thought changes . . . Capacities for linking and abstraction develop.' She points out that 'psychic reality is experienced and differentiated from external reality, the symbol is differentiated from the object . . . in contrast with symbolic equation in which the symbol is equated with the original object giving rise to concrete thinking.' I believe that this latter state, characteristic of the paranoid-schizoid position, is linked to a greater tendency to action rather than thought; a more wholesale 'acting out' as Rosenfeld describes (1965) and a greater tendency to evoke action in others.

The implication is that families whose mode of mental operations are characteristic of the 'paranoid-schizoid' position (Klein 1975) rather than the depressive position are not only unlikely to see themselves as the agents of their own disturbances but are likely to evoke unconsciously determined action in those around them. The process of projection or projective identification within the family leading to the perception of one member as the source of difficulties is familiar as the scapegoat phenomenon and may lead to referral of this person. In many other cases, however, the principal manifestations occur around the family rather than in it. The members of a family whose relationships are experienced in the main in the paranoid-schizoid position as opposed to the depressive position, are likely to feel persecuted rather than guilty; ill rather than worried; enmity rather than conflict; desperation rather than sadness. They are liable to be triumphant or if not to feel squashed and to see others as either allies or opponents. Their tendency to take flight (e.g., by moving, changing partner, changing schools, etc.) is linked to their belief that psychic experience can be split off and left behind: by the same token there is a sense of being hunted and a fear of being cornered.

For people with these characteristics a place like a clinic where problems are focused on seems threatening and even the collation of information is felt to be unwelcome. It is not surprising therefore that they shun clinics; avoid meeting teachers and become the chronically unsatisfactory cases of social services if, as is by no means always the case, they are in the lower social classes. If the family are amongst the more affluent or educated groups the dramatis personae tend to be different but the kind of happenings are similar. The professionals then may be solicitors, private medical advisers; family friends or relatives; colleagues or partners at work; divorce courts; Members of Parliament and so on. The risk of them becoming unknowingly involved in an enactment is as great with even less likelihood of it being recognised.

It is recognition of these provocative or paralysing effects in such cases which at least gives pause for reflection. This often produces the painful discovery of the limitations of help or the constraints involved in the situation. In turn it may lead to the possibility of taking uncomfortable but necessary steps or accepting small, significant changes rather than cherishing unrealised hope for a transformation. The thesis which is argued here is that 'realisation', and change as a consequence of 'realisation', rather than change as an alternative to 'realisation' may prevent patterns which cross not only individual but generational boundaries.

Theoretical discussion

The clinical phenomenon described in this chapter is of the reproduction amongst professional workers and agencies of a pattern of 'object-relationships' which resemble those of some families with which they have contact. The repetitious pattern or event may take place between family members; family member and professionals; professional and professional; professional and social agencies.

It is argued in this chapter that the phenomenon of repetition compulsion first described by Freud (1918) may be analogous to this and that an essential element in this concept is replacement of recollection (or any form of mental realisation) by a blindly repeated pattern of events. In the instances referred to, the events transcend the individual's and his family's lives and reverberate amongst those associated with them. It is suggested that some of the processes grouped under the concept of projective identification, first used by Melanie Klein, may underlie the phenomenon. Since it appears to occur even where there is no direct contact (as may be observed in groups who simply discuss these cases) the mode of operation would seem to be by identification and replication, mobilised by something psychic analogous to 'resonance'. That is to compare it to the physical phenomenon by which vibrations in one object can induce sympathetic vibrations in another at a distance, e.g. musical instruments. This would seem to be a feasible metaphor if the assumption was made that certain basic internal object relationships are ubiquitous. Freud speculated in 'The Wolf Man' (Freud – 'From the History of an Infantile Neurosis') that a knowledge of the 'primal scene' might be phylogenetic, thus implying that a rudimentary form of the Oedipus complex would be innate. It is implicit in Melanie Klein's writings that some basic phantasies are innate concerning good and bad objects for example; and the 'primal scene'. Roger Money-Kyrle with his description of 'imageless expectations' and Wilfred Bion with his notion of 'innate preconceptions' make this explicit.

In the passage of Freud's referred to above where he considers the possibility of 'instinctive knowledge' as a hereditary endowment, he uses the German word 'instinktiv' where the word he usually used which translated into the English as 'instinctual' is 'triebhaft' which is open to the substitution of 'drive'. This is of some significance in view of the later development of the concept of unconscious phantasy, particularly in Kleinian writing. Susan Isaacs, in her definitive paper, 'The Nature and Function of Phantasy', considers unconscious phantasy as the mental expression of instincts; all impulses, all feelings, all modes of defence are experienced in phantasy (1952, p. 83).

Authors influenced by Melanie Klein, such as Bion, Jaques and Menzies have described how groups may share such phantasies and collectively react to them. In his paper on 'Social Systems as Defence against Persecutory and Depressive Anxiety' (1955), Jaques describes institutions as having beneath a manifest structure and function an underlying 'unconscious function'. He sees this as the maintenance of shared belief and activities which collectively defend against basic anxieties. He describes this as based on shared projections, i.e., 'when external objects are shared with others but used for common purposes of projection, phantasy social relationships may be established through projective identification with a common object . . . further elaborated by introjection' (p. 482).

Thus in the first example in this chapter the fundamental anxieties associated with the Oedipus complex would be mobilised in phantasies of those in contact with the case. Then the defensive configuration mobilised of a sterile couple and a defeated third party, enacted unwittingly. Whilst repetition prevailed and unwitting re-enactment continued, realisation could be avoided, constancy maintained and conflict averted. In the second case described, change is threatening the family in the form of the emergence of a sexually mature young woman and provoking basic anxieties about such an object or past object. 'Malignancy' is suspected and the 'malign object' sought in various anatomical organs before being perceived by the professional group as the mother herself. Here the shared phantasy of a dangerous, disordered, female object was collectively defended against by action designed for removal.

Events involving families, and the elements of society in contact with them in such cases as I have described are thought about by many family therapists in terms derived from 'General Systems Theory', 'Cybernetics', and 'Information Theory'. General Systems Theory (GST) was grounded as a general science of organisation and wholeness by Ludwig von Bertalanffy in 1940; it has a great deal in common with Cybernetics, a subject with dates from 1942 and was named in 1947 by Wiener and Rosenbleuth to describe the science of control and communication in the animal and machine; it emphasised particularly that the laws governing control are universal and do not depend on the classical dichotomy between organic and inorganic systems. This is expressed in GST in the concept of 'structural isomorphism' or with an assumption of 'dynamic equilibrium' (Schanck 1954); that is the maintenance of an overall 'steady state' by any fluctuation in subelements being compensated so the system remains in total balance. Thus 'a systems approach is an approach to the study of physical and social systems which enable complex and dynamic situations to be understood in broad outline' (Ackoff and Emery 1972). Systems may have recognisable subsystems and the improvement of one of these to the detriment of the system as a whole is described as 'suboptimisation', hence the warnings from some family therapists about treating individuals; and from some sociologists about treating particular families rather than society. The ascending order of systems inside larger systems like 'Chinese boxes' is often referred to as 'hierarchies' and the rules governing patterns of behaviour which is reproduced at different organisational levels are called 'recursive'. This is a term borrowed from linguistics to describe language rules which can be applied an indefinite number of times in generating sentences. The phenomena which I have referred to could perhaps be described as 'recursive' in this sense. It is not my intention to describe the application of these theories to family therapy in this chapter or to place the concepts which I am endeavouring to describe in relation to a 'systems approach' to families. There is, however, one fundamental question raised by the notion of 'dynamic equilibrium' whether applied to individuals or families which has a place in psychoanalytic theory and I would like to pursue that as it influences the way the social system (whether it be a family or an institution) is perceived.

This notion of 'dynamic equilibrium' is enshrined in a very influential 'systems approach' to sociology in the work of Talcott Parsons in the 1950s and the related school of 'structural-functionalism'. This is a mode of theorising in which particularly features of social structures are explained in terms of their contribution in maintaining a self-equilibrating system as a viable entity. I find it of particular interest that sociological critics of this approach object to it on three particular grounds; one, that it is tautologous; two, that it explains stability and not change; and three, that it ignores essential conflict. Critics of other schools who particularly make this last point are know as 'Conflict Theorists' and may in general be either 'pluralist' or 'Marxist' sociologists who regard conflict as inherent in society.

It is of interest to a psychoanalyst, I think, because it covers similar ground to that which Freud explored in the 1920s; in particular in 'Beyond the Pleasure Principle' (Freud 1920) and 'Civilization and its Discontents' (Freud 1930). In these two books he re-examines his earlier ideas about the basic forces underlying man's behaviour and social relationships. He had previously followed the idea that the basic determinant was the 'pleasure principle' – this he derived from Fechner's 'constancy principle' or 'tendency towards stability'. Activity was therefore directed to restoring an earlier state of things. It looked like movement but sought quietude: the dominance of the pleasure principle was opposed, he had suggested, by the reality principle. He realised therefore that if this – which we could perfectly describe as 'dynamic equilibrium' – was the only force the 'elementary living entity would from its very beginning have no wish to change; if conditions remained the same it would do no more than constantly repeat the same course of life.' He linked, therefore, the 'compulsion to repeat' in the behaviour and experience of people with this tendency which he described as 'the inertia inherent in organic life'.

> The dominating tendency of mental life . . . is the effort to reduce, to keep constant or to remove internal tension due to stimuli – a tendency which finds expression in the pleasure principle.

This he named the 'death instinct', since he saw its ultimate goal as returning in ways 'immanent in the organism itself' to inorganic existence. He was careful to point out that self-preservation and mastery were component instincts whose function it was to ward off any other possible way to death and were themselves manifestations of this status-quo-seeking instinct. There was only one inherent source of opposition which existed because it was a living system and that was the urge to reproduce. The disturber of the peace therefore in the case of the human being was Eros, his capac ity for object love, which in the individual stood in opposition to his narcissism. As Freud put it, object instincts were in opposition to ego instincts.

In 'Civilization and its Discontents' he went further, more clearly equating the life instincts with the disturbers of the peace within the individual and the death instincts with a 'primary mutual hostility of human beings' which he saw as perpetually threatening civilized society with disintegration. The satisfaction, he thought, which derived from the exercise of this destructive urge lay in the fulfilment of the ego's old wish for omnipotence; aim inhibited, i.e. 'moderated and tamed', he saw its satisfaction lay in control over nature.

Freud, therefore, came to see conflict as inevitable and expressed in ambivalence towards love objects who were both the source of desire and dissatisfaction; the origins of hope and the end of omnipotence. Melanie Klein later was to describe in the 'depressive position' the attempts of the individual to resolve this basic ambivalence to the primary object and its consequences. An object relations theory which incorporates this basic conflict and its attendant persecutory and depressive anxieties sees social conflict as inevitable and social institutions as attempting to contain them.

As Freud described it, the compulsion to repeat unthinkingly was an expression of that tendency to constancy, to inertia, which he thought innate. The counter tendency – to experience, to seek, to relate – he associated with the life instincts and the urge to change. We could argue therefore that the struggle to 'realise' rather than 'repeat' takes place within this basic conflict and that an element of discomfort, strain or anxiety is inevitable in the process. When professional workers therefore are called upon to resist unconscious collusion in order to become aware of the existence of an underlying dynamic configuration, they will find themselves 'going against the grain' of their own emotional inclinations.

References

Ackoff RL, Emery FE (1972) *On Purposeful Systems*. London, Tavistock Publications.

Bion WR (1967) *Second Thoughts*. London, Heinemann.

Bion WR (1970) Attention and Interpretation. London, Tavistock Publications.

Bion WR (1974) *Bion's Brazilian Lectures I*. Rio de Janeiro, Imago Editora.

Freud S (1914) *Remembering, Repeating and Working Through*, 'Standard Edition XII'. London, Hogarth Press and Institute of Psychoanalysis (1958), pp. 147, 156.

Freud S (1918/14) *From the History of an Infantile Neurosis*, 'Standard Edition XVII. London, Hogarth Press and Institute of Psychoanalysis (1955).

Freud S (1920) *Beyond the Pleasure Principle*, 'Standard Edition XXI'. London, Hogarth Press and Institute of Psychoanalysis (1961).

Freud S (1930/29) *Civilization and its Discontents*, 'Standard Edition XXI'. London, Hogarth Press and Institute of Psychoanalysis (1961).

Isaacs S (1952) *The Nature and Function of Phantasy*, 'Developments in Psychoanalysis'. London, Hogarth Press, Chapter III.

Jaques E (1955) Social systems as a defence against persecutory and depressive anxiety. In: M. Klein et al. (eds) *New Directions in Psychoanalysis*. London, Tavistock Publications.

Joseph B (1978) Different types of anxiety and their handling in the analytic situation *International Journal of Psychoanalysis* 59: 223–228.

Klein M (1946) Notes on some schizoid mechanisms. In: M. Klein (ed.) *Developments in Psychoanalysis*, London, Hogarth Press and Institute of Psychoanalysis (1952), pp. 292–320.

Klein M (1975) *Envy, Gratitude and Other Works, 1946–63*. London, Hogarth Press and Institute of Psychoanalysis.
Lagache D (1964) La Méthode psychoanalytique. In L. Michaux et al (eds) *Psychiatrie*. Paris.
Laplanche J, Pontalis JB (1973) *The Language of Psychoanalysis*. London, Hogarth Press.
Rosenfeld H (1965) *Psychotic States: A Psychoanalytical Approach*. London, Hogarth Press, Chapter X
Schank RL (1954) *The Permanent Revolution in Science*. New York, Philosophical Library.
Segal H (1973) *Introduction to the Work of Melanie Klein*. London, Hogarth Press.

Part 4

Professional stresses and supports

14 Who cares for the carers? Work with refugees

Maureen Fox

Some years ago a telephone call to the clinic from a school nurse described a situation in which a refugee pupil had collapsed in the playground. The child was rushed to hospital amid anxieties that she had stopped breathing. The call described how this incident had induced a feeling of panic and represented the teachers' growing anxiety in their ever-increasing work with refugee children. The request was for support for staff in their handling and management of refugee pupils. The girl survived and nothing physical was found to be wrong with her but that is another story. The purpose of this chapter is to investigate the impact of working with refugees and asylum seekers and the need for support for staff undertaking this work.

The teachers' anxiety was that there was something they had or had not done that had threatened the survival of this girl. Poignantly, they talked about feeling helpless and at times irritated when confronted with these young people, a situation exacerbated by the fact that they would often arrive in class unannounced. Frequently, teachers knew nothing about these youngsters or where they had come from but their minds were filled with media images of awfulness. Over the years since that first telephone call, I have frequently heard social workers, psychologists and psychotherapists express this feeling of helplessness. In schools the same questions arise about how to respond when you feel so paralysed having listened to their accounts.

The aim of our work at the Child and Family Department at the Tavistock Clinic, has been to provide support, consultation and training on the needs of refugee children and on the needs of the adults working with them.

The particular case I would like to describe is a girl I have called Sophia, whose painful situation reverberated within and between all of us who encountered her. But in presenting this case I am mindful of our own experience in the Refugee Workshop at the clinic, a regular support group for those of us engaged in this work. I am thinking of the temptation to be drawn into unreflective action, a wish to do something or even blame someone, when we feel knocked off balance in the face of pain that is difficult to bear. It isn't that there is anything wrong with being moved to action, far from it. In fact those of us working with refugees find ourselves writing letters to housing departments and immigration authorities and providing testimonials in support of applications for further education. But here I am thinking more about the state of mind in which the action is undertaken and the purpose it serves.

We have come to recognise that, as with the teachers, conflicting states of mind can emerge in relation to material that is distressing and within the group these different states of mind can be represented by different people at different times, for example, those who feel overwhelmed and paralysed may become a source of irritation to those who feel impelled to do something; whilst those who remain thoughtful may be resented by both for their apparent complacency and lack of sympathy. In reality, each of these aspects belongs to all of us, but the rawness of the disturbance can temporarily leave us with a reduced capacity to hold in mind a range of different and conflicting perspectives. The task of the workshop is to hear these different points of view and provide a forum where such splits and attacks on linking can be investigated and their meaning understood.

Case study

The case I have chosen to describe is a vivid, if painful, example of these various forces at work. I am sure that her story is familiar to all those who have experience of working with this population.

Sophia was born in a refugee camp in the Horn of Africa. She was a toddler when her mother remarried leaving her father to care for her and her two older brothers which she recalled he did with love and concern. The war in her native land ended when she was 14 and her father set off alone to re-establish the family home, leaving her with her 16-year-old brother, her oldest brother having joined the jihad. After many months of waiting she learned of her father's death and she and her brother embarked on the journey to the family village to find out what had become of him. Some weeks later, they arrived safely and began to settle into their new life. But one evening some men, in plain clothes, came and took her brother away and he has not been heard of since.

A distant relative, living in another country, learned of her plight and arranged for her to travel to the UK providing her with the telephone number of an uncle who was living in London. Like many of the 6000 youngsters who arrive unaccompanied in the UK each year, she was taken by the escort who accompanied her to a community centre belonging to her own ethnic group, where she was left. No one there had heard of her uncle and the telephone number which she clutched proved to be unobtainable. Social services were contacted and she was placed in bed and breakfast accommodation. She was told that if she was lonely she could go to a local café or spend time in the park and she was given the address of the nearest school. At this time, she was just about to turn 16.

At the school, where over 15% of the pupils were refugees, she received a warm welcome from a small group of staff who were acutely aware of the needs of youngsters like her. They were aware of their need for a carer who would provide the safety and security of a home, take care of their need for food and shelter their emotional need for love, guidance and support. But, as with so many of these young people, the teachers were aware that the burden of concern would most probably fall on them, and Sophia was no exception. They contacted the local authority concerning her need for care, the Home Office concerning her immigration status, they found her a solicitor and referred her to the Tavistock Outreach Refugee Project: a project that had been set up in the school to provide counselling to refugee children.

The reason for Sophia's referral was that although she sought contact with those around her, she spent most of the day crying. It was becoming increasingly difficult to be near her, not because she was disliked, but because the pain she communicated was difficult to bear. They worried about her state of mind and about the effect she was having on her peers. Other teachers, too, were finding her tears disturbing and some expressed anger and resentment at having her in class. At the clinic we felt moved by her situation and, like her teachers, were concerned about her distress, about her living situation and the lack of provision being made for her care. We were also exercised by the impact of her pain on staff.

Support to teachers working closely with refugee children has been a core aspect of our work, creating a space within the busy day where some reflection can take place upon what is known and what is not known about the child's situation, the circumstances of his arrival in this country and his internal resources as they come to light through his interactions and expectations of those around him. In the absence of information about a child's history, we have found that exploring the observations of staff and listening carefully to their account of what it feels like to be with him, can add considerably to our understanding of the child and the possible meaning of his difficult, and at times baffling, behaviour. We believed that the teachers' experience of being overwhelmed by Sophia's pain and their difficulty in bearing it, told us not only about what had been evoked in them but also let us know something of the quality of the mental pain that she herself was experiencing.

We agreed to offer help in a number of ways: to support the specialist teachers working closely with her, make contact with the local authority concerning her need for care and arrange for a therapist from the clinic to come to the school to meet with Sophia for an assessment. This assessment would enable us to gain an understanding of Sophia and her capacities but it would also serve to inform our support work with the school and our discussions with social services.

The therapist met with Sophia in the comfortably furnished room that the school had set aside for this purpose. She arrived for her session on time and sat on the edge of the chair, her eyes directed towards the floor. She sobbed quietly in a way that was difficult to bear, conveying the immensity of her grief. They sat together for some time before the therapist broke the silence and began to talk gently, acknowledging the little she knew about her situation. The therapist understood that something powerful was being conveyed at a primitive level and she reached into her own mind to search for what it might mean, in much the same way as does a mother in response to the deeply disturbing cries of her newborn baby. She found that her mind was filled with feelings of anxiety, fear, dread and confusion, leaving her in no doubt about the nature of Sophia's distress. She realised that for Sophia the awfulness of the past and the present were as one and that the resilience that had carried her from country to country had finally broken down. Tentatively, she began to put what she was thinking into words and she suggested that Sophia wanted her to know just how terrifying it was to be on her own in a strange country, without a home, and without anyone to keep her safe. At this Sophia made eye contact for the first time and her look seemed to will the therapist to go on talking, which she did. It was towards the end of the session that Sophia found herself able to speak and she stated that she wanted to live with a family. The therapist acknowledged her wish and they arranged to continue to meet weekly in school.

Later, in supervision, the therapist reflected upon the appropriateness of Sophia's wish for a new family but realised that the family she was seeking was a family that was lost to her forever and that no new family could replace. The idea occurred that what was difficult to bear was not only the tragedy of her external situation but the disaster that had taken place in her internal world as a consequence of abandonment by all those she had loved and depended upon for her survival and wellbeing, who had subsequently let her down so badly. She had lost contact with the feeling that there was anyone or anything good inside or outside of her that could sustain her.

In the 1920s Freud drew our attention to the shattering effects that certain life-threatening events had on the functioning of the mind. Indeed, in investigating war neurosis after the First World War he recorded symptoms of irritability, insomnia, anxiety, depressive moods and feelings of insufficiency, post-traumatic stress symptoms with which we are all very familiar. Freud suggested that in trauma, the ego, whose job it is to regulate the amount of excitement impinging on the mind from both external and internal sources, becomes itself so overstimulated, that normal psychic activity is devastatingly reduced or paralysed. In other words, the protective barrier that enables us to cope with anxiety within normal limits and that prevents the mind from being overwhelmed, has itself been breached. Without this protective membrane the normal psychic systems of mastery, control and defence that we rely on for our equilibrium, are blasted away leaving the individual unprotected, disintegrated and suffering acute mental pain. I believe this is an apt description of what Sophia and the teachers were experiencing. It is how we as professionals respond to this breach in our own capacity to cope with anxiety that I want to explore.

Together with the school we made the strongest possible representation to the local authority concerning Sophia's need for care but were informed that such a resource was not available for 16-year-olds and we were reminded that all young people were treated similarly, irrespective of nationality. Following persistent lobbying two concessions were gained. She was eventually provided with a place in a hostel which was staffed overnight and she was allocated a social worker, a student on a 3-month placement: the idea being that such a person would be able to give her much more time and attention than a worker carrying a heavy case load.

Servicing as an avoidance of mental pain

The sensitive and keen young woman who was appointed did, indeed, give Sophia a great deal of time and attention, helping her with shopping and cooking and finding her way in a new country. She liked Sophia but found her suffering and loneliness difficult to bear. She was confronted by a child whose needs were insatiable, suggestive of the early deprivation that predated her arrival in the UK. No matter how much she provided she was left feeling inadequate and guilty. With every good intention, she invited Sophia to the cinema in the evenings and on outings with friends and as a consequence of these actions, she was severely reprimanded and her placement terminated. She was punished for failing to depersonalise (Menzies 1988) her relationship with Sophia and ensure that it remained devoid of contact with her human suffering. Instead of concerning herself solely with practicalities, she had been receptive to her mental pain and responded to her need for care and companionship. Waddell (1989) describes:

> . . . how difficult it is to tolerate mental pain. The personality is structured around the different ways of processing that pain, or failing to do so. The range extends from the unconscious strivings of the infant to evacuate its distress, to the large scale social and political structures which conceal casualties, or at least avoid tak-

ing direct responsibility for them, by attempting to deal with them by a process which I shall call servicing, as prevalent personally as it is professionally.

(p. 12)

Waddell helpfully makes the distinction between *servicing*, responsive action focusing on material and practical help in a way that militates against contact with mental pain, and *serving*, a response that involves engaging with and tolerating psychic pain as a means of transforming it into something more bearable. However, these functions are not mutually exclusive and the needs of refugees are most helpfully addressed by workers who remain open to what is being communicated psychically whilst attending to the practicalities in hand.

I believe this description of how agencies and individuals engage in protecting themselves from exposure to pain was what Lord Laming (2003) had in mind in his Summary of the Victoria Climbie Inquiry:

Many of the procedures that I heard about are self-serving, supporting the needs of the organisation, rather than the public they are set up to serve.

(p. 13)

My intention in recounting this incident is not to scapegoat the local authority. The reality is much more complicated for all of us and in any case, the other agencies are in the fortunate position of not having to decide which children get parents or social workers and which don't, when there are so few resources to go round. Instead, I would like to use this example to consider the dynamics operating within the system, in particular, the management of psychic pain that threatens to overwhelm and the management of limitations imposed by reality. We might speculate on the way in which the local authority dealt defensively with the painful consequences of its decision not to provide Sophia with a family. Whilst it was true that the time the student had available was considerably more than Sophia would otherwise have received, nevertheless, this allocation to the most junior, unqualified and temporary member of staff served to protect management from experiencing the anxiety and guilt that the social worker was left with. I believe it was the local authority's fear of being overwhelmed, we could say of having the institution's protective membrane breached, that led them to turn a blind eye and deny the consequences for Sophia of the loss of another attachment figure, a re-enactment of her abandonment by her father to the care of her brother who, like the junior social worker, then disappears. I am sure those of us working in health and education can supply our own examples of this kind of institutional splitting.

Sophia attended the sessions with the therapist regularly and on time and she became more able to put her fears into words. Before her transfer to the hostel, she described her terror at night when she would move furniture against her bedroom door to keep out intruders. Concretely, she struggled to erect a barrier against the other residents who would wander into her room but symbolically, she was also struggling to erect a barrier that would keep out the pain that threatened to take over the room of her mind. She was frightened by the loud voices and the footsteps that came and went in the corridor evoking memories of the men in plain clothes who had taken her brother. She pleaded with the therapist to find her a family and felt let down when she failed to do so. At times the therapist felt that Sophia experienced her as the persecutor, a kind of conglomerate figure representing all those who had abandoned and deprived her: her country, mother, father, brothers, aunt and the local authority.

Melanie Klein described the process whereby psychic pain that is experienced as intolerable can be got rid of through a mechanism of projection, a means of putting unwanted feelings into someone else. This manoeuvre, which takes place unconsciously, is resorted to in the face of overwhelming danger and fear. The more threatening the impending danger is to one's survival, the more forcibly these feelings have to be expelled. Under these circumstances the experience that is being evacuated can come to be felt deeply by the recipient as it was by all of those working with Sophia.

Sustaining therapeutic contact

You will not be surprised to learn that the therapist experienced a similar temptation to provide more than she could appropriately offer. But unlike the social work student, the trainee therapist had the benefit of a substantial support system to help her when the pain of the work threatened to overwhelm. She continued to find Sophia's anger and disappointment difficult to bear and at times felt useless and impotent. To supervision she took her struggle with the temptation to find a family for Sophia herself. She explored feelings of anger and guilt at enjoying the pleasures of life and family, feelings intensified by the projection into her of Sophia's own guilt feelings about surviving, and enjoying opportunities for care and support denied her brothers and father. She questioned the worthwhileness of what she was doing and wondered if she was making things worse by encouraging her to talk. But with the support and containment available to her she was sustained in her therapeutic task and regained her equilibrium. After a few months the value of the work became more apparent. The teachers reported that Sophia was much less tearful in class and had made friends with a few of her peers.

Wilfred Bion described how an infant at birth has neither the capacity to tolerate or think about the pain he experiences, for example, of hunger, cold and fear. He explained that all he can do is rid himself these feelings and he does this through his cries which alert his mother and bring her to his side. Her response is to become preoccupied by what is upsetting him, using her own mind to discern the source of his pain. Once this is understood she relieves his discomfort, addressing his physical need for food and warmth and his emotional need for relief from anxiety. It is the mother's sensitivity to what is being projected that enables her to understand the nature and origin of his distress. For the infant these projections represent his earliest means of communication but they also serve to reduce the intensity of the pain that his mind is not yet equipped to manage. Bion called this process containment which he described as mother's capacity to think about her infant's anxieties without finding them overwhelming and becoming caught up in them herself. Eventually, over a period of time and through much repetition, the infant takes in this capacity to tolerate and manage anxiety without having to feel unduly alarmed. Babies with mothers who can take the panic out of their anxieties gradually internalise some version of a mother who can manage psychic pain. In this way the infant develops the resources inside himself to transform his experience from something that is profoundly disturbing into a capacity for resilience. Bion linked the mother's containment of her baby with the work of the therapist in transforming an experience that is unbearable into something that, whilst still painful, can be endured and thought about. It is the internal presence of a mother who can tolerate mental pain that enables the individual to move from a state of disintegration to one of integration.

On arrival at the school Sophia had been unable to manage her sadness and fear which spilt out in tears affecting everyone around her. The specialist teachers responded appropriately by activating the network but found themselves drawn into identifying with her mental state rather than containing it. They endeavoured to provide for her needs in every way possible and her suffering became their suffering and they felt as helpless as she did. However, they recognised this unsatisfactory state of affairs and sought help for both themselves and for her.

The support sessions with the teachers provided a safe space for thought and reflection. What they had found difficult to bear was her aloneness which stirred up in them primitive anxieties about separation and abandonment. They expressed sadness and guilt, feelings they had previously been unable to apprehend or investigate. With deep regret they came to acknowledge the limits of what could be done. But in acknowledging their limitations, they were free to consider what could realistically be provided and their personal and professional confidence returned. Released from feelings of hopelessness, they were able to endure her acute suffering and focus on securing her place at the school and confronting colleagues who sought to rid themselves of her and the discomfort she represented. They changed from thinking of her as a distressed child with no hope to a distressed child for whom there could be hope.

I believe the local authority was not unmoved by Sophia's situation but had felt the need to defend itself against the painful consequences of their decision, projecting its unwanted anxieties into the most junior and temporary member of staff, and turning away from the difficulties that ensued. The impact of Sophia's distress proved too much for the student social worker and she was knocked off balance. What she was unable to manage, and needed support to achieve, was the capacity to bear the pain and limitations of Sophia's situation, an achievement that would have helped her feel sufficiently separated from Sophia, to know about her suffering, without having to join her in it.

It is interesting to consider some of the similarities that existed between the two key workers: both were in training, enthusiastic, generous, and moved to breach professional boundaries by providing more than was appropriate. What was different was the support and containment available to the trainee therapist sustaining her in reflection rather than action. Consequently, she was able to tolerate Sophia's distress without seeking to take it away. By enduring it, she provided her with the experience of being with an adult who could survive it. Gradually, Sophia came to internalise this capacity and slowly develop these resources within herself. She continued to bring her tears to the sessions but outside the room her despair was no longer evident and she was able to find some satisfaction in her relationship with her peers.

Conclusion

This case brings into focus the need for a helpful partnership between agencies representing a containing couple with the capacity to support each other in providing what is realistic and tolerating the frustration of their own and each other's limitations. There was a danger of a split taking place between the services, for example, of the clinic being idealised as the good father and social services decried as the bad, neglectful mother, a re-enactment of the break-up that had occurred between the actual parents. Such dangers require a toleration of different and conflicting perspectives and a capacity to see things from the other's point of view. In meeting Sophia's needs the school, social services and the clinic were each required to bear pain and frustration that was both individual and institutional. The development of a capacity for containment enables agencies to make creative use of the resources available rather than squander them on rivalrous splits and recriminations, like self-preoccupied parents who readily lose sight of the child. The need for support for the carers was evident within each agency. In this example support took the form of supervision, but it need not always be so formally constituted and may be achieved, more informally, through work discussion or peer consultation. Support for workers is an essential aspect of any service for refugees as the survival of one is dependent upon the survival of the other.

References

Klein M (1946) *Notes on some Schizoid Mechanisms in Envy and Gratitude*, London, Hogarth Press, 1987.
Lord Laming (2003) *The Victoria Climbie Inquiry: Summary and Recommendations*. HMSO.
Menzies Lyth I (1988) *Containing Anxiety in Institutions*. London, Free Association Books.
Waddell M (1989) Living in two worlds. *Free Associations* **15**: 11–35.

15 The containing function of supervision in working with abuse

Dick Agass[1]

A skilled and experienced social worker was counselling a female client with an extremely violent family history, which included having been sexually abused by her father. After one particularly harrowing session with her client the worker was returning to her office when she was alarmed to find herself driving through a red light. On another occasion, again after a very gruelling session, she went back to her office, wrote up the session and then went home for the weekend. Over the weekend, however, she became convinced that she had inadvertently put the case-notes in the waste-bin, or perhaps posted them to someone, instead of putting them in the filing cabinet, and she had a strong urge to go back to the office to make sure the notes were safe.

I begin with these incidents because they illustrate a key aspect of the subject I want to discuss in this chapter – namely the impact on any professional worker of severe disturbance within an individual or family, and the extent to which this disturbance can be contained, thought about and worked with in a way which not only safeguards the worker's sanity but also offers some alleviation of the client's distress. As this worker's supervisor, it was clear to me that the appalling events of her client's life and the acutely painful feelings stirred up in the counselling sessions were steadily getting under her skin, affecting her sleep and her personal relationships and making her feel, in her own word, 'contaminated'. She had come to feel so invaded and poisoned by what her client was communicating to her, both verbally and in less easily identifiable ways, that she had developed a strong and largely unconscious urge to rid herself of the case altogether (bin the notes), which troubled her greatly because it conflicted with her professional responsibilities, as well as with her view of herself as a conscientious and caring person. The incident of going through the red light, which she reasonably ascribed to 'overload', could perhaps be understood at a less conscious level as a warning to herself that in working with this client she was having to override her own internal danger signals, thus putting her own mental and physical wellbeing increasingly at risk.

Such experiences are not uncommon in any area of work closely involved with human suffering, and there are some classic studies of the impact of physical illness

1 This paper draws on two previously published papers: 'Containment, supervision and abuse' in *Psychodynamic Perspectives on Abuse: The Cost of Fear* edited by Una McCluskey and Carol-Ann Hooper (London, Jessica Kingsley Publishers, 2000, pp. 209–222. Copyright © Jessica Kingsley Publishers); and 'Countertransference, supervision and the reflection process' in *Journal of Social Work Practice* 2002; **16**(2): 125–133.

or mental disturbance on professionals and professional systems (e.g. Main 1957; Menzies 1959). One very experienced mental health social worker on a training course I was conducting said she found it remarkable how one or two of her clients seemed to 'discharge a whole load of disturbance' into her, so that her normal ability to leave her work behind her when she went home was completely undermined. She added: 'I've no idea how they do it.'

It is this whole question of 'how they do it' that I want to examine first – how workers can come to feel so disturbed by their clients without necessarily understanding what the disturbance is or how it got in. This means looking beyond the consciously distressing aspects of any particular case to a deeper level of interpersonal process that is largely unconscious. Unless we have a way of thinking about and understanding such processes they are likely to have an adverse effect on our own psychic balance as well as on our work, leading either to some kind of retaliatory acting out towards our clients or to illness and burn-out.

My discussion will focus on the psychoanalytic concepts of projective identification (Klein) and containment (Bion), and the main concern of this chapter is the vital role of supervision in helping the worker to contain and understand the client's experience as a necessary step towards rendering that experience more understandable and manageable for the client. I have drawn my examples from cases involving physical, emotional or sexual abuse because such cases are frequently the most challenging and disturbing we are called upon to deal with. Encountering such abuse presents special difficulties for the worker, who is likely to feel abusive or abused, and in some degree contaminated (as the worker above put it) by exposure to the client's experience. What one hears most often from social workers is that they hardly ever have the opportunity or the help to examine their work in any depth, still less its effect on themselves, beyond the purview of administrative and statutory requirements. In writing this chapter I therefore have in mind the large number of practitioners who spend their working lives exposed to their clients' disturbance and who cope as best they can with its impact.

Projective identification and containment

The concept of projective identification originates with Melanie Klein (1946) and describes an unconscious defence mechanism of very early development (belonging to what she termed the paranoid-schizoid position) in which the infant deals with intense primitive anxieties by segregating its 'good' and 'bad' objects[2], together with the good and bad parts of the self linked to these objects, and then doing its best, in phantasy, to ensure that these good and bad aspects of its experience remain separate. In this way everything unconsciously perceived as bad and harmful is split off internally and may then be projected into the external world. As Feldman (1992) helpfully summarises:

> Klein came to use the term 'projective identification' to describe this process
> whereby the infant projects (primarily) harmful contents into his object (for

---

2 The analytic term for the *person* who is the object of one's impulses or feelings (external object), or the intrapsychic version of that person (internal object).

example, into his mother), and by the same token projects those parts of his mental apparatus with which they are linked. In so far as the mother then comes to contain the bad parts of the self, she is not only felt to be bad, as a separate individual, but is *identified* with the bad, unwanted parts of the self.

(p. 75)

Klein (1946, p. 8) described this as 'the prototype of an aggressive object-relation', in that the hated parts of the self are now hated *in the object* – they are no longer experienced as belonging to the self. Good parts of the self are also projected into an object as a means of keeping them separate, and therefore safe, from the bad – though, as Spillius (1992) points out, the emphasis both in Klein's work and that of subsequent analysts has been on the projection of bad feelings that the infant or patient cannot contain. In normal development, through a constant cycle of projection and introjection, the projected parts of the self, both good and bad, are taken back in, together with parts of the object, and the ego gradually becomes stronger and more integrated, more able to tolerate the co-existence of good and bad feelings towards whole, separate objects – in Kleinian terms, a movement towards the depressive position. However, if there are problems in an individual's early development, he or she may fail to develop any cohesive sense of self or any clear ego boundaries, with the consequence that splitting and projective processes become established as the primary mode of relating to others, perhaps operating in an increasingly rigid and irreversible way. Some severely disturbed individuals – referred to as 'borderline' in a way that highlights this problem with their own internal and external boundaries – live in a more or less permanent state of identification with their objects so that they no longer have any clear sense of 'who's who'. Through projective identification the painful reality of separateness can be avoided by the illusion of being part of another person or being inside them. Projective identification may also be used as a means of taking over and controlling an object or acquiring its properties, turning it into a possession or an extension of the self.

If Klein's original emphasis was on the *defensive* nature of projective identification – especially ridding the self of its unwanted parts – then Bion developed the notion of projective identification as the infant's earliest means of *communication* with the mother. According to Bion (1958, 1962a,b) the infant projects its confused and frightening feeling-states into the mother, who, in favourable circumstances, 'contains' them, and then, in her emotionally attuned handling of the infant, gives them back to him in a more manageable form – a function which, over time, the infant introjects and becomes more able to manage for himself. It is stressed that this is a normal aspect of human development which continues to be refined throughout life as an essential component of human relating. However, if something goes wrong with this process in infancy, if there is no 'container' for the unmanageable feelings, or one which cannot contain them but only push them back at the infant in an unmodified state, then these feelings are rendered even more frightening and may give rise to states of overwhelming anxiety and disintegration.

It is this concept of projective identification as a communicative process which now underlies any psychodynamic approach to interpersonal process, especially in relation to the intensely powerful feelings that can be stirred up in therapists or other helping professionals by their clients or patients – the countertransference. By analogy with the containing mother, professionals need to develop a capacity for what

Bion calls 'reverie', a state of mind in which painful, confusing and sometimes unbearable feelings and impulses can be contained and reflected upon so that the client may be able to re-introject them in a modified form, along with the capacity to deal with them internally rather than by projecting them into, and repeatedly acting them out with, other people. In practice, even when projective identification is being used largely to evacuate unwanted feelings into the worker, it is hard not to see this also as a form of unconscious communication. The following example illustrates some of these processes.

Approaching the summer break, a therapist I was supervising changed her holiday plans at short notice and wrote to her client informing him that their next session would now be the last one before the break (he had been expecting one more after that). The client then arrived late for his session, and, to the therapist's surprise, sat in a different chair to his usual one. He then talked about his determination to give up smoking, and pressed the therapist to tell him whether she had ever been a smoker. When she at first refused to tell him he complained that he was 'sick and tired of being at the bottom of a power imbalance here', adding that he could be 'rude' and 'get into her bag' to see if she had any cigarettes. After holding out for a while she eventually succumbed to his interrogation. To her credit she did manage to ask him whether he felt affected by her change of holiday dates, but this predictably drew a contemptuous response. Overall she felt controlled, threatened and undermined by the client, and desperate to make contact with me after the session to talk about what had happened. It was only several weeks later, when she brought all this to supervision, that we were able to think about the client's behaviour and its effect upon her. In the preceding weeks he had begun to open up to her and to reveal some of his vulnerability. Clearly he had found her letter unbearably hurtful and dismissive, and it triggered a powerful defensive reaction. We were then able to look at the therapist's feelings (which had stayed with her during her holiday) as a clear projective identification of the client's own internal state. He was subjecting *her* to a sudden disorientating change (the chair), to feeling bullied, belittled (the interrogation) and intruded into (her bag), whilst also getting rid of his dependency (the smoking) into her – it was she who felt in desperate need of someone (her supervisor) after the session.

We can see how the client aggressively projects his bad feelings into the therapist, making sure (in this case by rather crude means) that *she* experiences them instead. This client had a childhood marked by rejection and sexual abuse, and his response to the wounding letter is unconsciously to recreate the abusive dynamic, casting the therapist in the role of himself as child victim. The reference to being 'rude' and 'getting into her bag' is unmistakably sexual, and it made the therapist feel quite threatened. It also had the effect of actually 'getting into her' in the sense that she remained troubled by him during her holiday. He had ensured that she kept him very much in mind. In effect the stirrings of neediness and dependency engendered in him by their recent work, and intensified by the break, were now hated, and hatefully expelled into the therapist. In supervision she quickly found relief in being able to think about and understand what had happened, learning to view her countertransference as a projective communication of the client's internal state. She was able to recover her empathic feeling for the client's hurt, and in subsequent sessions helped him to reflect on the mobilising of his defences in reaction to her abrupt change of plan. The episode became a growth point in the therapist's own learning as well as in the therapy.

We can see from this example that what happens is not simply the 'transfer' of a set of feelings from one person to another, but rather the re-creating and re-living of an object-relationship. This relationship, or aspects of it, may then be re-enacted not only between client and worker but also within or between different parts of the professional system. The result, in Freud's (1914) original terminology, is that an earlier situation is simply *repeated* rather than *remembered* and *worked through* – in other words re-enacted as an avoidance of any conscious recollection, reflection and resolution. Britton (1981; see Chapter 13 of this volume) gives a lucid account of this phenomenon.

The following example was given by a mental health social worker on a course I was facilitating. The client she presented was described as having borderline personality disorder – an immediate clue to the likelihood of splitting and projective processes as a prominent feature. The client was said to be unable to care either for her children, who were both up for adoption, or herself. She had a history of sexual abuse, both in her family and in residential school, but had only recently disclosed that the original abuser had been her father. Her dealings with her siblings were described as 'very confused and dishonest', and she had a consistently hostile relationship with her mother, by whom she felt rejected. The worker described her struggles with this client, particularly during a period of inpatient psychiatric care, when the client would constantly complain about the worker not visiting enough, but then, when she did visit, would either refuse to speak to her or else simply ask her to carry out minor tasks or errands. The worker said she was constantly aware of the client's hostility, and felt she could never give her what she needed. She also felt denigrated by the ward staff, who knew 'their' patient very well from her frequent admissions, and who made it obvious in various ways that they shared the client's view of the worker's lack of experience and commitment.

Listening to the worker it was obvious that the pressure of her client's behaviour towards her was taking its toll. She had been obliged to take some sick leave (quite probably, though not consciously, related to this client), and had contemplated getting the case transferred to another worker. Above all she felt used by the client, who seemed intent on devaluing her by keeping the relationship on a menial level whilst complaining about the lack of any real help. Clearly there was an abusive dynamic at work here, with its familiar noxious blend of favouritism and degradation. The worker's sense of being trapped in something confusing and demeaning that could hardly be called a relationship but was the only thing on offer, combined with her desperate desire to escape – by going off sick or transferring the case – could certainly be viewed as projected elements of the client's own early experience of abuse and neglect. In subjecting the worker to this treatment the client seems to have been unconsciously repeating her early experience with the roles reversed, recruiting the nurses to join in the abuse of the worker.

This is a clear example of the way in which key elements of a client's internal world not only transmit themselves to an individual worker but may also be enacted between that worker and other professionals. In fact the situation here is reminiscent of Main's (1957) classic investigation of a group of psychiatric patients who were remarkable not only for the intractable nature of their problems but also for the 'special' status they acquired in the course of their treatment careers. Main found that these patients (whom we would now consider 'borderline') somehow managed to stimulate superhuman efforts (to the point of burn-out) and intense rivalries among the nursing staff for the honour of being admitted to a dedicated 'in-group' of carers. Within this inner circle the patient would bestow confidences in such a way that each nurse thought she alone enjoyed a privileged intimacy. Although Main does not go into individual case histories, the dynamic he describes is strongly suggestive of an abusive family system in which the abuser deploys a divisive strategy of favouritism and secret alliances, deluding his victims into feeling 'special' for being thus exploited. Main also points to the blurring of professional roles and boundaries that always occurred with these patients, and this again reflects the breaching of personal and generational boundaries in sexual abuse.

To return to our example, the social worker's painful experience (no doubt shared with the client's children) of longing for some acknowledgement, some flicker of warmth, whilst being used, pushed out and treated as worthless, may be understood as a projection by the client of her own early experience of rejecting and abusive parents. In the hospital setting the client had managed to reverse the situation so that she was now getting special attention from a loyal group of carers whilst *someone else* was being left out in the cold and abused.

Containment, supervision and the capacity to think

One striking feature of these examples is how the workers became so caught up in their clients' defensive systems that they found it virtually impossible to think. The development of an infant's capacity for thought is a key aspect of Bion's theory of the container and the contained, and though the details of this theory are beyond the scope of the present chapter (see O'Shaughnessy 1981; Spillius 1994), it will be helpful to summarise its essential elements.

Following Freud (1911), Bion (1962 a,b) viewed thinking as a developmental achievement in which the illusion of omnipotent control of one's object world is gradually abandoned in the face of reality. At the risk of drastic oversimplification we might say that projective identification, if it is adhered to as the primary mode of relating to others, becomes a way of *not thinking* about, or learning from, experience. Thinking involves difficult psychic work, and the toleration and working through of painful and conflicting emotional states. Through projective identification of these unwelcome states can be evacuated into other people as raw, unprocessed matter (Bion's 'beta elements'), the psychic equivalent of eliminating unwanted substances from the body. In this way painful experience can be avoided by repeatedly getting other people to experience and enact it, so that they, and not the subject, are obliged to suffer its effects. The result may be that very little in the subject's internal world is ever really engaged with or worked through before it gets discharged in some kind of activity – 'acted out', as we usually put it. Once something is being re-enacted, either with an individual worker or involving other professionals (as in the last example), the client can simply repeat it rather than try to think about it or resolve it. For thinking to become possible, and to be sustained, there has to be the experience of a containing object which can detoxify the projected elements and render them (by a process Bion calls 'alpha function') more susceptible to symbolisation, thought and mental work.

My thesis here is that, even with some of our most damaged and disturbed clients it may be possible to bring this function into play, to contain and process elements of their experience so that they can begin to take them back in and work on them internally, instead of constantly getting rid of them, and in the process depleting themselves, by projective identification. I will now present two rather more detailed examples to show how supervision can fulfil this containing role for the worker or therapist whilst they themselves are struggling to contain the client's projections. When successful, this process can result in emotional growth for both client and worker.

The first example concerns a 19-year-old female client who referred herself to a social work team specialising in drug and alcohol abuse. Her presenting problem was her drinking, but the focus of the work quickly settled on the fact that she had been sexually abused by her paternal grandfather from a very early age, often while her mother was in the house. Up to the age of seven she knew she did not like what her grandfather did to her, but did not realise it was wrong. When she was nine he moved away, but she continued to live in fear that he would come back and get her. It was not until she was thirteen that she told her mother about the abuse, and then only because she thought the grandfather was going to move back in with them. To their credit her parents believed her straight away (it seems likely he had abused others in the family too) and banned him from the house. Despite her relief she could not deal with the abuse and its effects on her, and as she got into her teens her behaviour went more and more off the rails. She drank excessively and was recklessly promiscuous. Sometimes she stepped off the curb with her eyes closed to see if she was 'meant' to die. She was aware that intensely violent feelings built up inside her, but the only way she could deal with them was by some sort of blood-letting, either cutting herself or getting herself injured in fights, which felt to her like getting the abuser out of her system. By the time of her self-referral she had at least found some stability and support, sharing a house with a number of other women whom she seemed to regard as a surrogate family.

The reason the worker approached me for help with this case was that she felt she lacked the mental health experience to deal with some of her client's rather strange ideas and experiences. For example, the client said she had 'presences' that were with her in varying combinations and with varying intensity. One was described as a short and hostile male presence, while another was a benevolent female presence. She also believed that she consisted of seven parts, and that the presences could take these parts away. She could feel reasonably well with five, but knew that if she went down to three she would be in dire trouble. Once the parts were lost she had to find them again. She was apparently convinced that she would die at twenty-five, and had a vision of someone driving past in a car and shooting her in the head. She also suffered from sleep disturbance and perceptual distortions, for example doors appearing to be the wrong size when she looked at them. All these things, together with the fact that she still talked to her cuddly toys, made her afraid that she was mad. Several years previously she had been sent for an EEG and remembered being told that it showed 'something wrong with her brain'.

I could see that the worker had made a good relationship with her client, who seemed very committed to their weekly sessions. The main business of supervision was to contain the intense anxiety stirred up in the worker, who was quite sure she had no means of understanding, let alone alleviating, her client's disturbed mental state.

It is a familiar feature of abuse victims that their mental capacities are shut down by their experience because it is quite simply too traumatic to take in. The only way they can survive is often to dissociate – to split themselves internally in an attempt to safeguard some part of the ego in which they can hope to take refuge. The resulting loss of parts of themselves and their mental functions can be catastrophic. I think some such internal situation is evident here in the client's description of 'parts' of herself which are constantly under threat from malevolent internal objects ('presences'), with the presence of good objects apparently maintaining a precarious balance. It was notable that the worker, a very capable practitioner, was quite sure she lacked the mental capacity to deal with this case, as though, like her client, she had 'something wrong with her brain' or had metaphorically been shot in the head. Becoming stupid, sometimes to the point of severe intellectual impairment, is a well-documented intrapsychic defence among victims of abuse (Sinason 1992). Seemingly the worker had become incorporated into the same defensive pattern. This meant it was vital for supervision to provide a space in which she could recover her own intuitive and intellectual skills so that the horror of her client's experience could be thought about and processed.

The client's behaviour was alarmingly self-destructive, representing a perverse 'solution' to the original abuse (Milton 1994). In supervision we considered her dissociative response to the trauma, which had split up her internal world, played havoc with her development and left her in a very weakened state. The malevolent male presence almost certainly represented the abuser, whilst the perceptual disturbances might be understood as involuntary flashbacks to a child's-eye view of a (bedroom?) doorway. As for the seven 'parts' of her that could be taken away, I suppose there is an obvious association with seven days of the week, and seven was also the age at which she said she realised the abuse was wrong. What more poignant lament for the time stolen from her by her abuser?

It emerged that the worker had kept her own collection of cuddly toys well into adulthood, and this helped her to identify with the child inside her client who longed for contact but who was also frightened and mistrustful of the grown-up world. The worker was aware of an unspoken appeal from her client to care for her, and at times to make physical contact. She felt uneasy about this, but at the same time anxious that she might damage the client by withholding something vital. She was able to use supervision to think about this and to strengthen her own personal boundaries. This undoubtedly led to a strengthening of the client's boundaries as well, and to a deepening of the relationship. As for fears about brain damage, a simple check with the appropriate medical team revealed that the client's EEG had been within the normal range, which came as a great relief to the client as well as opening up new pathways in the worker's own thinking. As the worker grew in confidence, the client too began to change. In analytic terms, the worker was being taken in as a good object, which led to a strengthening of the ego. The client's relationship with her mother, whom she had always blamed for letting the abuse happen, improved considerably, and she managed to bring her drinking more under control. Follow-up contact a year after the end of sessions found the client in a stable, nonabusive relationship as well as in employment. She was generally feeling much better about herself and more in control of her own life.

My final example brings us back to our starting point – the worker who became anxious about what she might have done with her client's case-notes. I cannot give a full account of this case, but I want to discuss certain aspects of it that have a bearing on our theme. This client's experience was so traumatic that it had been expelled from awareness, together with vital parts of her mental apparatus, leaving her in a severely dissociated and under-functioning state. As in the previous example, the worker played a vital role in helping her client to recover these traumatised parts of herself, using supervision to contain and work through the countertransference which was at times almost unbearable.

The client's family history was dominated by her father's violence, and there had been changes of name and even changes of continent, evidently to avoid detection. The biggest uprooting occurred after the death of her mother while they were living abroad. The client was not told directly about this but remembered her father dropping her off at school and saying to her: 'Tell your teacher your mother's dead.' Three days later they were back in England with a different family name. As with the previous client, but this time in a more literal sense, her life had been broken up in pieces, and then any connection between the pieces destroyed, so that her internal world had become a completely dark and terrifying place. As well as witnessing her father's assaults on her mother, she had herself been beaten and sexually abused by him, and it soon became clear that the acute anxiety symptoms which had prompted her referral were part of an internal crisis caused by fragments of this early experience breaking back through into her awareness.

Looking back, I think that from the outset the worker was under intense unconscious pressure from the client *to have this awareness for her*, to contain the knowledge of what had happened in her life, together with all the unbearable feelings associated with it. This seemed to be confirmed at one point by the client dreaming that she was being abused by her father while the worker was in the room watching and being disgusted. Disgust, however, was only part of what was being projected. As the client recalled witnessing her mother being beaten up and raped by her father, the worker felt completely overwhelmed, out of her depth and unable to help. What emerged here was the client's unbearable sense of helplessness and guilt that as a child she had not been able to protect her mother. This internal state was also being projected into the worker, reinforced by the comment that, in telling her about these events she was trusting the worker with her life, as she still feared her father would kill her if he found out. An atmosphere of extreme danger was thus recreated in the sessions, with the worker in the role of a helpless onlooker, paralysed by fear and disgust, and feeling totally responsible for a life poised on a knife-edge.

There were times when the worker felt so overwhelmed by what she was being required to contain – such as the chilling intimation that the client may well have witnessed her mother being killed by her father – that she longed for the whole experience to go away. She felt abused by what was being projected into her, which had something of the force and impact of a rape, invading and contaminating her and making her feel barely able to inhabit her own internal space.

But then, at first bewilderingly for the worker, the roles were reversed. In the build-up to describing the details of her abuse, the client began to feel that the worker could 'make' her do anything, whether she wanted to or not. This had the effect of making the worker determined to push the responsibility back onto the client for deciding when and how she should talk about her experience. The problem was that the client found she had no words with which to describe it, and only the vaguest idea of body parts and functions. The worker duly helped her with the terminology, but reported in supervision that it felt rather like forcing something down the client's throat. A situation then developed in which the client felt more and more 'made' to do something against her will, and had moments of seeing her father's mocking, triumphant face superimposed on the worker's. At this point the worker felt she had 'become' the abuser and that the therapy was lost. This needed to be contained and worked through in the supervision, and the client was eventually able to put into words her father's abusive acts, which included putting his penis in her mouth.

What I want to emphasise here is that at first the client could only deal with her unbearable early experience, once it had started to break back through into her consciousness, by projecting it into the worker and by engaging her in re-enactments of the original trauma. The worker experienced an inrush of this unprocessed 'beta element' material, and was at times very nearly overwhelmed by it. With the help of supervision she was able to use her sensitivity and receptiveness to transform this evacuative process into a powerfully communicative interaction. This was especially problematic here because the original trauma had left the client with no internal container for her own experience, and hence no capacity to deal with it symbolically in language and thought (see Garland 2002). The worker's attempt to supply the missing words was itself experienced in a very concrete way as a repetition of the original abuse.

This example shows how complex and challenging such situations can be, because even in the midst of this defensive re-enactment of her trauma I think the client was unconsciously probing the worker in a desperate search for containment – for a mind which might help her retrieve the lost parts of herself and somehow make sense of and come to terms with her unbearable early experience. Supervision provided the containing environment in which this horrific raw material could begin to be processed. With great difficulty the worker managed to communicate her own processing of it back to the client, not just through verbal comments and interpretations but through her whole way of relating, as well as through the containing structure of the sessions themselves. Most importantly, she survived the experience and communicated to her client that it could be survived, understood and worked through. The outcome of this case, as with the previous one, was very satisfactory. Several years later the client was found to be much happier and more stable, coping better with all aspects of her life and catching up on her lost education by studying for a degree.

Conclusion

In this chapter I have tried to demonstrate the vital importance of understanding the unconscious processes involved in working with disturbed and traumatised clients. In particular I have highlighted the role of supervision in helping the worker to cope with, make sense of and then put to therapeutic use his or her own emotional responses to the client – the countertransference. Analytically the concepts of projective identification and containment are at the heart of this process. If projective identification involves an unconscious attempt to induce in the worker the very state of mind the client is trying to eliminate in him- or herself (Carpy 1989), then how the worker responds to its impact is crucial for both of them. Defensively the worker may react by withdrawing, or by some kind of retaliation. Either way the client is not helped to change, and the worker may well feel, over time, worn down, drained and disillusioned. If the worker can contain these projections, then it may be possible to help the client 'transform the unbearable into something that can eventually be thought about, held in the mind and considered, rather than responded to as an overwhelming experience that causes a further breakdown of the ability to think' (Garland 2002, p. 110).

To 'contain' in this context is not simply putting up with or absorbing whatever uncomfortable or unpleasant feelings the client stirs up in us. It is a much more active and demanding process of tolerating, understanding and working through our own emotional responses in the hope that this will enable our clients to do the same for themselves. It may then be possible for the client 'gradually to re-introject the previously intolerable aspects of himself . . . (along with) the capacity to tolerate them which he has observed in the (worker)' (Carpy 1989, p. 292). If patients or clients find themselves confronted by someone who seems either totally unaffected by what they project into them, or else totally taken over and disabled by it, they will have no real experience of being understood and helped, and perhaps no real hope that this could ever be the case. There may be a conscious sense of relief or even triumph if they manage to neutralise the worker's effectiveness, but in terms of the client's own internal plight it leaves them stuck in exactly the same place. Defensively this may suit their purposes, but it may also leave a trapped and desperate health-seeking part of them more isolated than ever.

To function therapeutically in such circumstances makes considerable demands on any professional. Undoubtedly the most important factors here are still the personal attributes and professional skills of the worker. However, these attributes and skills are unlikely to be effective without the availability of a good-enough experience of supervision as a space for containment and psychic processing. I would add that a specialised training in counselling or psychotherapy is highly advisable for anyone involved in these areas of work, and that having a personal experience of therapy is invaluable in helping us to utilise what is, after all, our most potent and yet most fragile resource – ourselves.

I am grateful to the practitioners who allowed me to use their supervision material for this chapter, and to the clients featured in the two extended case examples for also giving their consent.

References

Bion WR (1958) Attacks on linking. In *Second Thoughts*. London; Heinemann (1967).

Bion WR (1962a) A theory of thinking. In *Second Thoughts*. London; Heinemann (1967).

Bion WR (1962b) *Learning from Experience*. London; Heinemann.

Britton R (1981) Re-enactment as an unwitting professional response to family dynamics. In S Box (ed.) *Crisis at Adolescence: Object Relations Therapy with the Family*. New Jersey: Jason Aronson, Inc. (1994). Reprinted as Chapter 13 of this volume.

Carpy DV (1989) Tolerating the countertransference: A mutative process. *International Journal of Psycho-Analysis* 70: 287–294.

Feldman M (1992) Splitting and projective identification. In R Anderson (ed.) *Clinical Lectures on Klein and Bion*. London; Routledge.

Freud S (1911) Formulations on the two principles of mental functioning. *Standard Edition* 12: 215–226.

Freud S (1914) Remembering, repeating and working-through. *Standard Edition* 12: 145–156

Garland C (2002) Issues in treatment: A case of rape. In C Garland (ed.) *Understanding Trauma: A Psychoanalytical Approach*, 2nd edn. Tavistock Clinic Series. London; Karnac.

Klein M (1946) Notes on some schizoid mechanisms. In *The Writings of Melanie Klein. Volume 3: Envy and Gratitude and Other Works 1946–1963*. London; Hogarth Press (1975).

Main TF (1957) The ailment. *British Journal of Medical Psychology* 30(3): 129–145. Reprinted in *The Ailment and other Psychoanalytic Essays*. London, Free Association Books (1989).

Menzies IEP (1959) The functioning of social systems as a defence against anxiety: A report on a study of the nursing service of a general hospital. *Human Relations* **13**: 95–121. Republished as: The functioning of social systems as a defence against anxiety. In *Containing Anxiety in Institutions: Selected Essays. Vol 1*. London, Free Association Books (1988).

Milton J (1994) Abuser and abused: Perverse solutions following childhood abuse. *Psychoanalytic Psychotherapy* 8(3): 243–255.

O'Shaughnessy E (1981) W. R. Bion's theory of thinking and new techniques in child analysis. In E Bott Spillius (ed.) *Melanie Klein Today, Vol 2*. London, Routledge (1988, pp. 177–190).

Sinason V (1992) *Mental Handicap and the Human Condition*. London; Free Association Books.

Spillius E Bott (1992) Clinical experiences of projective identification. In R Anderson (ed.) *Clinical Lectures on Klein and Bion*. London, Routledge.

Spillius E Bott (1994) Developments in Kleinian thought: Overview and personal view. *Psychoanalytic Inquiry* 3(14): 324–364.

Appendix 1   Helpful organisations

The Tavistock Centre,
120 Belsize Lane,
London, NW3 5BA
Tel: 020 7435 7111

Offers social work training at all levels based on a psychoanalytic approach. A prospectus can be obtained from academic services. Tailor-made courses can also be delivered to local authorities.

GAPS

Group for the advancement of psychodynamics and psychotherapy in social work. Publishes an excellent journal, 'The Journal of Social Work Practice' which is included in the price of the subscription. Also has an annual lecture and other events.

Secretary: Judy Toasland, NSPCC, 28 Addiscombe Grove, Croydon, 5LP, UK.

NP3

A network of social work teachers and educators dedicated to developing relation-ship-based practice. Holds regular meetings.

Contact: Adrian Ward. Email: *adrian.ward@uea.ac.uk*

Personal Therapy

BPC – *The British Psychoanalytic Council*, West Hill House, 6 Swains Lane, London, N6 6QS.
A national organisation of psychotherapy training which has very high standards of training. Members and organisations cover the whole country. There are reduced fee schemes run by member organisations including:

- The Lincoln Centre
- The British Association of Psychotherapists
- The London Centre for Psychotherapy

Index

Abraham, Karl 8–9
acting out 169, 190; in BPD 146;
  complementary 167, 168; in double
  deprivation 92; of sexually abused girls
  78, 80, 82
addiction: addicted parents 131–4; and child
  care 129; psychodynamics 128–31; see
  also substance abuse
addiction services 135
addictive vulnerability 129, 131
adolescence of disabled child 110
Adolescent Separation Anxiety Interview
  (ASAI) 24
agency, development of 67
aggression 7; in children 9; in double
  deprivation 90
agro–claustrophobic dilemma 144
alcohol abuse: affective responses 132; in
  families 127–8, 131; identifying children
  135; in manic defence 10; in mothers 64;
  normalisation 131; see also substance
  abuse
Alcoholics Anonymous 133
Analysis Terminable and Interminable 31
anthropology 20–1
anxiety in children 9
assessment: in family assessment centre 49;
  observation in 47; parenting abilities
  115–16, 121–6
attachment: of disabled child 107; loyalty to
  parents 67
attachment research 23
attachment theory 3
attachment theory, contemporary 23
attacks on linking 96–8, 99
attention 49
attention seeking 49
avoidance 23; of collaboration 120; of
  mental pain 180–2; in parenting
  assessment 124, 125; of reality 117

babies: 'at risk' study 24–5; depressive
  position 10; paranoid schizoid position
  10; projective identification 9; quiet
  50–2
belief systems: of clients 64–5; of workers
  64–5, 66–7
'beta element' material 190, 194
Beyond the Pleasure Principle 8, 172
Bion, Wilfred 6, 11–12; on BPD
  development 146–7; on containment 26,
  146, 155, 182–3; history 5–6; linking,
  attacks on 34, 96, 97–8; 'nameless dread'
  11, 147; on projective identification
  166–7, 187–8; reflective space 33;
  thinking under fire 134
blame over disabled child 105, 106
'bombardment' of workers 4, 11
borderline families 160
borderline personality disorder (BPD) 6,
  12, 139–51; analytic perspective 140–1;
  caring for 141, 142–3; clinical work
  143–6; description 140; development
  146–7; DSM-IV categories 140;
  engagement with patients 144; in gang
  families 160; manipulation of
  professionals 139, 142–3, 149, 150, 161,
  189–90; parents 147–8; projective
  identification 187, 189; psychiatric
  perspective 140; research 148–50;
  self-harm 141–2; splitting in 140–1, 144,
  149, 161; treatment 19, 148–50;
  uncertainty of identity 141
borderline states 12
Bowlby, John 6
BPD see borderline personality disorder

Caldwell, Maria 49
carers: in BPD 141; of sexually abused girls
  83–4, 85; support for 177–84
change, resistance to 31
child abuse: family, chronic long-term
  153–66; see also physical abuse, child;
  sexual abuse
childhood developmental model 65–6
childhood sexuality 7

psychoanalytic therapies, efficacy of 19
psychodynamic work in Probation service 18
psychosis 11–12
psychosocial research: evidence-based practice 18; quantitative/qualitative 24
psychotherapy: keeping family in mind 135; substance abuse 135–6; *see also* group therapy
psychotherapy with sexual abused girls 71–88; attachment/family history 85–6; carers' views 86–7; carers, work with 83–4, 85; clinical analysis 72–3; findings, general 73–4; girls, discussion with 81–3; impact of abuse 84–5; introduction 71; literature 71–2; parenting issues 84, 85–6; parents 84, 86; parents' workers 84; psychodynamic inferences 74–81; structure of therapy 72; support work 83–4; workers, effect on 86–7
psychotic illness and childcare 6

quiet babies 50–2

racism 31–43; case material 34–42; defence against curiosity/thinking 33–4; in double deprivation 92; matching patient and therapist 41–2; sexual imagery 34
random controlled trials (RCTs) 17, 19, 20; NICE recommendations 19–20
raters 22, 24
re-enactment 56–7; as avoidance 188; as defence 194; as professional response, unwitting 165–74; as therapy 193
reality: acceptance 117; children's 66; internal/external blurring 76, 123; in pathological organisations 163; in psychosis 12
reality evasion: in couples 117–21; and projective identification 119–21
reflection in sexually abused girls 80–1
reflective space 20, 27, 33, 42; for curiosity 39–42; in observation 47; parents/carers of abused girls 83; for sexually abused girls 82
Refugee Workshop 177
refugees, work with 177–84; case study 178–83; different perspectives 177–8; supporting staff 179
relationships: mother–child 39, 50, 85–6; of sexually abused girls 77–8, 81, 82–3, 85–6; transfer of pattern across 166
repetition compulsion 8, 154, 156, 172, 173; and professional 're-enactment' 166, 167, 170
research practitioner model 16

responsibility: for children at risk 61–2; evasion 12; personal *vs* relational 61; projection 161
reverie 187
risk assessment 121–6
Robertson, James 6

secondary handicap 110
self-destructiveness 7–8, 191, 192
self-harm: in BPD 141–2, 144, 145, 146, 147, 148; psychoanalytic psychotherapy for 19; RCT recommendations by NICE 19–20
separateness: case material 38; and racism 31, 32, 33
servicing 181
settings for work: external 13–14; internal 13
sexual abuse: blurring of generations 118; in BPD development 146; and childhood sexuality 7; effects on professionals 77, 78–9, 86, 185, 193; impact of 71, 72; inability to manage experiences 76–8; multigenerational, treatment of 162–3; outcome studies 71–2; psychoanalytic psychotherapy for 19; re-enactment 56–7; risk assessment 121–6; unconscious complicity of mother 120–1
sexuality: Freud on 8; Sigmund Freud on 7
sexually abused children: outcomes, likely 72; physical appearance 74, 77; psychotherapy 71–88
shame 33, 106
sibling rivalry 57
Social Care Institute for Excellence (SCIE) 16–17
social development, delayed 53
social policy application 27
social work: abuser/abused split 157; comparison with other professionals 15–16; organisational setting 13–14; reprofessionalisation 17, 26–7; therapeutic potential 4
social work research 15–17; application to practice 16–17; methodology 17–18; plurality of influences 16; problems with 15
social work values 13
social workers: effects of clients' behaviour 4, 157–8; effects of sexual abuse cases 86, 185, 193; feelings/beliefs 64–5, 66–8; feelings during observation 47, 48, 56–7; frame of thought 59; new 63; threats to 157; turnover of staff 63
space for thinking *see* reflective space
'specialist team model' 149